STUDENT TO STALAG

Robin P Thomas DFC. RIBA

A POD BOOK

Published by POD Publishing
52 Parkwood Road, Wimborne, Dorset
England

On behalf of

ISBN: 0 9531737 3 9

This book was designed and produced by POD
Publishers on behalf of the copyright holder and
printed in the UK by:

The Basingstoke Press
Hampshire, England

Cover design by Christopher Stobs-Stobart

DEDICATION

The British Red Cross Society is pleased to acknowledge the generosity of Robin Thomas, in donating the profits from the sale of this publication to its funds. The part the International Red Cross played in 'Student to Stalag' is a familiar one in times of War and relates specifically to sustaining P.O.W's in their desperate time of need. The seemingly ordinary day-to-day activities, like communications, obtaining reading material and so on are made profoundly more difficult by incarceration. The Red Cross also played a significant part in alleviating concern for those at home and the sheer boredom of P.O.W's living in a stalag.

Today the International Red Cross and Red Crescent movement plays an increasing role in times of conflict, but at the same time provides a range of much needed services to vulnerable people in our own community.

By donating the proceeds of this book in 1999 Robin Thomas is helping to make a further contribution to the welfare and well-being of the Country and the People he fought for so bravely in the 1940's.

John Derben, OBE, FRICS
British Red Cross
Hampshire Branch

STUDENT TO STALAG

INTRODUCTION

At the tender age of eighteen Robin Thomas, like so many of his peers, faced the prospect of war with Germany with a mixture of determination, dread and even a little excitement, but how best could he serve his country in its time of need? Having lived all his life in Portsmouth, a city with centuries old naval traditions and association with generations of seafarers, it was logical that his first steps to joining up were directed in that quarter. But more by accident than design he found himself in the RAF.

After many months of training to be a Navigator, in England and Canada, he finally joined the active war machine - at a time when the famous Mosquito Bomber came into service.

Three years after the outbreak of war his plane was shot down twenty-six thousand feet above the Dutch city of Utrecht. He and his pilot managed to bail out, at a height that was considered likely, without an oxygen supply, to cause death by asphyxiation. But survive they did and Robin spent the next two and a half years as a prisoner of war in Stalag Luft 3, the camp made famous by the book and film of *The Great Escape* – and the horrific massacre, on Hitler's personal orders, of fifty of the prisoners that were recaptured after a mass breakout through a tunnel dug beneath the perimeter fence.

Robin Thomas, Portsmouth born, bred and living in retirement, was awarded the DFC for his service to King and Country. He recounts the events that took him from *Student to Stalag* in a humorous style, making light of the suffering and hardship that war brings to the lives of those involved. He has graciously dedicated this, his first book, to *The International Red Cross*, an organisation that did so much to help him and his fellow prisoners survive and return home to enjoy the peace they fought and sacrificed so much to secure.

STUDENT TO STALAG.

CONTENTS

Chapter

	FORWARD	1
1	September 1939.	2
2	War Damage Commission.	7
3	Reception and I. T. W.	11
4	On the Atlantic.	19
5	Port Albert, Ontario.	26
6	Air Navigation School.	31
7	Into the Air.	40
8	Picton.	46
9	Bombs and Guns.	50
10	Halifax and Montreal.	55
11	Gander, Newfoundland.	62
12	Over the Atlantic.	67
13	O.T.U. Upwood.	76
14	105 Squadron. Swanton Morley.	83
15	Horsham St. Faith's	90
16	Mosquitoes.	98
17	Contact with the Army.	108
18	The Navy, etc.	114
19	My Car.	122
20	Operations.	131
21	Attack of Gremlins	144
22	Shot down - First time.	153
23	Gas Holder and Gas Masks.	162
24	Utrecht. Oct. 11th. 1942.	172
25	Now a Kreigie. Preliminaries.	183
26	By Train - 4th Class.	194
27	A New Compound.	203
28	The Theatre.	216
29	Tin Bashing.	224
30	Escaping.	237
31	Day by Day.	251
32	Good-bye Luft 3.	264
33	Hallo Marlag-Milag Nord.	280
34	Stalag to Student.	291

R.P. Thomas, 31 Air Navigation School, Port Albert,
Canada - Winter 1941

A Mosquito Bomber of 105 Squadron

FORWARD.

It is more than fifty years since most of the events I have attempted to recall in the following pages, took place. Events outside of my sphere of control, such as the progress of the war, dates, times etc. are mentioned only in their context to my memories, and I have made no attempt to check their accuracy. Occasionally there has come my way, more by fortuitous accident than through any effort on my part, factual detail which I have been glad to use. This does not happen often, my overall intent has been to set down my memories of what I consider to be memorable in that exciting time of my life when I set out, with most of my generation, to win a war.

CHAPTER 1

September 1939

According to an article in the Readers Digest I died at approximately five-thirty-five on the evening of the 11th October 1942 over the Dutch city of Utrecht when my parachute opened at around twenty-six thousand feet above that city.

The article, which appeared in about 1960 announced, with its customary and well deserved authority, that to entrust oneself to a parachute at an altitude above seventeen thousand feet, without a supply of oxygen, was to invite death by asphyxiation. The fact that both my pilot and myself had exceeded this critical height by some nine thousand feet promotes one to speculate on the scientific integrity of the author of the theory who had not the dedication to put his calculations to the test. Indeed, it would have been pointless for him to have done so, for in the first place had his calculations been correct then he would have killed himself and NOT survived to enjoy the congratulations due to him. In the second place, had he not been asphyxiated, but survived (as we did) then there would have been no point in propounding the theory in the first place. Let this be a lesson to all inventors of untested theories.

As I began the twenty-minute journey back to earth my whole life did not flash before me, as of course it should have done if the theory had been correct. It is, however, a convenient device to pretend some of it did, thereby enabling me to explain, I fear at some length, how I came to find myself in this predicament.

It may be safely assumed the war had quite a lot to do with the situation. It, the war that is, started, as is fairly well known, on the 3rd of September 1939, three weeks before my eighteenth birthday. A few days after the outbreak of war the Portsmouth Evening News reported that the magnificent steam and motor yachts moored at Gosport by their wealthy owners had been requisitioned by the Government to be equipped as minesweepers, (or was it submarine chasers?).

Volunteers from the local boating and yachting fraternity were invited to offer their services as crew members - as civilians, not Royal Naval sailors, albeit in Naval uniform and under the command of RN Officers. The pay, including a messing allowance, was astronomical, or so it seemed to me compared with the half-crown a week I was receiving as a pupil in my fathers office learning, without a great deal of enthusiasm, how to become an Architect.

It all sounded great fun so next day I paid the penny fare on the steam launch to Gosport, known locally as the Gosport Liner, which left from the jetty some one hundred yards from our front door, and presented myself aboard one of the Yachts. I was interviewed by an officer who, I am sure, detected the guilt I know I felt when I lied to him that I was over eighteen, resulting in a 'Don't call us we'll call you' parting. Had I been truthful and admitted my eighteenth birthday was only a fortnight away, it is very likely I might have become an Acting Able Seaman on a minesweeper and this would have been a very different story.

As I was leaving, to spend another penny to get back to Portsmouth, I met the son of an Isle of Wight boat-builder from whom my father had bought a houseboat. He was well known to me, a year or two older and a very experienced small boat sailor. Not surprisingly he was enlisted on the spot and survived the war with distinction, achieving the rank of Commander by the end of the war.

Our houseboat had been, (the past tense is unfortunately necessary for we were never again to stay in it,) a splendid structure surmounting an ancient hull securely fastened to the shore of Bembridge Harbour. It was optimistically named 'Wander Bird' and for my brother and me made possible the most wonderful summer holidays from school. Mother looked after us and Father made the tiresome journey, via ferry and train from Portsmouth, to spend each night, and, of course, the weekends with us. Sometimes, when the weather seemed settled, he would make the journey in the 'BOBIL', (derived from Bob, me and Bill, my brother) a comfortable four berth motor boat converted, at Father's instructions, from a clinker built harbour boat about twenty-five feet long. We had sailing dinghies, bicycles, youth and virtually nothing at all to complain about.

Father loved boats and had commissioned a new rather luxurious motor cruiser, to his own design, which was ready for it's maiden voyage at the outbreak of war. The maiden voyage was all we ever did, up the harbour to Portchester and back to the boat builder's yard where it was given a copper bottom before the Navy took it away. It was seen by a cousin serving in the Merchant Navy off the Gold Coast and that was the last we ever heard of it.

Having apparently failed to get into the Navy by the 'back door', I became eighteen and continued to scan the Evening News in the hope that I might find some other way of getting afloat in a small boat at Government expense. Actually enlisting and then having to be trained for something at which I considered myself to be fully competent and able to rank as an expert at the drop of a hat was a tiresome business.

One day this turned up:-

AIR-SEA RESCUE LAUNCHES
CREWS WANTED.
Volunteers with small boat
experience call at the RAF
recruiting office in Victoria
Buildings Southsea.

I cut out the advertisement and at the first opportunity, without telling my parents, went along to the Victoria Building, which up to now I had only known as the Victoria Cinema, or local 'flea pit'. Sure enough, around the back were offices on several floors, including a Recruiting Department of the RAF. I was welcomed by a man in uniform with sergeant's stripes who showed interest in the advertisement but was entirely ignorant of any such requirement, or of any authority for the placement of the article in the paper, let alone the involvement of his recruiting office. He would, however, go and see the officer, who, in turn, was most agreeable and asked if I had ever considered joining the RAF as aircrew.

I had, very briefly, thought about flying but was under the impression that flyers were superior beings mysteriously selected by an almost Almighty. I never dreamt you could go and say 'I would like to fly an aeroplane' and be taken seriously. However I was prepared to change my mind to the extent that, perhaps, I might be one of those superior beings after all.

Flying had, in fact, fascinated me ever since the time my brother and I had been strapped, with the belt from someone's raincoat, into the front cockpit of a Westland Widgeon. It was piloted, and I believe owned, by Mr. Harold Penrose, the chief test pilot with Westland's at Yeovil, a friend and neighbour of my Aunt with whom we were staying at the time. The aeroplane was a high wing, open cockpit, two-seater monoplane and we were particularly cautioned not to put our arms over the side and touch the very hot exhaust pipe.

I have since designed and built model aeroplanes as a hobby and am gratified to recall that some actually flew. I did not build kits because then I would have to share the credit for any success achieved. There was, and still is, a great deal of satisfaction in designing and building something that actually works as intended. If it doesn't work you don't have far to look to know who the damn fool is.

So when the officer asked if I'd thought about flying, I replied, 'No not really but it doesn't seem a bad idea'. A doctor was produced to check my physical (or could it have been mental?) condition. The officer then asked many questions, one of which has stayed in my memory. He asked me to solve $(a-b)^2$ the answer to which, being fresh from school, I knew but still managed to produce the wrong answer. He did not appear in the least concerned and said something like - 'We need people of your education as Observers'. Then, sensing my disappointment that I was not going to be a Pilot, went on – 'The Observer, or Navigator is the brains of the crew and is shortly to be considered the Captain of the aircraft.' He was half right. Observers never did become the Captain of the aircraft.

I was given a railway warrant to go to Uxbridge in about a week. I had been a boarder at school and in the OTC and was not, therefore, completely unfamiliar with the goings on in military type establishments, or even with the discomfort of a bed made of very hard stuffed cushions, known as biscuits. Their sole virtue seemed to be the tidy pile they made when placed one upon the other for the daily barrack room inspection.

I remember little of that trip to Uxbridge, except that we were sworn in, en-masse, chanting out the words read aloud by someone or other, and that the discomfort of the night was made worse by some of the older rookies who, I suspect, were making the most of an unfamiliar experience by playing cards, very noisily, all night. I recall a large fat young man, with an expensive complexion, who came from the doctor's room complaining indignantly that they had found traces of urine in his alcohol.

I was given my service number and dog tags to wear round my neck on a piece of string. They also gave each of us a silver lapel badge to tell those who approached close enough that the bearer was a member of the RAFVR (Royal Air Force Volunteer Reserve). I was proud of my little badge and wish I had been as dishonest as some of my colleagues who pretended to have lost theirs and no doubt have them to this day.

We were then all sent home and told we would be sent for when required.

CHAPTER 2

War Damage Commission.

After the excitement of being sworn in, without actually becoming anything different, the fact had to be faced that a state of war was not at all a good thing for the practice of Architecture. I recollect producing drawings for a few Air Raid shelters, measuring basements and designing a strengthening structure sufficient to carry the building above should it be knocked over by a bomb. It should not be supposed that we, or others in our profession, had this sort of expertise at our fingertips. There were government publications concerned with 'Air Raid Precautions' covering all such matters with, if my memory is not at fault, remarkable competence and forethought.

Father became employed by the War Damage Commission, administered, at that time, by the District Valuer and I was taken on as a sort of office boy with fairly modest duties like checking the, already opened, mail to ensure the contents of each envelope had been completely removed. I also operated the incredibly primitive Gestetner where, instead of winding a handle, it was necessary to squirt ink upon a flat plate before attacking it with a small rubber roller to ensure it was covered with ink of a uniform thickness. I usually succeeded in adding numerous blots, blobs, smears, fingerprints or other imperfections to the intended document, not to mention returning home impersonating a Black and White Minstrel.

The first 'casualties' of the Balloon Barrage in Portsmouth were not marauding German aircraft but my brother and me. Whilst freewheeling on our bicycles down the steepest hill in Southsea, (a slope of about 1 in 40) we were so intent on admiring the balloons flying high above the Common that we failed to notice that our 'flight paths' were converging. My pedal went through the spokes of my

Brother's front wheel and we became airborne, resulting in somewhat bent and bruised bikes and bodies.

Driving a car in the Blackout was not too bad when you could see the curb, but half way across a large road junction was like being in limbo. I once had to abandon the car to go in search of the curb. I was to experience the same feeling sometime later in an aeroplane, without the option of that same solution.

Our house had a roof top balcony, and being five stories high enjoyed a splendid view, across to the Isle of Wight, and over most of the city, including the dockyard wharves, alongside which were the battleships, cruisers, destroyers and other warships of the Royal Navy. On one occasion, soon after the Air Raid Sirens had sounded, we went up on the roof to see what was happening. A large formation of some twenty or thirty German bombers came in from the East, not very high, perhaps six or seven thousand feet, presumably heading for the dockyard where there were a large number of warships presenting a very enticing target. The seemingly tranquil scene was suddenly interrupted by a roar of noise and the sky in front of the formation turned black with shell bursts from the warship's Pom-Poms. It was a very dramatic sight, and, it appeared, the Germans thought so too, for the whole lot turned about and, apparently, went home. It was not always to be thus. Portsmouth suffered severely from bombing, both by day and night, much of it while I was still at home. I clearly remember seeing the Guildhall like a giant Roman Candle, flames squirting out of the clock tower, and the rest of the building a seething mass of flame; likewise the Harbour Station.

It was not unusual on returning from a visit to the Cinema that I would have to find an alternative way home, or sometimes pick my way over the newly shattered glass and other debris which a short time before had been someone's home. During one of the raids our two sailing dinghies were destroyed when the building where they were stored was burnt to the ground.

It was, apparently, not a simple matter to take on an Office Boy in the District Valuer's office. The difficulties associated with persuading the Treasury to part with his wages were nearly insurmountable. It was about three weeks before I was paid, but the ten pounds was wealth beyond my wildest dreams. My girl friend was amazed and impressed when I turned up in a taxi to take her to a dance at the Clarance Pier that evening and, subsequently, took her home in another.

One of my duties as office boy was to go around to the various Centres in the City and collect, wheedle or steal from them, the forms people had to fill in to obtain compensation for bomb damage. These forms were in very short supply and it says a great deal for my powers of persuasion, charm or downright dishonesty, that our Centre, (it was after all the Head Office) always had a sufficient supply. That is until some hopeful from another Centre came to us with a sad story of how they had run out, when we would deny having any at all.

A bicycle was my only means of transport and because it was mine, I was paid three pence a mile. On one occasion I was returning with a stack of looted forms when some road hog failed to see me joining the main road. What is more, he also failed to stop for at least twenty feet after scooping me up onto his near-side front mudguard, where I sat looking at him through the windscreen grasping my bent bike in my left hand and holding it clear of the road. I felt rather sorry for the driver who was as white as a sheet and who, it might be argued, was not entirely to blame. I dismounted from his mudguard, examined his car for scratches, reassured him that there were none and sauntered nonchalantly away pushing my bike and hoping he would remain in his state of shock long enough for me to get safely away. The bike only needed the pedal crank bending back away from the frame.

Sometime about then a letter came from the Air Ministry to tell me there was very little likelihood of them wanting to start my training as aircrew for some time yet. Whilst I was welcome to stay on the reserve until they did want me, I could, if I wished, opt to pass the time as an Airman engaged on General Duties, such as Airfield Defence. This, though obviously not what I wanted, sounded better than being a wealthy office boy. At least I would be in uniform and Airfield Defence, with visions of machine guns and brave deeds, sounded a great deal better than exploding tubes of Gestetner ink. The offer was accepted, a Railway warrant turned up and I set off for Babbacombe, taking the minimal amount of luggage specified in the instructions attached to the Warrant.

By some miracle of confused administration I never did any Airfield Defence, or any other kind of General Duties. I later discovered from some who did, that these were euphemisms for cleaning out the latrines, and other lowly tasks. No, I am happy to relate my arrival in Babbacombe on the 11th October 1940 was the beginning of my training as an Air Observer.

CHAPTER 3

Reception and I.T.W.

After the first night in Babbacombe, spent in a guesthouse and paid for by the RAF, all the new recruits assembled in the car park of a Hotel. We were welcomed into the Air force and made aware, by he who did the welcoming, that there was some considerable doubt, in his mind, as to what the Royal Air Force was coming to. He instructed all those who had been selected to be trained as Observers to line up on the right, and those who were to be Pilots on the left. This was not only the first intimation that maybe we were not going to fire machine guns at German Bombers, but also left me, even to this day, speculating on what might have happened if I had joined the left group rather than the right. I am sure there was no documentation for anyone to check whether we had joined the correct group. They were relying on our honesty and ignorance, and I was too honest and too ignorant, for I would still have preferred to be a Pilot in spite of the blarney of the Recruiting Officer.

We were billeted in hotels, issued with uniforms and all the other kit, and then subjected to our first Kit Inspection to make sure everything we should have, we did have. An afternoon was spent cleaning buttons and boots and blancoing webbing etc. I was given a good tip on new brass buttons - to pour on a liberal amount of Brasso and then set light to it, thus burning off any corrosion resisting treatment or lacquer put there by the manufacturer. Another was to heat a spoon to as near red hot as possible and then, with the hot spoon, burnish the toecaps of your new boots. These two very useful tips nearly resulted in the Hotel being burnt down.

Our new uniforms were devoid of all insignia, except for a white flash in our forage caps to show we were Trainee Aircrew Cadets, not common or garden Erks or AC Plonks. We were very proud of our flashes and rushed off to the nearest photographer to have a picture taken to send back home. Rushing into the town presented us with a new hazard. We had been given a lesson on saluting and now every time an officer loomed up you either; saluted him, took a consuming interest in the nearest shop window or quickly crossed the road. As future experience was to teach me most of the officers were well aware of, and very grateful for these evasive tactics. They were, for the most part, rather new themselves, and the older hands were very bored with having to return the fascinating variety of salutations they were receiving from nearly half the population of Babbacombe, composed of ever-changing intakes of brand new Aircrew Cadets.

We were assembled in, what had been, the Drawing Room of the Hotel one sunny summer afternoon either waiting for or recovering from the effects of having large needles forced, not always gently, into arms and bottoms. They either draw out blood or squirted in some innocent looking fluid destined to cause considerable discomfort in the next few days.

The needle sticking procedure was carried out in an adjoining room, out of sight of the potential victims, though it did seem a little tactless to allow the recently treated patient to return past those waiting to find out what was going on. Most of us managed to survive without due hurt to ourselves or our dignity, but one fellow, who might reasonably have been supposed a good match for Joe Louis or Frank Bruno, came from the adjoining room with a glazed look on his face. He declined the help that was offered, muttering that he was quite alright, he only needed a little fresh air and would go out and sit in the garden. He walked carefully across the room towards the open French doors, gaining confidence at each step, only to miss the opening by a good three feet and collide with the wall. He was led gently outside to sit upon a low wall and give a fairly realistic imitation of 'The Thinker' by Rodin.

Before leaving Babbacombe I was not the only one to purchase a steel pocket mirror in a leather case, to be kept in the left-hand breast pocket of my uniform tunic. A newspaper story told of the rear gunner whose life had been saved by just such a mirror deflecting a potentially fatal bullet. I still have that mirror, having carried it, in that pocket, throughout my time in the Air Force.

Next came Newquay , and my promotion to Leading Aircraftsman (LAC). This, unfortunately, did not set me above my fellows for they all received the same preferment. We were given a pair of arm badges depicting a propeller to denote our new rank and these were sewn on with varying degrees of skill, at the Beachcroft Hotel, my new home, on top of the cliffs. I had a splendid room, complete with hot and cold running water, on the second floor looking out over the Bristol Channel. The snag was that I had to share it with two other characters during the next five or six weeks. The quality of the furnishings fell well below that of the room, with its three iron bedsteads and the, by now familiar, three-piece biscuit mattresses. It nevertheless became a comfortable and peaceful billet - after we put an end to the raids mounted by the occupants of a nearby room. They thought it great fun to visit us in the middle of the night to tip our beds over leaving us, half awake, on the floor, under the bed. They did not think it so funny when we did it to them. Anticipating a revenge visit, we bought screws and fixed the beds to the floor. Some nights later the revenge raid was a complete failure and the owners of three strained backs returned painfully and unfulfilled to their own room.

On the second day we were issued with full flying kit and items of equipment not received at Babbacombe. In the afternoon there was to be the inevitable kit inspection resulting, for me at any rate, in two memorable happenings. In the room next to ours some character decided his flying kit would be displayed to best advantage if it was stuffed with pillows and clothed to resemble a fully clad airman reclining on his bed. He made a very fine job of it, even the face was utterly realistic with none of it visible behind the oxygen mask, goggles, and the all-enveloping leather helmet with its great bulbous ear pieces. These were to contain the earphones, or in this case the ends of the Gosport tubes forming the speaking tube type inter-com used in a Tiger Moth or similar aircraft.

We did not see what happened when the Inspecting Officer, preceded by the Sergeant, entered the room, but we did hear something like this:

"Atteen-shun! Stand by your beds!" Short pause. "GET UP THAT MAN!" By this time the Officer had entered the room and in more cultured tones inquired of the sergeant "Why is that man not standing up and why is he dres....." the voice died away as the truth sank in. The subsequent conversation, as overheard, was decidedly one sided, leading us to conclude that the humour of the episode, found by the majority to be considerable, was entirely lost upon the Officer and even more so upon the Sergeant.

They then came to our room to find it in immaculate condition, but by now eagle eyed to discover the slightest imperfection they pounced with glee upon the unhappy fact that I did not have a Ration Bag. I had no idea what a Ration Bag might be, but to lose one appeared to be akin to treasonable sabotage. The fact that I had never been issued with one was no excuse for losing it. Next day I trembled before the Flight Sergeant who filled out a form in triplicate and hit it three times with a rubber stamp. Deaf to my protestations of never having been issued with the confounded thing he callously told me the cost of the item would be deducted from my pay.

Our Flight Commander, a Flying Officer who had escaped from school mastering not many months before, and would never fly anything except a desk, countersigned all three copies with visible disapproval as if to say 'what on earth is the Air Force coming to?' He directed me to the Wing Commander, whose office was in a five-star hotel and who was, as is so often the case, charming, friendly and even sympathetic. He too counter-countersigned the form in triplicate. I picked up my stamped, triple signed form, in triplicate, and anticipating bankruptcy, took it to the stores where a bored Corporal glanced at it, went to a shelf and threw on to the counter a little cotton bag about eight inches by six with a string. I had to sign for it, in triplicate I dare say, and on inquiring was told the cost was a penny halfpenny. It is things like this that inspire a reluctant respect, and even admiration, for the British Bureaucratic system. It makes a lot of sense when considered in the context of the Sergeant Pilot who lost his greatcoat, quite an expensive item, so he carefully crashed an aeroplane, made sure it burnt, and claimed his coat had also been burnt with the aircraft. He received a new coat, at no cost, and a deal of sympathy and congratulations for his lucky escape!

It was by now November and early morning parades took place on a car park at the other end of the cliff top road. The march to get there in the dark could be quite hazardous. With a strong wind blowing in from the sea and a rubberised cape with ambition to become a sail, it was quite difficult to stay upright, let alone steer anything but a very erratic course. Two oil hurricane lamps, white at the front and red at the back, carried by the unfortunates on the outside corners of the squad did not inspire great confidence. They were not very bright and, most of the time, were covered by the flapping capes. One of the many advantages of being average, normal height became apparent in this situation. Normal people were placed in the middle of a squad and the taller freaks were at the front and back. This was achieved by some ingenious forgotten manoeuvre, starting with a line-up - tallest on the left, shortest on the right, which was carried out at the beginning of each posting. You kept that position all the time you were there.

Marching normally behind inconsiderate people with abnormally long legs made keeping up very difficult. One day, on the way back to our hotel, I conferred with the other two in our file who were equally fed up with having to split themselves in the attempt to keep up. We decided to reduce the length of our stride to the normal and watched with interest as a gap developed, and steadily increased, between the front portion of the flight and the part, now led by our file. It was quite some time before the Corporal, who was up with the front of the flight, looked around to find he was now in charge of a much smaller flight than he remembered starting out with.

"Flight halt!" he cried, which it did, including us for we were still within hearing distance. He came back to enquire, in fairly picturesque language, what it was we thought we were doing, where it was we thought we were going, and why had he been inflicted with such a mob of horrible people? With great respect it was explained to him how difficult it was for average sized people, however horrible, to keep up with the freaks in the front files. He was not an unreasonable man, apart from being over six feet tall so, muttering something about a disease associated with ducks, he sorted things out. Henceforth the front files marched somewhat stiltedly, as if their feet had invisible leg irons, whilst the middle of the flight looked smart, normal, and natural.

Having been in the OTC at school, the 'Left Right, Left Right! Halt! About Turn!' business was no stranger to me and I had, while taking my Certificate 'A', developed quite a good Parade Ground voice. If the truth be known the voice was a great deal better than the knowledge required to know what it ought to be saying, but this was a small matter only known to myself. I did not allow it to inhibit my willingness to boss around my colleagues when given the opportunity. And so it happened one day, for a reason long ago forgotten. I was bellowing out orders for the Squad (I seem to remember it was more properly called a Flight) to march up and down, delaying the 'about turn' until it seemed inevitable they would go on into the ditch, and enjoying myself enormously. An officer, attracted by the professional quality of my parade ground voice, came to congratulate me, but spoiled the effect by criticising my stance. Apparently I should not have been sitting on the wall, swinging my legs, quite obviously at my ease, and thoroughly enjoying the corrupting influence of absolute power.

Here it was we were introduced to the mysteries of the Vickers gas operated machinegun and its more modern counterpart the Browning. Their mechanisms are rather different but both invoke the standard function of having the 'firing pin strike the detonator, causing the ignition of the propellant, thereby encouraging the bullet to nip smartly up the barrel, hotly pursued by the gasses'.

Sometimes we played softball on the lovely empty beaches. I am not sure why it was not cricket but I suppose the equipment had come with some American, or Canadian, comforts for the troops. Someone, fortunately, knew the rules, rather like 'rounders', from which it may well have been derived.

Not so good was another idea - that we should go on a cross-country run. This turned out to be moderately interesting. Not having taken part in such an event before I took the precaution of bringing some money. A few of us found a Pub not far from the hotel and enjoyed the scrumpy until it seemed time to hitch a lift back on a passing lorry. We were dropped about a hundred yards short of the hotel thereby arriving convincingly breathless.

A guard was mounted outside the front entrance of the hotel at night. We all took it in turn to be on guard duty and spent the night in a room adjacent to the entrance, from where one did a stint, standing outside with an unloaded rifle, shouting at anyone turning up - 'Halt who goes there?' We hoped that the person would reply 'Friend!' so that you could say 'Advance friend and be recognised'. Inevitably a complete stranger would appear, undoubtedly one of the other two hundred inhabitants of the hotel you had not yet met. So, with complete confidence, and remembering the rifle was empty, you said - 'Pass friend'.

My parents had moved from our house at the mouth of Portsmouth Harbour to be out of the way of the bombing and at the same time allow the Navy to take it over as a billet for the WRNS (Wrens). Mother and Father, together with an Aunt and Uncle, had moved into a remote farmhouse in the Hampshire countryside some ten or twelve miles to the North of Portsmouth. It was very difficult to find, as I discovered when coming home for Christmas leave and having to rely on buses to the nearest village, from where a telephone call summoned Mother to come and fetch me.

It was a Christmas memorable mostly for being thoroughly splendid in every way including, with some reservations, a bicycle journey of some eight or nine miles to take a girl friend to the pictures. Coming back in the dark I found that the farmhouse had been moved from the lane I remembered and also from the one I thought it might have been in if it hadn't been in the first one. The trouble with wrong lanes is that you have to travel their full length before finding it is not the one you want and then having to return the full length to start looking for another one. It was exceedingly late and I was exhausted when I eventually arrived to be greeted by my very anxious parents.

Our ITW (Initial Training Wing) days were now over and on return to Newquay it was not long before we packed our kit, boarded trucks one freezing January morning and were taken to a railway station, to continue freezing until the train arrived some time later. We bade farewell to the Officers and NCO's who suddenly seemed quite likable, and were now facing the fearsome prospect of another intake just like we had been six weeks ago, but probably not so agreeable! We now knew our training was to continue in Canada and I expect someone knew how we were to get there. We had to wait and see.

CHAPTER 4

On the Atlantic.

The train stopped late in the afternoon at Wilmslow in Cheshire where there was a large Transit Camp. I do not believe it served any other purpose, but I could well be mistaken. It was not the sort of place to be remembered with affection. The heating arrangements consisted of iron stoves of minimum quantity and quality, with tin flues rising from the top of the stove and disappearing in a very loose fit through a hole in the roof. There were two of these in each hut, a hut being some sixty or seventy feet long by thirty feet wide and made of wood, with no insulation. The stoves were not lit when we arrived. Paper and kindling were eventually found, coke sprinkled on top and flames started rising after ignition, but not up the flue. In no time the room was full of smoke and smelling warm without a single degree rise in temperature.

Eventually a semblance of a fire was produced. An extroverted character triumphantly produced a chair and with much exaggeration, to prove we were now comfortable, opened a book and sat back placing his feet on the stove – which promptly caused the chimney to collapse and fall across the room, narrowly missing the culprit and, fortunately, everyone else. The damage to the tin flue was considerable, and the products of combustion were now exclusively within the hut. So the fire was decanted to the other stove, no-one was allowed to put their feet on it, and we all went to bed, that being the only place to keep warm.

The Airman's Mess was enormous and similarly heated, but with larger stoves. These were kept nearly, and sometimes actually, red hot, in which condition they were very convenient for making instant toast, thereby producing an agreeable smell and a feeling of warmth when you managed to push your way to the stove. My only other memory of Wilmslow transit camp was of utter boredom. (When visiting Wilmslow, the town not the Camp, some fifty years later it turned out to be a very pleasant place.)

Another train took us on to Greenock, or it might have been Gourock. (Both places were mentioned and I have never been sure.) We lined up on the quayside to await embarkation on a tender, which was to take us out to a large liner a couple of hundred yards off shore. A whisper went around suggesting the first ones on board would be put in the hold and when that was full the remainder would be put in cabins, starting in the tourist class and working up to first class. There was no attempt to get us in any sort of order so I ingeniously worked my way to the back of the queue and eventually arrived on the s.s. 'Duchess of York' - to find the rumour contained a large element of truth and an even larger element of inaccuracy. The filling up was started from the cabins down, and I finished up deep down in the hold.

Hammocks had to be collected from a hold in the stern of the ship, accessed via vertical ladders. On arriving at the bottom there were, as promised, great piles of hammocks and other necessities for sleeping in the bowels of a ship. I heard voices from the other side of a bulkhead and went to investigate, hoping to find a better way of going back with my hammock than up the vertical ladders. The people on the other side of the bulkhead were trying to settle into a greatly inferior hold to ours and I pleasantly mentioned to one of them that I didn't think much of their accommodation. He looked blank and muttered something in a foreign tongue. I had already thought there was something odd about them, now I realised I was amongst a batch of German prisoners, also on their way to Canada, and somewhat anxious about the whole business. They were under the impression that all ships in the Atlantic were being sunk by 'U' boat torpedoes, a thought that had also occurred to us! I returned the way I had come.

There were lots of beams, hooks, pipes and rods from which to hang a hammock. Finding two such fixings at approximately the correct distance apart was a little more difficult, particularly if you happened to be fussy as to whether you slept fore and aft or athwartships. My hammock finished up fore and aft, with one end tied to a large steel beam and the other around a small rod, about one-inch in diameter, a little springy to be sure, but this would almost certainly add to the comfort. I discovered, a lot later and when it no longer mattered, that the rod was an element of the mechanism to close the watertight doors in the bulkhead in an emergency. Had there been such an emergency, or even a practice, then either nothing would have worked because the rod was a trifle bent, or the hammock would have been wound up around the rod and I would have been ejected to the steel deck some six feet below.

Generally there is nowhere to put things when your home is a hammock, except for the deck beneath it. The only reason likely to prevent the occupant from landing on his own possessions is if his neighbour, bent double and trying to find his own place, had kicked it into someone else's patch for him to land on. I was fortunate for alongside my hammock just below the deck-head was a large, square section of ventilation duct with enough room above it for all my possessions to be placed. Included with my things was a large, very precious, slab of just purchased chocolate. Waking on the first morning and deciding to lay in a little and enjoy a piece of this rare delicacy I reached up and found only a sticky puddle of molten chocolate. During the night the heat had been turned on and was distributed through my duct shelf.

The ship had been victualed in South Africa and we were able to buy, without coupons or other forms of rationing, such luxuries as chocolate, and tobacco. The only available brand of tobacco and cigarettes was called 'C to C'. On the tin, with a suitable illustration, you were informed this stood for 'Cape to Cairo' (it was that famous!), but was more commonly thought to stand for 'Camel to Consumer'.

Next morning the s.s. *'Duchess of York'* set sail down the Clyde and that was a truly beautiful sight as the mountain tops and heather turned red in the rising sunlight. Two or three miles out into the Irish Sea the ship stopped and other merchant ships began to gather around to form a convoy. A signal light started flashing from the shore and seizing this as a opportunity to practice our hard learnt Morse Code a friend, who was good at such things, read the lamp whilst I, who was quite competent to do so, wrote the letters down as he called them out. We supposed the message might be in code but it was in clear language and read, amongst other things - *'Return to Gourock'* (or Greenock). And that is what happened. All the ships turned around and went back whence we had come.

Next morning was more as one might expect a January morning on the Clyde to be like. There was nothing to be seen of the banks and braes as we set sail again for the Atlantic Ocean to join with a large convoy and its escorts bound for sunnier climes, it seemed, as we went steadily southwards towards the Azores. With great common sense an order was given for greatcoats not to be worn on the morning muster now that the weather was so warm. Unfortunately this seemed to exhaust the reservoir of common sense. A few days later when we left the convoy and were approaching (what felt like) the North Pole the order remained in force. By then the majority of us were not feeling our usual happy selves. Most were queasy and many rather ill, nothing like as ill as we were to become, but sufficiently so as not to give a damn about some stupid order requiring one to freeze by forbidding the wearing of greatcoats. So the majority wore their coats, others followed, and the order was either rescinded or failed by default, I do not remember which and none of us cared.

We were alone after leaving the convoy except for a single escort - the battleship HMS *'Ramillies'*. Northern mid-Atlantic was reached at the same time as the biggest storm that ocean had ever experienced. If this fact is not recorded by those whose duty it is to take note of such things, then it can only be because they were not there, or was it a matter of strict security? It was so bad that 'Ramillies' could make no progress at all and unhappily played at being a submarine, whilst the 'Duchess of York', creaking and groaning, lay hove-to and allowed us to be observers as the bows of the battleship repeatedly disappeared into a succession of monstrous waves. When a wave reached the middle of the ship the bows came clear of the water, and the propellers were clear at the stern, which explained its inability to make any progress. This went on for four of the most uncomfortable days it had ever been my lot, up to that time, to experience.

We felt sorry for the poor devils cooped up inside the battleship but I suspect they were more comfortable than we were. Whereas we rose, fell, rolled and crashed at each enormous wave they appeared to stay more or less level and go straight through whatever came at them. None of them were to be seen outside, unhappily lining the ship's rails, as we were. It has to be significant that two large targets, a battleship and a liner, stayed in the same place for four days in mid- Atlantic without being attacked by submarines. I suspect it was more comfortable for them well below the surface.

It is not easy to convey the additional utter misery from looking over the side of a ship rising and falling some thirty feet as we bashed into each watery mountain, producing a mass of bubbles, which remained completely stationary relative to the side of the boat, thereby clearly indicating a complete lack of progress.

The s.s. 'Duchess of York', they now told us, (it would have made not the slightest difference had they told us earlier,) was built for Canadian Pacific Railways especially to negotiate the St. Lawrence River. To do this a flat bottom was essential and, so they say, worked very well in the river but not at all well in mid Atlantic in January in the roughest sea ever experienced. For this reason it was fondly referred to as the *'Drunken Duchess'* long before we might have been tempted to call it something less endearing.

There was a large Dining Room euphemistically called a Mess (or should that be the other way about?) where they offered an unending supply of meat and two veg. and tripe and onions. I had never met Tripe and Onions before and there was no way I was going to change that happy state of affairs, nor was I going to renew my acquaintance with Meat and Two Veg. I settled for a diet of bread and butter with tea and thus dis-enjoyed six meals a day, three up and three down. I was fascinated to see the bread being buttered by covering the counter with sliced bread and then, with a large whitewash brush, painting on the butter (which was kept at a suitable temperature). As the butter became cold so its thickness increased, unfortunately I did not feel up to exploiting this.

To alleviate the boredom I read, and enjoyed, Raphael Sabatini's 'Sea Hawk', which upset no one, but this was not the case when three or four of us found our way on to the forecastle. Each time it seemed that a wave would come crashing on board we fled to get out of the way, either to something high, like a winch, or for preference a ventilation duct inlet, which had not only been turned so to face away from the oncoming waves but had also been closed off horizontally. It was therefore possible to curl up inside, some four feet above the deck, and watch the wave, about a foot deep, go swirling across on its way to the scuppers. This was positively not boring. It was not very sensible, either, but above all it made the people on the Bridge rather cross. They conveyed this to us from a distance, so we disappeared before they could reduce the distance and were thereby never identified to suffer the consequences of our little adventure. After which I very likely returned to suffer meal number four - even numbers were always up!

One morning we awoke to find all motion had ceased. On reaching the deck we discovered that the ship was covered in snow and tied up alongside a pier in Halifax, Nova Scotia.

CHAPTER 5

Port Albert Ontario.

The train was one of those wonderful bell ringing monsters, until then only seen in pictures, and was to be home for a couple of days while it steamed and whoo-whooed its way to Goderich, Ontario, on the east shore of Lake Huron. It was a very comfortable journey with full waiter service, even for us lowly people. I don't think they had yet found out that you just didn't treat 'other ranks' like that. There were proper bunk beds made up for us when it was time to retire, meals were served to us at our seats on de-mountable tables, and such meals they were. They would have ranked as magnificent even if not being compared with tripe and onions; not to mention the reverse meal affliction! I remember being concerned that the black and sticky smuts from the engine seemed to get in everywhere and were particularly noticeable in the morning, on the no longer immaculate white sheets and on the faces of its passengers.

The train stopped many times at small towns. There were no stations, as we knew them, and the main street had little or no physical barrier between it and the railway lines. We mostly stayed on or near the train but the children, most of whom wore skates, came to investigate these strangers from another land. Having relieved us of as much British coinage as we were prepared to give, they would skate off down the snow packed surface of the street as if on an Ice Rink.

Goderich was, and is as I have recently been back to check, a pleasant and attractive town of moderate size, circular in plan with the streets radiating from the central Park like the spokes of a wheel. The Park, once a largish area of grass, trees, benches and a World War 1 cannon, is now much less of those things and a great deal more of a very large Court House/Civil Offices type building, most necessary no doubt but hardly an improvement. Not surprisingly, being on the shore of a very large lake, some of these radiating roads tended to be rather shorter than might normally have been expected. Someone, we were told, had dropped a Victorian clanger when sending the plans out from England. Goderich ought to have been in the middle of that part of Ontario, or at least the city plan should have been, and had it been where it should have been it would have been called Guelph. Being thus informed, it comes as no great surprise to find Guelph is a long thin town with a straight main street ideally suited to run parallel with the shore of the lake, which isn't there, it being about a hundred miles to the west.

In my opinion Goderich came out of this mistake very well. It not only has a story, but is aesthetically a great improvement on Guelph which, on the only occasion I went there, I found to be rather dull despite being named for the British Royal Family, before they had a good idea and changed their name to Windsor. Nowadays it is just about swallowed up in Toronto.

Ten or fifteen miles North of Goderich was an almost non-existent village on a small creek feeding into the Lake. Close by had been built RAF Station, 'Port Albert', (that being the name of the village,) complete with airfield and the base for No.31, Air Navigation School. This was to be our home for the next three months or so and where we became, No.34 Astro Course.

Here was quite the best place the RAF had found for us so far. Forget about hotels with three in a room, huts with wonky stoves, ships (most particularly ships) and even trains with waiter service. This place was brand new, some parts indeed were still under construction. The living quarters were large 'H' shaped blocks with the ablutions in the linking piece between the two barrack blocks, equipped with multiple shower cubicles and basins on tiled floors within tiled walls. The water was so hot there was a distinct danger of being scalded before one learnt to avoid the jet of steam, which usually preceded the water. The single-storey, well insulated, double-glazed timber-built barrack blocks were furnished with comfortable double-decker bunks generously spaced apart on polished maple strip flooring, which would have been better appreciated had it been someone else's responsibility to keep it clean and polished like a mirror.

Polishing could be made an interesting, and sometimes risky, chore by wrapping a concrete block in an old blanket and then hurling it the length of the block, as in the Scottish game of curling. This called for strength, skill and accuracy, all three attributes rarely being available at the same time.

The heating arrangements consisted of three automatic solid fuel stoves in each block. Each stove was about six feet cube and attended to once a day by an orderly, who filled the bunker and cleared away the ash. Everything else was done by electricity and thermostats, set so high that if you came in after doing anything energetic, (bear in mind the outside temperature was around ten or fifteen Fahrenheit or lower,) it was quite impossible to breathe. Out you had to go again until all panting was finished and the hot air could be persuaded into lungs accustomed to the sub-zero temperatures.

The food was perfectly marvelous. Each morning for breakfast there was every type of cereal, eggs, almost unknown at home, and the American style very thinly sliced bacon, including the rind, which one did not notice it being so thin. Bacon was also not too common at home although the Services did not do too badly with the tinned variety, usually served with tinned tomatoes. This bacon was a novelty and a very agreeable change but I think I still preferred the way it was done at home.

Having provided every imaginable creature comfort an 'other-rank' could possibly desire, they also provided aeroplanes of the Anson variety. This was a gentlemanly type of aircraft, slightly reminiscent of an airborne conservatory, being continuously, but certainly not double, glazed from about two foot six inches above the cabin floor up to the ceiling. This was most convenient for the practice of learning navigation. Even when lost you had a very good all round view of where it was you didn't know where you were.

I believe the Anson was designed to be the first monoplane to carry passengers for Imperial Airways but was rejected on account of its high landing speed, around seventy m.p.h. This was low by the standards of 1941 and ridiculously low compared with the landing speeds that became commonplace by the end of the war. It had two endearing characteristics. If the ailerons, that is the control surfaces at the ends of the wings by which the lateral levelness of the aircraft was maintained, or altered, were waggled up and down then the engines nodded in sympathy. Should the aircraft have just taken off, or was intending to land, and it became necessary to raise or lower the undercarriage, this was done by winding a handle situated and projecting from under the pilots seat. A great number of turns were necessary requiring considerable exertion. It was not a job to be sought after but at least it induced some bodily heat, except in high summer when it must have been quite grim, but by then I was no longer in Ansons so it no longer mattered. Because of the position of the handle it was possible for the Pilot to do the winding himself. It is unlikely, however, that this has ever been seen to be done because, had anyone been there to see, he would instantly have qualified for the job.

The less endearing features of the Anson were its total lack of insulation, coupled with a heating system of which I remember nothing. This was very likely because it had none. It also had toilet facilities of remarkable simplicity, consisting of a rubber tube, not much more than a half-inch in diameter, projecting from the bottom of the fuselage at one end, and connected to a funnel at the other. It was not a large funnel, perhaps three inches diameter at the widest, and clipped to a convenient post alongside the wireless operator's seat towards the back of the cabin. It was not often used, for some very good reasons: (1) The rubber tube always seemed to face into the slipstream and the air coming in usually overcame anything trying to get out. (2) It took a long time, to say nothing of the effort, required to prepare, or even think of, using it when wearing sufficient clothing to stay alive in an aircraft where the temperature was probably ten degrees lower than outside, where it was already way below zero. And, if having overcome all obstacles, fluid entered the funnel it would freeze before reaching the other end of the rubber tube, even if it did, for once, happen to be pointing backwards.

I retain the happy memory of watching an Erk, whose job it was to go into the recently landed aircraft and clean out the cabin, walking cheerfully away towards a source of warmth grasping the outer end of the rubber tube, having detached the whole contrivance. He was swinging the funnel around his head, confident that the frozen contents, in this case the leftovers resulting from an attack of air-sickness, would stay firmly put until he arrived at wherever he was going.

CHAPTER 6

Air Navigation School.

We were taught in large comfortable classrooms. For the most part our class stayed in the same room and for many of the subjects we had the same tutor, a big rather imposing blond Flight Lieutenant of the regular RAF. He was a qualified Pilot and Navigator and quite the most important person we had ever come across. He very soon made it apparent he could be perfectly agreeable but that would rather depend on us.

I still have the exercise books, with all the notes of the different subjects we were meant to assimilate. The subjects covered were surprisingly many. Apart from the obvious knowledge required to persuade an aeroplane to finish up where you wanted to go, there were such seemingly unconnected lessons as - Air Force Law, the Command structure of the RAF, Kings Regulations, detailed knowledge of the working of the flying instruments. Likewise the mechanisms of the innards of bombs, guns etc. and Air Force Medicine. I have always been mechanically minded so I rather enjoyed knowing about guns, bombs and instruments but it was difficult to conceive a situation where the knowledge might have a practical application either airborne or, presumably accidentally, on the ground.

The more obvious subjects were also rather numerous. Navigation covering Map Reading; Dead Reckoning, ('dead' as in deduced, not as in demised); Astro Navigation; Meteorology; Mathematics and Radio direction finding. Nothing to do with Navigation but conceivably very useful was Aircraft Recognition - taught by a Pilot who had flown a Hurricane in the Battle of Britain and could not conceive of a better fighter plane. He dismissed the Spitfire *as 'a rather pretty little aeroplane'*. Some of his other descriptions stay in my memory. The Skua – *'Not a very good aeroplane with a tail like a duck's arse'*. The Me.109 - *'Goes like a dose of weasel shit'*.

The Wellington – *'A portly aeroplane with ye olde Englishy windows.'*

Gremlinology, concerns, and is, the science of a strange little gnome like character, in whom we were all taught to have implicit belief. Nobody has ever seen a Gremlin, any more than anyone has seen an electric shock, but it is very certain that neither Gremlins nor electric shocks like people who do not believe in them. Gremlins can see by night, but have to use a dark lantern to see by day. They carry an umbrella to use as a parachute, which enables them to float around the clouds and hook it onto the wing tips of passing aircraft. The umbrella when it is rolled, works as the 1941 equivalent of a sonic screwdriver, familiar to all addicts of Dr Who.

They can get anywhere, some are good, but most are bad. They get into the compass and pull the needle round; into a sextant and move the bubble; into the wireless and eat away the insulation, to say nothing of bending cathode rays, turning dots into dashes and vice-versa.

They can make the wind blow in the opposite direction, move the aerodrome twenty miles sideways and when you do find it they are able to lower it twenty feet just as you touch down, or conversely raise it twenty feet just before you touch down. There is a reliable method of getting rid of Gremlins. A large number of Daily Mirrors must be collected into a big pile. Also required is an enamel chamber pot and a robust stick. The Daily Mirrors are then lit and when blazing fiercely the enamel Jerry must be beaten continuously. Gremlins cannot resist the sound of a beaten Jerry and the flames from Daily Mirrors are uniquely fatal.

Unhappily both good and bad Gremlins are attracted and destroyed. The good Gremlins do not like this, neither do the 'baddies' but one tends to be not too concerned about them. The surviving good ones, incensed at the destruction of their mates, change into bad ones and the surviving bad ones become even worse so you end up more disastrously than you began. It is probably not possible to assemble enough Daily Mirrors to consume all Gremlins, and if we did the world would be a sadder place with no one to take the blame. The best thing about Gremlins is their enthusiasm for taking the blame, it being similar to being mentioned in dispatches. The more successful they are the more blame they merit.

Gremlinology is not an exact science, there are many versions but I can only tell of the one I was taught, and remember, and there may well be some doubt about that.

In amongst all this learning business I achieved my ambition of being in command, of a flight quick-marching across the apron in front of a hanger, the only sort of parade ground provided, and halting them in the midst of an extensive area of ice. I was not the only one to enjoy the resulting chaos but I was in the minority.

Getting into Goderich along the gravel road at this time of the year could be fairly exciting. There was, of course, no gravel to be seen beneath the deep and hard packed snow, which behaved only marginally differently from a sheet of ice. The normal method of transport was a bus, which without chains, went carefully along at about fifty miles an hour. If the bus was missed there was almost always the chance of getting a lift in a car, van, or truck either of which tended to go rather faster than the bus. One time, whilst travelling in the laundry van, we passed a car stopped at the side of the road. A tow was offered and accepted but there was no rope. The laundry man had a good idea, why not use a wire coat hanger? Well why not? One was produced, as you might expect, without difficulty and hooked over the projecting ends of the opposing bumpers. This tended to bring the two vehicles rather close together. The man to be towed seemed not too convinced but the laundry man was full of reassurance, so off we went, slowly at first so as not to untwist the coat hanger, and then faster. When we were doing about seventy miles an hour the man in the car behind started to sound his horn. 'Must be something wrong', muttered our driver as he stopped and went back to discover the reason. 'Huh!' he grunted as he got back behind the wheel. 'Reckons we're goin' too fast and he don't like not being able to see what's out front.' No mention that being on a sheet of ice might have any bearing on the situation. We moved off again, more sedately this time, until, at the crest of the modest hill into Goderich, the coat hanger untwisted and we became free of our tow, who declined the offer to be re-connected having decided he could coast down the hill to the garage at the bottom. The laundry man went back to his van muttering that there were 'some folk you jest cain't please'.

I recollect nothing disagreeable about Goderich, quite the contrary in fact. My first ambition was to learn how to skate on ice and the man in the shop where skates were sold perfectly understood this, as he also saw that a low ranking airman might be embarrassed by cash flow problems. I told him I could only afford five dollars, either as a deposit or, hopefully, in full payment. I left his shop with a new pair of skates attached to boots plus a pair of long, thick, woolen socks, quite essential he said, thrown in as a free gift - all for five dollars. I was, and am, quite sure this was well below the true cost so I sang his praises to all my colleagues and I hope the business that came as a result made good compensation for his generosity.

Then there was the matter of the watch I didn't have. After the first payday I went to a jeweler in Goderich to purchase a completely reliable and accurate watch - at a cost of about a dollar. This was not as unreasonable as it sounds since it had been possible at home to buy a watch for around five shillings, which was not much more than a dollar at that time. Mind you, it was not always possible to get to sleep in the same room as the watch unless it was under a pillow and preferably on the other side of the room. The jeweler said he did have watches at around a dollar but the reliability and accuracy requirements were in doubt. One watch in particular took my fancy in the tray he showed me and I left the shop with it, having paid ten dollars deposit and a promise to return on successive pay-days to discharge the remainder of the debt, amounting to nineteen dollars fifty cents. This I duly did, he charged no interest and I wore that watch, occasionally renewing the strap, from five miles above the ground to five feet under water, for the next thirty years. It was still in perfect condition when my wife replaced it with an automatic Omega.

The skating rink was a large barn like structure down a side street from the central park. It was completely un-sophisticated, with a level floor, which was flooded each night, the outside doors were thrown wide and the next day's skaters had a splendid ice rink. I never became a competent skater. My determination to be able to go backwards resulted in my being able to skate better and faster backwards than forwards, but I never did learn how to stop. There was a public address system over which the Skaters Waltz was played continuously. Remember this was before the days of tapes and suchlike, so they must have had a room full of new records. We would go to watch the local teams playing each other at ice hockey where the rules, if any, tended to elude us but the broken sticks and blood resulting from the constant disagreements were well worth the entrance fee.

The Venus Restaurant provided meals and relaxation in comfort to the music of the Jukebox, a large and incredibly ornate contrivance of bright coloured translucent panels, lit up intermittently from behind. The best part was being able to see all the very complicated works. I suppose the Jukebox was the forerunner of the Disco, but not so noisy? It is surprising how often today we still hear the music that came out of that Jukebox in 1941.

After one evening of skating and feasting it began to snow very heavily and continuously. As soon as we became aware of this we rushed out to get the earlier bus, but it had already decided it was not going to risk it. So the local taxi firm was approached. 'Not likely!' they said, there was no way they were going to risk having to spend the night at Port Albert, should they get that far, or sleep in the car if they couldn't get back. Very conscious that we were on the verge of spending our first night AWOL (absent without leave) we telephoned the Guardroom and explained the situation, went to a local hotel and stayed the night. At the crack of dawn we went in search of a Taxi and followed the snow-plough back to Port Albert, where a summons awaited, requiring our presence before the Wing Commander. The possibility that we were going to be congratulated on our behaviour in the face of adversity soon evaporated. Somewhat unfairly, I thought, he gave us a sound ticking off for not having applied our recently acquired knowledge of meteorology to anticipate the blizzard!

When it thawed and the gravel came to the surface two things happened: large potholes and much mud appeared, into which the bus would stick and we had to get out and push. Where parts of the road had been concreted the slabs buckled upwards to produce monumental bumps. Notices were displayed on either side proclaiming the one word 'BUMP' and you ignored it at your peril and, usually, not more than once.

Being a round town, the townsfolk of Goderich liked to take their evening recreation driving around the central park, very slowly so as to be able to exchange the time of evening with their neighbours. (Unless they were teenagers in which case they drove much faster to impress their girl friends). Having been an enthusiastic, though unrecognised, poet for many years, I wrote a poem, quoted here exactly as it appeared on the front page of the camp journal, 'Compass News' No.6 of Volume 1, dated Saturday May 10th 1941.

GARDRICH.

(this being phonetically the way it
was pronounced locally)

When I first came to Goderich,
I heard the happy sound
Of lots and lots of motor cars
Just going round and round.

I really was intrigued,
To think that here I'd found
A Town whose occupation
Was driving round and round.

Since then I've been to cities
Where motor cars abound,
But I've yet to find another
Where the cars go round and round.

I've searched and searched with gusto
From Galt to Owen Sound,
But still can't find another place
Where cars go round and round.

I tried to hitch one Sunday,
But lo the dirty hound,
Had got as far as Goderich
Then went round and round and round.

Even when we're flying
High above the ruddy ground,
I still can see those blasted cars
Goin' round and round and ROUND

LAC. R.P.THOMAS.

I suppose it's not too bad if you don't linger too long. At least it made the front page - there are three other poems in the same edition and they are on inside pages! As an illustration of the sort of thing the Journal thought worth publishing:-

'*Dear Melting Pot,* (that being the name of the agony column) *How does Hitler manage to keep his arm stretched out, for hours on end, when reviewing his troops?*
A C Jenks.'
Answer:
'*It has been suggested that he has a patent gadget made of aluminium which fits inside his sleeve and clamps on the chest. Moreover it is worked by remote control. When the operator, some miles away, presses a button the arm flies up automatically. There are several fittings and accessories which he uses. The famous moustache is stuck on with glue. Also Hitler is completely bald. Lastly the voice which you hear really belongs to a ventriloquist for the Fuhrer is quite dumb.*"

It was possible to cover remarkable distances by hitch-hiking and it was a great deal cheaper than the train or bus. The money saved was spent, at least in the case of a friend and myself, in staying at the very best hotels. We could not afford to eat in them, but the local Drug Store or Chinese Restaurant was more than adequate, being at that time, one hundred percent better than its British equivalent. One Saturday afternoon I hitched approximately seventy miles to London (Ontario that is), went to the pictures and hitched back again with time to spare to meet the deadline of twenty-three fifty-nine hours. It had helped considerably to be lucky enough to be picked up by a Police Car on the outward journey. They had heard of the speed limit, but only for other people.

On some occasions when setting out on a forty-eight hour pass, and having no planned destination, I was picked up by people who invited me to stay the week end, or whatever, with them. I always accepted and thereby met some very charming families, but it was often difficult to find some common ground to form the basis of a conversation.   One time, having been picked up and accepted the invitation to go back home with my new found host, he, seeking a subject upon which to start a conversation, said something like 'I'm the President of the local association of Fruit Grower's Club'. That at any rate was what he turned out to be, but with the difficulties of the accent and the noise of the car I understood him to say he was the President of the local 'Association Footballer's Club'. The next five minutes or so witnessed a conversation of extreme and complicated non-understanding while we discussed the pros and cons of soccer, of which I understood very little and he nothing at all!

CHAPTER 7

Into the Air

When we first arrived, and for some time thereafter, the runways existed as a matter of faith. All that could be seen were long, straight, not too wide, stretches of hard packed snow flanked on either side by high banks of the same stuff. Some feet below these, as time was to prove, were tarmac runways. Until they were revealed the packed snow was kept clear of fresh snow falls by magnificent ploughs of the type that send vast plumes of snow soaring into the sky, and very beautiful it was in the bright sunshine.

The first flights came under the category of 'Air Experience', or something like that. We, the sprog trainees, duly experienced the sight of the ground from two thousand feet above it, the noise, the vibration and the oncoming signs of airsickness. Above all we experienced the cold that pervades mid Canada in February and is amplified by at least twenty percent in a draughty Anson moving at about one hundred and ten knots. We had to learn about knots because Ansons were used in Coastal Command and anything to do with the sea has to use nautical miles. When moving the speed is measured in knots, one knot being one nautical mile per hour. If you ever wish to appear knowledgeable in the company of Naval people it is only necessary to mention 'knots per hour' to establish your complete ignorance. For the purposes of navigation the nautical mile is a better measure of distance than the land mile because it bears a direct relationship to maps of whatever scale, being one minute of longitude at the equator.

After learning the basics of Navigation these were tested in the air, usually with considerable success. It was not difficult to map read in our part of Ontario which was well provided with towns, roads, railways and Lake Huron stretching North and South for hundreds of miles. But it was possible to get lost. Some of the exercises required one to navigate without a map, except for a piece cut from one showing about a one-mile radius with the airfield as centre. If everything was done properly, including the pilot flying accurate compass courses, all went well and on looking out of the window there was the airfield right where it should have been. On other occasions there wasn't anywhere recognisable, for instance, water in all directions. This could soon be solved by steering North East thereby being certain to hit the shore of the lake North of Port Albert and by flying South sooner or later you arrived home. If, however, the countryside was unrecognisable, then one headed South to a more heavily populated area, until a familiar town turned up or, best of all, a railway which would sooner or later have a station with a large name sign readable from a low flying Anson.

There were, of course, other ways of getting lost, such as flying above cloud, inattention and incompetence, but it says a great deal for the quality of our tutors that getting lost was never, in my experience, the cause of any serious mishap. This is not to say there were no accidents. I remember two at Port Albert, a mid-air collision in which a friend of mine was one of those killed, and another caused by engine failure, followed by a forced landing in which there were some injured.

Night flying was another kettle of fish altogether. It was not at all difficult provided one was allowed to use the same techniques as in daytime map reading. All the towns, and even farmhouses were lit up and although farmhouses seldom entered into the reckoning the lights of towns and villages made it easy to know your position. If there were no lights to be seen then it was odds on you were over the lake or so far north as to be way off any maps you had thought to bring along, and probably out of petrol anyway. The solution to the former was the same as in daylight, the latter could, at best, be quite embarrassing!

As the homecoming aircraft approached Port Albert a finger of light beckoned a friendly welcome, or more prosaically a powerful searchlight pointed vertically into the sky above the aerodrome to make as certain as possible that we did not miss it. It cost a great deal to train a navigator, to say nothing of the Anson and its Pilot and they just did not want to lose us.

Astro-navigation is a complicated and, in those days, an uncertain way of moving around in the dark. It required the measurement of the angle between a heavenly body and the horizon. The horizon from an aeroplane at night is in the wrong place, even if you could see it, which of course you can't because it's dark, so you use a sextant containing its own built in horizon in the form of a bubble, like that in a spirit level. The trick was to bring the star, or other heavenly object, via an ingenious optical system, visually into the centre of the bubble. Unfortunately an aircraft does not fly straight and level but follows a cyclic course completing each cycle in approximately two minutes. This confuses the bubble and for an accurate sight it is necessary to take a series of sights over two minutes and average the results.

The procedure for fixing the position of an aircraft by star sights is: (1) Identify the two stars you are going to use. There have to be two, because each will produce a line upon which you are - somewhere. If these lines cross then that is where you are. If they do not cross - start again. (2) Get your sextant, which should have some sort of averaging device. One kind had to be wound up and was semi-automatic, another had a large wheel engraved with degrees of altitude and a pencil arrangement which drew a line on the wheel each time the star was in the bubble and the Navigator pressed the lever. The middle of the bunch of pencil lines was the average of the sight and any rogue sights could be seen and omitted. (I much preferred the latter type.) (3) Poke your head out through the top of the aeroplane. Sometimes there was a perspex Astro-Dome capable of causing optical aberrations, if there was no dome you froze. (4) Take a careful note of the time to within a second, bearing in mind a minute is rather more than a mile. (5) Bring the star into the middle of the bubble, and press the button, as often as possible during the first thirty seconds and then change to the other star and do the same for one minute. Then go back to the first star for the last thirty seconds. The fiendish ingenuity of sandwiching the sights on one star between the sights on the other was to produce an average sighting of two stars both at the same time. (6) Take another note of the time and return to your table to do the calculations, or if a cloud had completely obscured the second star, or you had fallen over when the aircraft dropped a hundred feet in an air pocket - start all over again.

All these difficulties are compounded by the speed of the aircraft and the tedious mathematics which were required in those days, which sometimes meant that by the time you had done the sums you could have overshot where the place you wanted probably wasn't anyway. From my experience all this could be evaluated as follows:-

A good fix had an accuracy of about 1 mile.

A normal fix ......about 5 miles

A bad fix..........about 10 miles, or with a bit

of Gremlin trouble the wrong hemisphere.

Having become in such a short time an authority on Astro Navigation, and a published Poet, it is hardly surprising to find I had written another Poem. I cannot remember if this one was also printed in the Camp Journal. I believe it was, but it would seem I was becoming a trifle blasé and not bothering to save the publications.

<u>Astro</u>
Said Altair to Procyon,
If you care to look down there,
You will see some brave young airmen
About to take the air.

They intend to navigate my dear
By using you and me,
In conjunction with a bubble
And a book called A.N.T." (Air Navigation Tables that is)

So Altair smiled a mirthless smile
And said to Regulas,
"Move around a bit old man
And tell your friend Cirrus".

Cirrus thought the joke was huge,
And tho' a trifle stout,
Turned himself completely round
And put himself quite out.

Capella felt so tired,
She didn't want to play,
But if they all insisted,
Why, she'd change her S.H.A. (Siderial Hour Angle that is.)

One by one the stars were told
About the midnight frolics,
So when first Nav. shot Betel-geuse
All he got was Pollux.

There were books of star curves, the invention of a very clever man called Weems. I believe he was a Naval Officer, and his books certainly would seem to have been more use in a ship's cabin than in an aircraft in wartime. The trouble was that the curves were drawn in three colours, four if you count black, and one of these colours was red. There was nothing political about this, it was simply that the lighting at the Navigator's desk was also red and this made Mr. Weems's red star curve disappear entirely. The cleverness of these curves was that they represented the position line, that otherwise needed four figure logarithms and half a page of calculations to establish.

As Spring approached it was fascinating to see, from the air, day by day the snow line retreating to the North. I do not recollect any finite distance being noted but it must have been measured in miles per day. I do recall there was only a month between being able to walk on the frozen lake and being able to swim in it.

And so one day, having sat the necessary examinations, we all became competent, or near enough, Navigators and it was time to move on from No.31 Air Navigation School, Port Albert, and the friendly town of Goderich.

CHAPTER 8

Picton.

It was no great distance to Picton where we became members of No. 2 Squad, 19 Course, 31 Bombing and Gunnery School. Picton is a small Town in Prince Edward County, Ontario, on the coast of a deep inlet at the East side of a peninsular, (similar in shape and size to the Isle of Wight but more irregular) projecting into Lake Ontario about eighty miles East of Toronto. Again it was a splendid new RAF station only a few miles up a hill, out of the town.

By now it was summer and very hot, which was bad for sitting in a classroom, but not so when enjoying the swimming facilities. There were large sandy beaches and the little harbour and quay in the town where it was always possible to take a quick dip. Usually quick because the water was incredibly cold even in mid-summer. We were told that this was due to the great depth of Lake Ontario never quite allowing the water to recover from its frozen winter state. Without any perceptible tides in the lake the beaches did not get a good regular wash. There were storms, of course, and these tended to throw up large numbers of dead fish leaving them to litter the beaches in unending lines above the tide line where the storm waves had washed them.

Picton was no hive of activity. There was a Chinese Restaurant - where I was once charged twenty-five cents extra, a vast amount, for ordering fried tomato, with eggs, bacon and fried bread. It appears fried tomatoes were unheard of up to then to a Chinaman in Picton. His single thick slice of a large tomato covered in breadcrumbs and lightly fried was a disappointing alternative to Mother's whole, or half, tomatoes hot right through and squoodgy enough to spread over the fried bread.

The cinema did not open on Sundays and there was nothing to do - until a friend and I discovered religion. We were walking down the main street one Sunday when we heard the sounds of country style music coming from a church-like building. We turned smart right, went in and found it was indeed a Church of the Pentecostal persuasion. I am sure it was not their intention to provide entertainment to bored British airmen, but this is precisely what they managed on that, and many subsequent Sundays. The kind of diversions on offer included spontaneous (we assumed) prayers and confessions, of a personal nature, spoken out loud, but not always very clear, by members of the congregation. Thanks expressed by the Minister for the virtues of his congregation went something like this, very much shortened, version:

'Brother James has donated a hundred dollars, Praise the Lord, thank God, Alleluiah, Alleluiah, Alleluiah for Brother James'. 'Sister Martha has given fifty dollars, Praise the Lord, thank God, Alleluiah, Alleluiah, for Sister Martha.' 'Brother Will and Sister Ruth have given Five Dollars, Praise the Lord, Alleluiah, for Brother Will and Sister Ruth'. 'Sister Anna has given twenty five cents, Thank God for Sister Anna.'

Then there was the Hymn singing accompanied by a small enthusiastic band comprising, an accordion, fiddle, guitar, banjo and a saxophone. I expect there was a piano but it is not memorable. The Hymns were splendid, lots of rhythmic hand clapping to the, '...It's good enough for Father and it's good enough for me...' Clap, clap, variety. But best of all was the Sermon, not that we ever heard one right through as they tended to be very long and not always believable. I remember on one occasion leaving when we were assured by no less an authority than the Minister, speaking on behalf of God, that the '...Moon will turn to water and the resulting inundation will flood the world and wash away the sins of mankind'. This did not at all conform with our recent lessons in Astronomy and Meteorology and not wishing to be led astray from the teachings of our employer we quietly withdrew.

Best ever was the time when the Minister ascended to his pulpit and announced he had '... received a request to give a solo.' From beneath his voluminous black robe or cassock he produced a trumpet and proceeded to give a very competent and enjoyable solo performance. After which he, unfortunately, lapsed back into inventive sermonising. We usually put twenty-five cents into the collection plate, which, for my part, was better value than the poor substitute for a fried tomato in the Chinese Restaurant. It seemed remarkable to us that this Church was so well patronised by what had to be, judging by the large and expensive motor cars parked outside, many affluent members of the local community. After the sermon finished, most went home, but the more fervent went into the crypt to moan and groan into the small hours of Monday morning - so said the townsfolk and who were we to disbelieve them? We certainly never stayed to check.

Hitch hiking from Picton made going to Toronto hardly worthwhile, that city being so close, but there were other places of interest, like Niagara, and Ottawa the capital of Canada. Niagara I had already visited back in the winter when the falls were frozen, and the construction of the Honeymoon Bridge was well advanced. It was high summer when I made my second visit. All the fruit trees were in blossom and the 'Maid of the Mist' was doing good business taking oilskin-clad passengers around and under the falls. This was the nearest I ever came to setting foot in the United States. They were not yet in the war and servicemen in uniform were forbidden to land when the boat docked in Buffalo. At this second visit to Niagara I witnessed, and took a photograph, of the final central connecting piece being put in place in the Honeymoon Bridge. I saw it again nearly fifty years later and it looked as if a coat of paint would not come amiss.

In Ottawa my friend and I stayed in the Chateau Laurier, certainly the best hotel we had found so far. It had a swimming pool in the basement full of lukewarm water in which I found it possible to swim length after length almost indefinitely, or so it seemed. Ottawa is on the border of the Province of Quebec, with the dividing line being a river. On the Quebec side is the city of Hull, where the French influence did not conform with the 'nothing on Sunday' business. As a consequence a large proportion of the population of Ottawa made their way across the river every Sunday, to enjoy the more exciting surroundings of Hull.

The Government buildings in Ottawa were guarded by a Mountie in full dress uniform, without a horse but looking very impressive from a distance. On closer inspection he didn't seem quite the slim, fit, hardy type one might have expected; more plump, unhealthy and a bit elderly. This was forgivable, after all there was a war on and guarding the Houses of Parliament in far away Canada was more a ceremonial gesture than for security. When I approached with my camera, he spotted me and with much self-importance offered to move to a more suitable position and pose properly. This, I subsequently gathered, being the usual drill when approached by American tourists. It quite put me off and muttering 'No thank you, I've run out of film,' I went away. I never did get a picture of a Mountie.

CHAPTER 9.

Bombs and Guns.

At Picton they taught us to drop bombs in such a way that there might be a good chance of hitting the target, always assuming ones navigation had been adequate to find it. Having imparted the theory we took off in an aeroplane to put it into practice. The aeroplane this time was a Fairey Battle, a single engined low wing monoplane, rather like an overgrown Hurricane to look at, but there the similarity ended. It did not behave like a Hurricane being, I suspect, somewhat under-powered for its size. It had been ahead of its time when it first came into service but by the time it was needed to assume its role as a bomber in France during the 'Phony War' and the Blitzkrieg, it was outclassed by the opposition and suffered grievous losses. It suited our purpose very well, the Pilot sat in his cockpit up front and we, the trainees, sat behind him and whilst we could pass him messages that was the only contact possible, apart from speech on the intercom.

Our part of the 'Battle' consisted of an open cockpit, in which one usually stood, to see over the side or fire the gun, or lay on one's stomach between the open cockpit and the back of the Pilot's seat, peering through a hole in the bottom and using the bombsight. The Vickers Gas Operated machine gun was mounted on an ingenious swinging arm contraption (a modified Scarf Ring) which allowed the gun to be swung from one side to the other without shooting off the Rudder, or other parts of the tail unit. The gun was fed from a circular magazine holding, I think, one hundred rounds of .303 ammunition, forced out of the magazine casing and into the breech by a powerful spring. This I discovered when attempting to clear a jam, by foolishly undoing the retainer, resulting in a stream of live cartridges flying out of the magazine to be lost forever in the nooks and crannies of the fuselage.

The bombs weighed eleven and a half pounds and gave off white smoke when they hit the ground, or anything else for that matter. When the bomb dropping was done in the approved manner on a Range there were people in bunkers on the ground looking out over the target area. They were equipped with instruments to take bearings on the smoke emanating from the bomb. When these bearings were plotted they gave the position of the bomb relative to the target and you thereby scored the marks your good aim, or good luck, had earned you. Sometimes the bomb missed the target area altogether, which is why the takers of the bearings were in bunkers.

When preparing to drop bombs it is first necessary to find, as accurately as possible, the wind speed and direction. This was done by getting the Pilot to fly three different courses, each about sixty degrees different. The bomb aimer in the belly of the Battle, lying on his belly, would measure the drift on each of the three courses. Using a chinagraph wax pencil, he would plot each drift on the glass face of the compass, the three lines would cross, hopefully at one place, giving the vector for the wind speed and direction which could now be entered into the Bomb Sight. The whole procedure tended to be a little tedious but was not at all difficult, except when, on one occasion, the day was of the hottest (and that is very hot indeed). The hole in the floor of the Battle was positioned directly behind the engine radiator so, what might have been a cooling draught, was in fact more like an eruption from a blast furnace. All this heat added up to a very hot compass and a very sorry for itself wax pencil, which melted into a puddle when brought into contact with the glass. Such difficulties were sent to try us - and were very successful.

When the object of the flight was to fire the gun, each learner was issued with one or two drums of ammunition containing bullets with their tips painted a different colour for each learner. A small amount of this colour remained on the target drogue each time it was hit, which was not very often, so what might have been a task requiring keen eyesight and a certain amount of numeracy, could be done by anyone with a few minutes to spare.

One held the gun by the two pistol-grips, preparatory to firing. One grip had a trigger, for the right hand to fire the gun, and the other had a trigger, for the left hand to release the locking mechanism enabling the gun to be swung from one side to the other. The first time I went up to fire the gun I took a firm grip on both triggers, took aim at the drogue being towed behind another Battle, pulled the right hand trigger and immediately, in reaction to the noise and vibration, pulled the other trigger as well. The gun flew up on its way to the other side and being programmed to miss the tail unit became nearly vertical, all the time squirting a stream of bullets everywhere except where intended. I began to take a keen interest in a Harvard aeroplane a little above us and not noticed up to that moment. I am happy to recall it stayed above us apparently quite oblivious to the stream of bullets just gone by.

Another time, for some reason, I needed to move the gun to the other side and this time, of course, it stuck. Without thinking I caught hold of the barrel, which was as near red hot as makes little difference. It was the custom at that time to treat burns with butter to keep the air away. I had no butter but there was lots of air and I discovered that if I held my hand in the slipstream it diminished the pain, all the time aware that I was doing utterly the wrong thing and would undoubtedly suffer for it later. When we landed I went straight to the hospital, expecting at least a week's sick leave, only to be told it didn't look too bad. After smearing purple jelly over it they told me to come back next day if it was not better. It was better and I firmly believe I may have been the first to discover that the best thing for a burn is to keep it as cold as possible, with air or water or whatever, as soon as possible.

I have a Newspaper cutting with a picture of me and another fellow having been newly presented with our Observer badges. We're gazing delightedly at a trophy, held by the other bloke who had gained the highest marks, for bombing and gunnery, I was the runner-up. There was a knack to getting good marks for air-to-air shooting. It depended on the bored Pilot syndrome. Piloting a hot sweat-inducing aeroplane, on a hot July day, plodding up and down the same strip of Lake shore with a couple of dim sprogs in the back seat, who were obliged to get rid of two hundred rounds of ammunition before being able to land back at base for a lovely long cool drink, was conducive to great boredom and much impatience. This could be exploited. I would concentrate on only giving short, well aimed, bursts at the drogue some two hundred yards away, making it obvious I was not going to be hurried. This would result in the Pilots in both aircraft easing gently towards each other. When the drogue was nearly on the end of the gun barrel the magazine was emptied in one burst of concentrated fury, producing some very good scores.

Sharing the same airfield was an advanced pilot flying training school. It must have qualified as being 'advanced' because they flew Harvards, which were low-wing radial-engined fighter trainers, of very good performance and quite the noisiest aircraft ever constructed. It was said this noise emanated from the high tip speed of the propeller, and I have no reason to doubt this. It was certainly the only aircraft I could ever be entirely confident of identifying as soon as it came within earshot. If a school is categorised as being 'advanced' one is entitled to expect a modicum of expertise from its pupils. This was not always noticeable. One day a Harvard came into land without previously lowering the undercarriage, which is not an over-hazardous manoeuvre but is unpopular owing to the damage suffered by the underside of the fuselage and to the propeller which looks so sad all bent and folded back over the engine. There is, of course, always a good reason why landing like this is used as a last resort, such as failure of the mechanism or, hydraulics out of order. In this case, however, the 'advanced' pupil, who was flying solo, explained to his irate instructor, '...there was something very wrong with the aircraft and it was making a dreadful noise right by my head'. The noise turned out to be the klaxon horn designed to remind the pilot that he had forgotten to lower the wheels!

When flying a Harvard for the first few times a pupil was always accompanied by an Instructor. One such would tell his pupil, before taking off, to copy everything he did and thereby learn to become a good pilot. When this particular Instructor decided his Pupil was sufficiently competent he would unscrew the joystick, or control column, tap the pupil on the shoulder with it, and throw it over the side, thus indicating to the pupil he now had full control and was going to get no more assistance from the Instructor. One day a pupil, more conscientious than the others, and remembering his instructions, smiled delightedly, rapidly unscrewed his stick and threw it after the other. An unhappy ending was only averted by the Instructor who'd had the foresight to have in his pocket a short version of the stick. Somehow he managed to land safely by shouting instructions to his pupil who had to operate the rudder, flaps, and throttle while he crouched in the cockpit to control the lateral and fore and aft stability. I believe it was the pupil who leaked the story. There was no possibility the Instructor was going to confess.

Each of us went before an interview board to decide who should be awarded a commission and who should remain a Sergeant. It seemed sensible that one should emphasize such things as; having been in the OTC at a recognised school where rugger and cricket were played, and casually name-drop relatives who were commissioned in the armed forces, whilst carefully avoiding any mention of acquaintances who were not. Well it worked for me, as I was to discover some time later back in England.

When we all became Sergeants at the end of the course it was natural for us to move into the Sergeants Mess. This was embarrassing for us, and quite infuriating for the Sergeants, some of whom had taken years of hard and devoted service to earn their stripes, whereas it had taken us around nine months to catch up with them.

CHAPTER 10.

Halifax and Montreal.

The train taking us from Picton to the Transit Camp in Halifax did not have bunks or any other comfortable way of passing the night, as had the train bringing us from Halifax some six months previously. In the time it took us to become higher in rank so the railway authorities had learnt it was only Officers who warranted the luxury they had, previously and mistakenly, lavished on us. Being mid-summer it was very hot and the air-conditioning was not as efficient as it has now become, fifty years later, so when the train stopped in Montreal for a couple of hours some of us went in search of a drink. I was persuaded to have a gin and ginger beer, well iced and long. It must have been the first time I had tried gin, or any other spirit, with anything. I clearly remember being delighted with both the taste, its thirst quenching properties and the effect.

The Transit Camp at Halifax, in which we were to wait for an unspecified period until a boat turned up to take us back to England, was very boring indeed. There was nothing required of us except to turn up on the Parade ground each morning, there to be told if anything was likely to happen. The rest of the day was ours to do as we pleased. Our pay had not caught up with us and the last payday was a long time back, so it was very difficult to do as you please when you have no money with which to do it. The camp was close to the city, the tram (street car) stopped outside the camp and would take you anywhere in the network for ten cents, very reasonable, if you have ten cents. The fare was collected as you left the tram by dropping the coins, usually a dime or two nickels, into a glass sided box with a trap-door bottom. Before opening the trap to allow the fare to drop into the till the driver would look through the glass side to check it was the right amount. Some of the really poor among us would drop in six individual cents and before the clatter had died away we were off the tram and moving quickly down the street before the driver had been able to count our contribution.

Having thus deviously arrived in town it was only to find there was little that could be done when limited funds are available. One found how incredibly long a cup of coffee in the 'Green Dragon' could be made to last, all the time aware of the suspicious looks from the waiters, and eventually, the Manager. We tried explaining our predicament, promising when we had funds we would always come and spend them in the 'Green Dragon'. I think they gathered we were up to no mischief but the subtleties of the situation could not find expression in our 'pidgin' Chinese or their understanding of English. Although we were not asked to leave there seemed little doubt they considered that, by enjoying their chairs, tables and air-conditioning, we were getting good value for our money. There was no question of being able to afford a meal so these had to be taken in the Mess back at Camp.

Pay day finally came and was celebrated by putting the full fare in the tram's glass box, a fine meal at the 'Green Dragon' to the accompaniment of happy oriental smiles, and the purchase of an Air Pistol. This was no ordinary air pistol or purchase, being a .22 bore breech-loader, worked by compressed air stored within the gun, and put there by some energetic work on the built-in pump. It was quite powerful, made in the USA and named after Benjamin Franklin. I had to go to the police to obtain a licence before the store would part with the pistol. It came home with me and saw good service in rat hunts on the farm and later as a, rather to be regretted, plaything when discovered by my young son.

Now in funds, I hired a canoe from a reluctant owner. He was of the opinion there was (a) too much wind, (b) the waters of Halifax Harbour were a little on the choppy side, (c) it was most likely my experience of such craft might be limited and (d) above all, he did not want the cushions to get wet. I suggested we could dispense with the cushions. He declined on the grounds that if I were to do that I would certainly sit on the seat in the stern, which was level with the gunwhale, which would make the craft top heavy and increase the likelihood of capsizing. He wanted me to sit, or kneel, in the bottom to give maximum stability. To do this a cushion was desirable. I had long ago mastered the art of using a single paddle and steering at the same time, and very well I did too, until thinking to go faster I sat up on the seat. I quickly discovered this raised the bow out of the water, increasing the windage and requiring increased effort from me – which resulted in vindication of the owners reluctance and the saturation of his precious cushions.

Following the necessary rescue operations the owner quite forgot the respect due to a visitor from the Mother Country and evinced not a scrap of sympathy when I remarked on the extreme coldness of the water. Fortunately the sun was hot and I soon dried out.

After a week or so in the Transit Camp some of us were told that, as we had done reasonably well in acquiring a knowledge of Astro Navigation, we had been selected to navigate a new aeroplane across the Atlantic back to the UK. This was welcome, daunting and exciting, all at the same time. I was not yet twenty and my father had forbidden me to ride my bicycle in the blackout!

Next day saw the select few on a train again, heading back to Montreal where we were to undergo a refresher course in Astro Navigation. The train had observation type platforms at the end of each carriage and it seemed fairly obvious these were, if not quite intended, ideal places from which to test a newly acquired Air Pistol by taking pot shots at the cows interested in train spotting. A hit would cause the cow to jump a bit, which did not happen very often and the cows did not seem to mind. At a range of about thirty yards there was little energy left in the pellet, certainly not sufficient to penetrate the skin or even leave a mark. There was, however, someone who did mind and unfortunately he was a Red Cap or RAF Policeman. They are not the best-loved people in the Service, and there was no doubt I came positively to hate this one when he confiscated my pistol. It was not by bribery that it was returned to its rightful owner, let that be clearly understood, it was my forgetfulness in leaving a new packet of cigarettes on his table, and him not thinking to point out my oversight when I left with the pistol.

In Montreal, after visiting the Navigation School and being provided with a timetable of classes etc., we were issued with a sextant, Air Navigation Tables and the Air Almanac, then told to go and find accommodation. This would be paid for from our daily allowance of so many dollars a day. Following our usual custom, three of us took a taxi to the best hotel in the city, the 'Mount Royal', where we persuaded them to put a third bed into a double room, without extra charge. This made it possible to live within our allowance and have enough left over for some modest meals in the nearest Drug Store. On our arrival in the room I discovered I had left a small suitcase in the taxi. 'Phone calls to the taxi firm produced no result, either then or later, and it had to be assumed the taxi driver or his next fare had stolen the suitcase. This was very upsetting, particularly as it had contained, among other things, a new pair of shoes, my photograph album (but fortunately not the negatives) and worst of all, and quite irreplaceable, my Log Book containing the details of every flight I had made.

Being conscientious, the three of us approached the Hotel Manager to ask if he would allow us on the roof when it was dark. I do not believe he had ever had such a request before and, politely, explained that guests were not allowed on the roof. Of course, we agreed, it was perhaps a slightly unusual request but we wanted to look at the stars. Now he understood perfectly, we were not only unusual but very likely drunk as well. After impressing him with sextants and books full of incomprehensible figures he became most co-operative and had us taken up to the roof where we were able to take many practice star sights. We were able to assure the Manager on our return, whilst expressing our thanks, that by our calculations his hotel was not where he thought it was but not to worry too much over this.

Part of the refresher course was to go flying at night in a Hudson aircraft, the same type we were going to fly back to England, and thus gain some familiarity with the Aircraft and, hopefully, remember the skills of taking star sights whilst airborne. I have already explained the difficulties, and the ready made solutions, to getting lost in Canada when all the towns are lit up and the shore of Lake Huron runs North and South for a hundred miles or so. This time it was to be different. A few miles North of Montreal there were no lights, because there was nothing to light up, no large lake and what there was, was even worse than what there wasn't - no Astro Dome, just a large hole in the roof, about two feet in diameter.

There was no heating in the aircraft, which might not seem important when you remember it was mid-summer, but at ten thousand feet it was extremely cold and very draughty and we had not been warned to put on flying kit. The crew, pilot and wireless operator, were in a snug little heated cockpit sealed off from us by a door kept firmly shut. There was also no oxygen and whilst this was not critical at this height it made one very sluggish. One fellow sat at his desk with no ambition to do anything except watch his sextant judder slowly across the desk until it fell onto the floor, where, with considerable initiative, he put his foot on it. A lack of Oxygen can give a curious, and false, impression of well-being and there is no doubt the chap with his foot on the sextant was happy, convinced he had shown remarkable finesse in arriving at such an ingenious solution.

That flight over the undeveloped backlands of Quebec was mostly memorable for the extreme cold and the discomfort of having to carry out involved mathematics with the equivalent of half a brain. Above were the stars, to either side and below there was nothing. Had everything depended on our navigation there might have been some bother, but in the cozy surroundings of their little cabin, neither the pilot or wireless operator, had the least intention of landing anywhere except at St. Huberts Air Base from whence we had started out. They had done all this many times before and were only politely interested in the result of our calculations. Their greatest fear must have been that one night, when the weather was at its nastiest, the wireless might break down. Needless to say, all ended well and landing back at base we stepped out into the unbelievable heat of a summer's night.

Our tutors may either have had no alternative to us, or we had satisfied them as to our competence, and the time arrived for us to leave on this great adventure. When they issued sextants for the journey I discovered I would not be able to have one of the type they had let me use for practice. I have previously mentioned my preference for the type with the big wheel and the pencil marks to get the average, which I had to hand back. In its place they gave me the equivalent article manufactured in the United States. It was very neat with the wheel a third of the size, there was no spring loaded clip to hold the pencil and the eyepiece folded up to enable the whole thing to be put in ones pocket. I suspect this latter feature was the designer's fundamental conception of a sextant, which would appeal to the amateur aviator who could show it off to his friends and very likely never venture into the sky at night, even if he had learnt how to use it. What was to prove the greatest difficulty was that there was no locking device to hold the folding eyepiece in the unfolded position.

Our luggage was reduced to a minimum. In addition to a kit-bag containing flying kit, we were only allowed to take a pack containing a change of clothes, pyjamas, sponge bag, a pair of shoes and a few other odds and ends. Although I do not remember having it, there must have been a gas mask. Everything else had to go into a kit-bag, which would be sent by boat. We rated the chances of ever seeing the kit-bag again as pretty low, but I can assure anyone who might be interested that to send a kit-bag full of treasured possessions across a submarine infested Atlantic Ocean is a great deal more reliable than leaving it in a Montreal taxi.

CHAPTER 11.

Gander, Newfoundland.

There were five or six Hudsons in the batch we were to navigate. We took off, independently, from St. Huberts Air Base, Montreal, one sunny morning around the 4th July 1941 and set course for Gander in Newfoundland. The aircraft was not the one in which we would be crossing the Atlantic, but one which when delivered to Gander would have the necessary modifications carried out for the journey. I was to find out the nature of these in the fullness of time. In the meantime I was able to navigate without any difficulty, it being daylight, and the St. Lawrence River was going in the same direction. The pilot, a civilian in the Air Transport Auxiliary, flew the machine and the wireless operator, also a civilian, assured us the equipment was working well and would get us out of any bother if we should get lost. In the meantime he would tune into the local radio stations for some suitable music.

The aircraft behaved itself, the wireless produced suitable music and we did not stray over the border into the States. This was considered rather important, they not being at war with anyone and therefore entitled to shoot us down if we infringed their airspace. But the importance was, I think, more likely to have been the avoidance of an international incident, however minor, that might cause embarrassment. At about two hundred and twenty miles an hour we found our way across the provinces of Quebec and New Brunswick, skirting Maine to the south. We flew the length of Prince Edward Island to the northern part of Nova Scotia, from where a course was set to cross the Gulf of St. Lawrence, over the Cabot Strait, to the south coast of Newfoundland. This was a fairly long sea crossing, about one hundred and fifty miles, and it was decided it would be a good idea to check the wind speed and direction rather than go on using the predicted wind we had been given back in Montreal.

To find a 'wind' over water it is necessary to have an object on the water more or less still. There was, of course, nothing. Somebody had thought this might happen and had invented a marker bomb, which burst when hitting the water depositing a large blob of aluminium powder on the surface. This blob was visible from a considerable height and would remain so until the powder sank into the water sometime later. The marker bomb was not dropped like any other kind of bomb but was kept in a rack, with others, at the back of the fuselage, from whence it was necessary to carry it, carefully hugged to ones breast. As this was, most likely, the first occasion one had ever seen such a thing, let alone use it, it was necessary to search, whilst carrying it, for any instructions. There were some, though nearly incomprehensible, since first a 'flare chute' had to be found. Nobody had told us about these and an Anson certainly did not have one. I discovered a sort of inverted flue pipe rising from the floor and decided, correctly as it happened, this was the flare chute, into which the 'bomb' was inserted tail first. A piece of wire was attached to a pin which when pulled out would make the thing 'live', that is to say it would be in a condition where, if the detonator were struck, it would explode. I did not wish to be too close when this pin was pulled out, so I attached the wire to some convenient protrusion, which would, when the bomb fell down the chute cause it to pull out its own pin. It is even possible this is the correct way it should be done but I never found out for sure, and never again saw a marker, or, indeed, a flare chute.

The aluminium powder duly appeared on the water, which seemed a good time to discover we had no apparatus for measuring the drift as the aircraft flew over the blob. It is true someone had anticipated this little difficulty by painting lines at radiating angles in red paint on the sheet of perspex through which, with a suitable instrument if you had one, the drift could be read. I would like to say, but cannot, that in spite of these difficulties I obtained a reliable wind, but it was near enough to the one predicted in

Montreal, which had served well enough so far for me to feel secure in continuing to use it.

The coast of Newfoundland turned up as expected and I thought I would be back to map reading, but this was map reading like nothing I had ever seen before. Here was an immense profusion of lakes of all shapes and sizes and any attempt to identify a particular lake with what was shown on the map proved impossible. I was very relieved when after about one hundred and thirty miles of unrecognisable lakes we popped over the top of a hill and there was Gander right ahead of us. Gander had no runways, just a great big area of tarmac, I believe they said it was a mile square.

It had taken about five hours from Montreal and it was now late afternoon. The aircraft was parked, we were fed and I was taken to a bedroom where, for the first time since getting into uniform, I had a room to myself. Next day, after a good lie-in, lunch was followed by a briefing session to inform us about such things as the weather to be expected that night over the ocean and whether it would be better to fly a rhumb line or a great circle course. I think we settled on the great circle, for good reasons which now escape me; something to do with the winds being kinder if we kept further north. We prepared flight plans, assuming a height of eight thousand feet, which would put us above the clouds where the stars could be seen. We made a multitude of calculations based on winds, temperatures, magnetic variations, etc. predicted for each band of longitude from Gander to Prestwick in Scotland. Call signs, letters and colours of the day had to be noted to convince people on our side, should the occasion arise, that we were friendly.

It was back to my room after supper to have a snooze before being taken out to the aircraft in the early evening. But a short while later there was a knock on the door and in came some of my mates and a couple of strangers with a bottle of some reddish liquid. Glasses were produced and we, the soon to be navigators of the Atlantic Ocean, were persuaded, without much difficulty, that an essential beginning to such a hazardous undertaking was rum. Not your ordinary grog type rum that pours out of a bottle, but the real stuff which has the consistency of syrup and has to be almost shaken out. It turned out to be splendid stuff and the warm glow, sense of confidence and well being lasted all the way to the Hudson, now fully prepared and ready to be flown to Scotland.

The Lockheed Hudson was a portly aeroplane of modest performance with a good range, but this did not include the Atlantic. Originally designed to carry passengers in comfort, it had been modified to be a war - plane, then further modified to enable it to be delivered under its own power to England. It was indeed comfortable, highly unsuccessful as a bomber, but very useful in Coastal Command looking for, and attacking with depth charges and bombs, submarines or ships.

On entering our Hudson through the door at the back, there was obviously something missing, like, would you believe, the cabin. In its place was the biggest petrol tank I'd ever seen. It must have been built-in as there was no possibility it came through the door. Our aeroplane was now a flying (I hoped) petrol tank. It was a squeeze to get past the tank up to the cockpit where all seemed normal and where we the crew - pilot, wireless operator and navigator - took our respective places, mine being next to the pilot in, what would usually have been, the second pilots seat. Now I found out why there was this vast area of tarmac and no runways. The trick was to take maximum advantage by facing directly into any wind there might be. With one large area this could be done without having to make any compromise dictated by runways.

When lined up for take-off, and having received permission from the control tower, the engines bellowed, the brakes released and speed built up, alarmingly slowly by normal standards, the 'plane being a bit overloaded. The Pilot was looking hard at the Air Speed Indicator and when it reached flying speed he tentatively raised the undercarriage thus reducing the drag. The small increase in speed allowed a gentle pull on the control column, we went up a few feet and could now be said to be flying - just. Almost instantly we cleared the limit of the tarmac.

If anyone wants to argue about the use of this technique, as I have described it, I can only say it is what we were told. I was not a trained pilot and had no reason to question its accuracy.

CHAPTER 12.

Over the Atlantic.

The take off was towards China and the setting sun. Height was gained slowly until, at about five hundred feet, the pilot persuaded the 'plane into a gentle turn away from the setting sun and towards the East, the coastline of Newfoundland, some two thousand five hundred miles of sea, and the United Kingdom. The climb continued for two hours before reaching the intended height of eight thousand feet, well above the clouds. With the sun setting behind us it was very beautiful, turning the cloud tops red above their white valleys and hollows, against the background of a sky, deep blue above and tapering to a cobalt blue at the horizons. There can be no more spectacular sight than a sunset above the clouds, except maybe, a sunrise, and we were to witness that in about five hours time. Until then there were other things to be busy about, such as changes of course to make allowance for the altering winds at the different heights, trying out the coffee in the flask, and testing the radio. The coffee was quite good.

The wireless operator was finding it difficult to get bearings due, he surmised, to interference from the Northern Lights or some other natural magnetic source. He was in no doubt that things would get better and be thoroughly reliable by the time we really needed them, that is, after the stars had gone with the sunrise and only three or four hundred miles of ocean remained. He was, of course, one hundred per cent mistaken. If he had thrown the whole contraption into the Atlantic we should have gained slightly more advantage by having less to carry, due to the considerable weight of radios in those days.

It was time for me to identify suitable stars to give the best results for obtaining fixes. The ideal was one bright star immediately in front or behind and about forty-five degrees above the horizon, and another, similar in all respects, but to one side or the other. Two suitable stars presented themselves and I prepared to get my first fix of the journey. I took the sextant from my pocket and unfolded it and with a pencil I had, to mark the drum, I made a note of the time on my pad. As the star appeared in the telescope I turned the wheel to bring its image into the centre of the bubble. It was almost there when it went careering around the horizon, the star that is, not because of any galactic catastrophe but because the sextant had decided it was time to fold up.

Repeated attempts had the same result and it was impossible for me to get an average for one sight, let alone the two required for a fix where the two position lines crossed at the average time. I arrived at the inevitable compromise - I had to arrive at something. The news from the wireless department was not encouraging either, so I decided to concentrate on one star behind us, taking a large number of single sights with no attempt to average, and also take sights on the Pole star, again without averaging. These would give, in the first instance, an indication as to whether we were ahead or behind, in an East/West direction, of where we ought to be, and similarly, from the Pole Star, an indication of whether we were to the North or South of the intended track. The Pole star moves, or appears to move, only very little compared to the other stars and this makes the calculations simpler. In effect it gives the Latitude direct and this is most convenient when one is flying, nearly, along a line of Latitude.

The frequent sights were beginning to show a pattern indicating we were a bit North and a bit ahead of our planned position, but not enough to worry about. I intended to wait until the situation became more positive before making a change of course. In the meantime coffee and sandwiches were produced as a sort of early breakfast which it was not, or a midnight feast which it wasn't either. The pilot decided he had to visit the Elsan at the back of the 'plane and happily left me in charge of the controls. Sitting in the driver's seat for the first time in my life, and over the middle of the ocean, I received my first lesson as a pilot. The lesson took about thirty seconds and consisted of instructions as to which of George's knobs should be twiddled to keep the aircraft on an even keel, particularly as the nose might tend to rise as he went into the tail. 'George' was, of course, the Automatic Pilot. Here was power indeed, so I took the opportunity to alter course to the South a bit to compensate for the error indicated by the sights on the Pole star. All went well, my twiddling was successful, the pilot returned and resumed his seat, and then both engines stopped.

They, the engines, showed no signs of distress, they just, and in perfect unison - stopped. The propellers still continued to revolve silently, now assuming the role of windmills. Hurriedly, I tried to make up my mind about our estimated position to pass to the radio operator, whilst he, ever optimistic, hoped the wireless would be able to transmit even if it was incapable of receiving bearings. The pilot, after a startled moment, remarked; 'Oh dear, I forgot to change over the tanks'. The engines came back to life as he did so.

After a while the sun came up in front of us, which seemed a good moment to have another snack, identifiable this time as breakfast. All this time my sightings on the two stars were indicating that we were some sixty miles North of track, and forty miles forward. I gave the new course and ETA (Estimated time of Arrival) to the pilot and the three of us sat back to await the coast of Ireland. At the ETA all that appeared was a large oil slick, not in the least like Ireland, unless it had sunk. Twenty minutes later the coast hove in sight, precisely at the place towards which I had been aiming. This was of course very gratifying and demonstrated how clever I had been to use the Pole Star. The error in time was not so gratifying but was subsequently found to be just what could be expected when the Navigator forgets to turn over the page at midnight, to the next day of the Air Almanac!

Not only was Ireland where it should have been but there was, as might have been expected, masses of cloud extending down to within a couple of thousand feet of the sea. By the time we were under the cloud Lough Swilly was beneath us, and also a Destroyer. The Royal Navy tended to be a bit touchy about aeroplanes in as much as they were inclined to shoot first and apologise afterwards. It was unlikely that a lone German raider would be this far West in daylight, or so I imagined, which was probably why the Destroyer Captain decided to challenge our identity instead of shooting. A signal light flashed the code in Morse requiring us to identify ourselves. There were two ways to do this, either by shooting off a Very cartridge, with the colours of the day, or, by using an Aldis lamp to signal the letters of the day. 'Letters, or Colours, of the day' were listed on a rice-paper 'flimsy' showing the periods for which they were valid during each twenty-four hour period. Being of a highly confidential nature they were to be eaten if it should appear likely the enemy would capture them. I am happy to report the only time this became necessary, I forgot.

The 'flimsy' was found, in its inedible cellophane case, the correct colours were identified, the cartridge containing the right colour combination selected, and inserted into the breech of the pistol. The pistol was a permanent fixture in the roof of the cockpit and nothing could be easier than to load it and fire. As it turned out it would have been a lot easier if the cartridge had fitted the breech! I struggled with the wretched thing but could find no way to make the cartridge go far enough into the pistol to allow the breech to close. While this was going on, the pilot was circling the destroyer deeming it prudent not to make a run for it, which might be interpreted as unfriendly, and encourage a burst from a Pom-Pom. At the height we were flying it could hardly miss.

It had to be the Aldis lamp! I knew we had one, I had seen it stowed by the door when we boarded, so I wriggled back past the, now empty, petrol tank, retrieved the lamp, brought it through to the cockpit, plugged it into a convenient socket, aimed at the destroyer and switched on. One brilliant flash of light, nothing more - the inevitable consequence of plugging a twelve-volt bulb into a twenty-four-volt socket!   They don't tell you about these things. The Pilot, with what I thought was great presence of mind, lowered the undercarriage, on the assumption that an aeroplane with its wheels down would be recognised as the equivalent of a man with his hands up. And so it was.

Leaving the Destroyer behind and going lower and lower to keep beneath the cloud, the aircraft suddenly lurched up into the clouds and I obtained an exact fix of our position - right above Ailsa Craig. If it had not been for the quick reaction of the pilot it would not have been above, but into. We landed rather heavily just around the corner at Prestwick, eleven hours and ten minutes after taking off from Gander.

It is not a good thing to land a Hudson too heavily, as I was to see some time later when one bounced so hard the undercarriage legs punched up through the wing, fracturing petrol tanks and severing many wires. The resulting fires in each wing were well fuelled by petrol from the burst tanks. The magnesium alloy used in the construction of the aircraft was also highly flammable. This particular Hudson was taking off when this happened and I had a bird's-eye view having just taken off in another 'plane at the time. All the crew got out, very quickly, and ran to the four corners of the airfield. When we arrived back there was a nasty black smudge, littered with bits, on the grass where the middle of the fuselage had been, the nose, the tail unit and the wings had each been pulled about fifty yards away by tractors to limit the conflagration.

After we landed at Prestwick there was a de-briefing in which much interest was expressed in the oil-slick as a possible indication of a disaster or a submarine, and why had we not radioed the information immediately and given the position? To us it had only been a disappointment for not being Ireland. After six months in peaceful Canada it was going to take a while for it to sink in that I was now back in a country at war and such seemingly insignificant things as oil slicks were of great significance. We were able to fluff over this obvious incompetence by mentioning the trouble with the wireless. This also avoided confessing that if we had radioed the position it would have been found to be some fifty miles in error. We were told that one of our number had run into the Mull of Kintyre. There were no survivors.

I have only vague memories of Prestwick. There must have been some rest facilities, but I only recollect visiting a colleague who had hired a hotel room, (he had lots of money) where I sat on the bed and woke up four hours later. How kind and generous it was of him to allow me to stay there and, hearing of my lack of funds, to give me half a crown, thus doubling my hoard of sterling and supplementing the three dollars in my wallet. This is the second time my poverty has intruded into this tale, not so much as a complaint, more a fact of life, and I hope it has not escaped notice that the fault was never mine. It is interesting to recall that the radio operator of the Hudson received five hundred dollars for eleven odd hours spent sitting in front of a defective wireless. The pilot was paid rather more for ensuring 'George' functioned throughout the same period, and I, with all the cares and responsibilities of a useless radio, a new aeroplane and, certainly not to be forgotten, looking after 'George' while the pilot went to the loo, was paid less than four dollars.

Both the pilot and radio operator had said they were going to fly back to Canada immediately, to pick up and ferry another Hudson to the U.K. Their return journey was to be in a Liberator, which would enable them to catch up on their sleep. I heard some time later that a Liberator, carrying ATA passengers, had crashed killing all aboard. I had no way of knowing for certain, but it was very likely that my two were in that aircraft.

With a rail Warrant to Portsmouth, three dollars and two half crowns, plus a kit-bag full of flying kit, a pack and a gas mask, I was deposited at the local railway station. It was a local station and this was the first time the Station Master had been faced with a pass to a distant place such as Portsmouth. He had no proper ticket to exchange for the warrant. He gave me a piece of white paper, in the nature of a receipt, not looking in the least official, and kept my Warrant. He entertained no doubt whatever that there would be no difficulty in exchanging the piece of white paper for a genuine ticket in Glasgow. As it turned out this was never put to the test. The train journey to Glasgow is about thirty miles and on the train I met an ATA pilot (Air Transport Auxiliary) also making his way to London via Glasgow on the same train as I hoped to catch.

Our arrival in Glasgow left almost no time at all for the connection let alone time to exchange my piece of white paper for a ticket. My new friend had no intention of missing his train, so we ran all the way and boarded the train within seconds of its departure. Being incredibly wealthy and important my friend had a reserved two berth, first class sleeper, and as the designated occupant of the other berth had decided to fly back to Canada, he invited me to take his place. This I duly did, and after only a brief skirmish with the ticket collector, who did not appear over impressed with my piece of white paper, we arrived next morning at Euston.

I took my piece of white paper to the ticket office and asked them if they would exchange it for a proper ticket to see me through the rest of my journey. They said it was not possible to issue a ticket for a trip on the 'Southern Railway' they being LMS, and told me to go to Waterloo. I broke into the very limited funds available to me and, with all my baggage' went to Waterloo on the Underground. There, they were even less helpful.

'This piece of paper purports to be a receipt for a warrant instructing the issue of a third class ticket from Prestwick to Portsmouth, it is written on LMS paper and as far as we are concerned was very likely written by you on a piece of stolen paper. Go to an LMS ticket office and see if they will believe you.'

So I made further inroads into my funds and went back to Euston where they refused, for the second time, to admit the validity of my piece of, now not so white, paper. Back again to Waterloo. By now one of the half-crowns was about gone, and even counting the Canadian Dollars, I could not afford the train fare. I desperately needed to find someone to feel sorry for me. I had vaguely heard of the RTO, which I think stands for 'Railway Transport Officer', but was not too clear on their function. I had a sneaking feeling they were rather akin to the Military Police, who I did not like following my encounter with them on the train to Montreal. Nevertheless it was to them I went.

They too took some convincing but the combination of the unlikely story of having been in Canada less than twenty-four hours ago, a bag full of flying kit, three dollars and my traitorous piece of grubby white paper eventually convinced them. They agreed to do everything in their power to get me on my way. This sounded impressive but turned out to be an exercise in pragmatism.

'I'm going over to the barrier,' the RTO man said, 'and I will open the gate to the right of the one where the Ticket Collector is collecting tickets. When I have the gate open - we have keys you know - you saunter in the vicinity and as soon as the Ticket Collector is looking the other way nip through the gate and get on the train. After that it's up to you.' Apart from a whispered: 'Good luck, mate', as he closed the gate behind me, that is what happened.

I had worked out that if an Inspector discovered I was without a ticket I would promise to pay at the end of the

74

journey, when I was in funds. The two did not necessarily coincide as I would have to borrow the fare from my father. There was no Inspector, but Portsmouth is a closed station and tickets are collected at the barrier. The train arrived on the high level platform where the barrier is at the top of a long flight of steps. I exploited this by putting my kit-bag under one arm, gas mask slung round my neck, and the bulging pack under the other arm. Thus burdened, obviously in a hurry and incapable of using my hands, I went straight past the Ticket Collector, eyes fixed on something in the far distance, and completely deaf to the cries of - 'Hey you, come back here! Hey, Hey.....etc', interspersed with clicking sounds as he went on snipping return tickets, gradually fading into the distance behind me.

I had accomplished the journey from Scotland to Portsmouth without a valid ticket, in a First Class sleeper but with more hassle than the flight from Gander and in slightly longer time.

CHAPTER 13

O.T.U. Upwood

My parents had moved to another farmhouse near Denmead, I did not have the telephone number and, anyhow, I wanted to surprise them by turning up un-announced. I had enough money for the bus fare and duly arrived in the village of Denmead, some four to five miles north of the City. No sooner was I off the bus when I spotted Mother's car parked outside the Post Office, where I was heading to find her telephone number. I knew it was her car because she had taught me to drive in it. 'What fun,' I thought, 'I'll get in and wait for her to get back', which I did - and she didn't, having sold the car to the man who wanted to know 'What the hell I thought I was doing sitting in his car with all that baggage on the back seat.'

My embarrassed explanations were received with understanding, and since he knew where my parents lived he offered to take me. I gratefully accepted and, although I had never been there before, I was home at last.

Mother and Father had adjusted to the new house, Father still worked for the War Damage Commission and received an extra petrol allowance for being in an essential occupation. He had become quite enthusiastic in the garden as a producer of vegetables, and as a breeder and keeper of chickens. Mother did not qualify for extra petrol, and since the basic ration would have been inadequate even to get to and from the village, let alone the city, they had decided to sell her car. She used a bicycle to go shopping in the village and for visiting the farms and surrounding homes to sell National Saving Certificates, and stamps. My Aunt and Uncle were partners in these agricultural activities. Some of the heavy digging work was sub-contracted to a farm labourer, living in a cottage close by, in his spare time. He was paid the going rate and thought he was doing well to be getting a supplement to his weekly wage. At the end of the war, in 1945, the rate was a shilling an hour, it may well have been less in 1941.

The new farmhouse was a great improvement on the last, being larger with a splendid garden, but was still up a very long lane. The front door faced into the garden at the back, and the back door - the one always used - was at the front. There was no electricity or gas and the water was pumped from a well, up into a tank on a high tower outside the back door. This was accomplished by a noisy, single cylinder petrol engine via a belt drive to an iron crank mechanism some seven feet high, located in a room across the hall from the kitchen. Water pumping time - every three or four days, (it also supplied the farm buildings) - was a good time to be somewhere else. My parents were still with my uncle and aunt, and there was now enough room for another couple with a 'teen-age son and daughter. It all seemed to work very well and did not seem overcrowded. My uncle, who ran a heating and electrical business, had put in a small solid fuel boiler to provide hot water. He could not, of course, do anything electrical until some years later when the mains arrived and the lovely smell of oil lamps was banished forever.

After a few days I received a Rail Warrant and a request to report to RAF Upwood, near Ramsey about ten miles South East of Peterborough. RAF Upwood was an OTU, that is an Operational Training Unit. It was here that we were to be trained to fly operations against the enemy. Up to this time it was not known in which type of aircraft we were to fly, and by the same token, the kind of operations in which we would be engaged. Upwood was a '2 Group' OTU and they tended to fly Blenheims and similar aeroplanes on frightening things like daylight low level bombing raids and lethal shipping strikes. Pilots and Wireless Operator/Air Gunners(Wop A.G.'s) also arrived from their different training courses, and we formed ourselves into three man crews.

Something had to be done about my missing Logbook. I had difficulty persuading the flight commander, to whom I took my problem, that the reason a replacement had become necessary was because the original had been stolen in Montreal. He preferred to say it had been 'lost', which I did not like to have on my record. It is pleasing to recall that my persistence eventually paid off.

Hardly had we begun to settle into a new regime when I was summoned by the Adjutant and told my Commission had come through. I was to have four days leave and eighty pounds, I think it was, to get kitted out. I had warned my parents of this possibility and they had made advance arrangements with the Master Tailor who was, fortuitously, the occupant of the other half of the farm-house. At the end of the four days I returned to Upwood as a Pilot Officer resplendent in a beautifully tailored uniform, including a greatcoat, raincoat, caps etc. He, the tailor, was sorry he had been unable to finish the second uniform in time, but it would follow by post in a day or so. There were not many new officers who had tailored uniforms, as indeed, I do not suppose there are many tailors able to accomplish so much in so little time. The majority, when newly commissioned, would go to Moss Bros. to get fitted out off the peg. Some kind of suitcase was necessary and I was lucky to get an all leather Cricket bag at a give away price - on account of the small holes, one on either side, caused by shrapnel hurrying from one side of the premises to the other when a bomb hit the shop.

I decided to take my bike back with me as, I had been warned, I would be billeted out in the village. To me it remains memorable, but there was nothing really exciting, or even interesting, in manouvering a cricket bag and bicycle, with little time to spare, across London in a taxi, in the blackout and with a driver who was slightly less than enthusiastic about the whole business. He only agreed when I said I would travel on the space by his side holding on to the bicycle. This, he assured me, was against the law, which I hope was reflected in the size of tip he received. The bike had to be left in Peterborough to be delivered to Ramsey by rail, from whence I collected it a day or two later.

My billet was a detached house in the best part of Ramsey. My hosts were a charming couple who made me welcome and comfortable, but I saw little of them. I left early in the morning and returned late in the evening, after closing time. My first experience of having too much to drink was in Ramsey. It was not an occasion I remember with pleasure. Someone asked if I liked rum, and remembering the rum I was given in Gander, I replied 'Oh yes!' Rum and Pep is not at all the same thing, and we stayed on those for the rest of the evening. I was rather ill and have disliked rum to this day, with or without 'pep'.

The pilot, with whom I was crewed, was a most agreeable chap named Pete Rowlands. We had an equally agreeable Wop/AG, and that, I am afraid, is all I remember of him. Pete, at that time a Sergeant, later received a commission and served with distinction, being decorated and becoming an airline pilot after the war. He was a very good pilot, never having wanted to be anything else, but sometimes his enthusiasm got the better of him. On one occasion we discovered a Blenheim has a nasty habit of losing its cockpit canopy when diving at high speed, intent upon persuading a farmer to fall off his hayrick! This was a frightening experience, because of the loud bang and sudden inrush of air which stirred up all the dirt, dust, and I'll swear, hay, which had been accumulating since the aircraft was built, creating the illusion that we had, in fact, hit the rick. I think the farmer was probably also frightened, he certainly was not to be seen when we went back to see if we could spot the canopy.

On another occasion, a newly acquired branch, from a tree, hooked on the Pitot Head projecting down under the nose (to measure the air speed). This made it difficult to persuade the flight commander that it was not us who had been the cause of a lady ringing to complain of a low flying aircraft over her house.

Pete thought it would be a good idea if I knew how to take over from the pilot and fly the aircraft. I was all in favour, but the Blenheim was not equipped with dual control and on one occasion, when I was doing the piloting, it was nearly the end of us, and the Blenheim. We were changing back into our respective seats when a foot, mine I think, jammed against the control column and we began a side slip which only came to an end when Pete regained control at about two hundred feet above the ground, or so he said. It seemed to me a great deal nearer.

A vital part of the training was to drop practice bombs at a range on the shore of The Wash. This was not far away and took place so frequently I was completely familiar with the route and knew exactly which road, railway, river, dike or water- course, to follow. So much so, one day I didn't bother to take any maps. Pete decided to follow Paul and John who were going to the same place but not, it turned out, by my route. It didn't matter since they knew where they were going and we intended to follow them. The aeroplane thought differently. One of the engines stopped. A Blenheim will fly on one engine, but not very quickly, so John and Paul disappeared into the distance and we had very little notion of where we were. Fortunately our Victorian ancestors had anticipated this very circumstance by building railways. By flying West we came across the London to Peterborough line, turned right up to Peterborough, from where I knew the way back to Upwood. By complaining bitterly about the faulty engine no one ever found out how foolish I had been to fly in the face of the advice implied in the 'famous last words' – 'I don't need a map, I know the way well'.

One evening, returning to my billet from a forty-eight hour pass, somewhat later than usual and knowing the family to be asleep in their beds, it seemed a good idea to break in without waking them. The kitchen window came open with a little persuasion from my penknife, my foot went into the sink, on to some crockery, but the noise was not too bad and nothing broke. As I gently eased my feet down to the floor the refrigerator started up, and frightened the life out of me. My hosts admitted to a similar shock when, next morning, they realised there was someone in my room which couldn't, they supposed, possibly be me.

One of us had been given a ticket to a dance in Peterborough. We rustled up another four to make a taxi load of six, thereby sharing the cost six ways. The dance turned out to be by ticket only and we had but one ticket between the two of us who wished to go dancing. The problem was solved by first going for a drink, then tearing the ticket in two and returning to the dance claiming each half as a pass-out ticket. It worked very well!

Being billeted out, whilst having some advantages, had some snags, particularly in the matter of getting up on time in the mornings without the assistance of a Sergeant Major, Batman, or alarm clock. One morning I overslept when I was supposed to be attending an early exercise at the crack of dawn, requiring me to put in an appearance somewhat before that time. It was still dark, at least half an hour later than it should have been, when I peddled furiously into a pitch-black hanger and was suddenly knocked off my bike by a blow on the head, leaving me dazed and bleeding on the concrete floor of the hanger. There was no one around to take the blame and it appeared my head had collided with a chain block suspended from the roof of the hanger at just the right height to clout me. I was now even later than I would have been and sympathy was in short measure when I eventually turned up for duty as a blood stained apparition. I was reminded of the heinousness of being late for a scheduled flight and the extreme inconvenience caused by keeping three aircraft waiting, to say nothing of their crews. This could easily be a Court Martial offence.

I was told to report to the Squadron Leader, who was uninterested in my good reasons, and the extenuating misfortunes attending them, which, in my opinion, mitigated the episode to an extent where sympathy was the only proper reaction. He observed that 'this is much too serious to be dealt with by me, go and see the Wing Commander'. The Wing Commander was of the same opinion and said to go and see the Group Captain. Now it seemed to me that a humble Pilot Officer does not approach a Group Captain, he waits to be sent for. He must have been a very busy man as I have now waited fifty years!

On a cross-country exercise there was a great deal of cloud and we were, to put it as nicely as possible - lost. It was reasonable to suppose that the Midlands ought to be somewhere beneath us. Eventually there appeared, over to port, something different to the unbroken cloud, soon identified as being a Balloon Barrage consisting of a great many balloons and likely, therefore, to be protecting a place of some substance. Consulting my crystal ball I entered in the Log: 'Balloons to Port, Derby - I think'. The Instructor did not take kindly to the 'I think'. After reminding him of a reason he had given for keeping a Log, i.e. 'to leave a record for any person who might have to take over if the Navigator was unable to continue with his duties', I explained that it had seemed, to me, less misleading to hint at some uncertainty than to give the impression there was no doubt in the matter. He agreed with some reluctance, and asked if I now knew whether it had indeed been Derby? I had to admit that it turned out to be Sheffield.

CHAPTER 14.

105 Squadron, Swanton Morley.

I did not find the Blenheim to be my favourite aeroplane. Originally it had been well ahead of its time but it was, by now, getting on a bit and was being outclassed by the opposition and superceded by the new American light bombers like the Boston. Imagine, therefore, how delighted some of us were to learn of our posting to 105 Squadron, and to hear it was to be equipped with an aeroplane of which almost nothing was known. It was still on the secret list only having had its maiden flight on the twenty-fifth of March 1940, nineteen months before. The aircraft, of which much was expected, was called 'The Mosquito'. It was built of wood, beautifully streamlined, with two Rolls Royce Merlin engines, no guns but able to carry a greater bomb load than the Blenheim and fast enough, it was hoped, to outstrip enemy fighters. It had a crew of two - pilot and observer - there being no requirement for a gunner in an aeroplane with no guns.

It is probably because our WOP/AG was with us for such a brief time that I remember so little about him, not even his name, but perhaps better than his name he remains in my memory as a thoroughly pleasant person. It was, I clearly recall, a sad moment when he went out of our lives, as well as the other crews we had got to know. I remember something of a send-off party, in the Local Pub, of fairly dramatic proportions! The gunners went to join Squadrons flying conventional bombers with gun turrets and wireless sets. You might well assume, from this comment, that the Mosquito was without a wireless, or that, like in a fighter, it was operated by the pilot? The answer was to be made quite clear when we reached Swanton Morley, the home of 105 Squadron. Yes, it did have a wireless - no, it was not worked by the pilot, and there are no prizes for guessing who the operator was to be.

Pete had a car, not a very new one, but adequately reliable if you knew its peculiarities, and it was to be our transport to Swanton Morley. Large baggage, such as my bicycle and my camp kit went on a lorry. When receiving a commission an officer is given a 'kitting out' allowance to cover the cost of clothing himself in the manner becoming an officer and a gentleman. But there is one item issued to him that becomes his, or his next-of-kin's, property forever, indeed I have mine to this day. The 'camp kit' consisted of a camp bed, folding stool, folding canvas wash basin, canvas bath and blankets, all contained in a leather strapped canvas cover to produce a bundle about three feet long and one and a half feet in diameter, and extremely heavy. It was, and is, a wonderful thing as long as it does not have to be carried. I actually only used mine once.

There was a petrol allowance for going on leave and postings and suchlike. The amount was calculated from the length of the proposed journey, in our case the distance from Upwood to Swanton Morley, say sixty miles, or about two gallons. Pete said this was not going to be enough because he intended to stop off on the way to spend the night at his parent's home in Bedford. Somehow, without disclosing this intention, he spun some yarn, begged, borrowed, or quite likely stole sufficient coupons to make possible the proposed 'stop off on the way'. The distance of sixty miles from Upwood to Swanton Morley, and a fairly comfortable two to three hours drive, increases to about one hundred and forty miles if you call in at Bedford on the way. Even without the declared intention of spending the night in Bedford, the time taken would have become six or seven hours. An average of thirty miles per hour was considered very good in the nineteen forties.

'How, I enquired, 'do we explain to the people in Swanton Morley that we shall arrive a day late?' It was a silly question prompted only by the newfound conscience, which came with my commission. Pete, still a Sergeant, had no such qualms. He telephoned from Bedford, without saying where he was, and explained that the car had broken down. The garage could not mend it until the following day and we were going to have to find somewhere to stay the night. Listening to this tale of woe, I felt quite sorry for us, and it came as no surprise that the explanation was not only accepted, but induced an offer to send out transport to collect us. This disastrous generosity was regretfully declined on the grounds that he wanted to stay with the car, but, 'if it could not be made to go we would ring again and accept the offer'.

Bedford remains a mystery to me. It was dark when we arrived and still dark early the next morning when our journey was resumed. Before getting to bed we had spent an over enthusiastic evening in the local, where Pete was hailed joyfully by his old acquaintances, and I was viewed with some suspicion, it not being obvious to any of them why it was not Pete who had the commission instead of me. It would have needed a more complicated explanation than I could offer to convince a Pub full of 'loyal friends' that the exuberance of a young talented pilot, with a relish for flying lower than stipulated, had not impressed the selection board. The impression I made was not improved when I substituted force for skill and threw a dart, which hit a wire on the board, bounced back, and stuck in the leg of a lady sitting behind me. She accepted my profuse apologies and agreed that, in the circumstances, it was a foolish place to be sitting. Not so her husband, who was not so easily appeased, in fact he was extremely angry, even accusing me of doing it on purpose. I found this rather flattering as, usually, I could not be certain of hitting the dart board let alone of being able to aim for, and hit, a wire as a preliminary to obtaining a ricochet, precisely calculated to arrive at his wife's leg! Pete smoothed it all over and everyone parted on the best of terms with good wishes for the future.

All the signposts had been removed for the duration. Although we had the very best of maps and, arguably, the best of navigators, there came a time on the way to Swanton Morley when we were more than a little uncertain where we were. In a small town we drew up alongside a Policeman to ask the way. The Policeman was standing at the summit of a fairly steep hill, or it may have been the crown of a hump-backed bridge over a railway or canal. He was anxious to help and appeared not to notice that in doing so he had to walk alongside the car to keep up as we juddered slowly, backwards, down the hill. There was nothing very remarkable about this, the brakes simply did not work when going backwards, a well known problem with the type of brakes in which the shoes were hung in the drums to 'dig in' going forwards, and trail in reverse. If properly adjusted they worked well going forward, and well enough going backwards. In our case they worked inadequately forward and almost not at all backwards. I had to learn this all over again when I bought a second-hand car after the war.

On the eleventh of October 1941, a year to the day since arriving in Babbacombe, we turned up at RAF Swanton Morley, which was and is, about four miles north of East Dereham, a country town some sixteen miles west of Norwich in the county of Norfolk. Another Squadron, No. 152 who flew fighters, was already in residence and occupying all the bedrooms. We were billeted in a large country house known as Bylaugh Hall. It has possibly since been demolished as I could not find it when, some twelve years ago, I re-visited the area. I remember it with affection. I shared a large room with another pilot officer of some distinction, who was not only decorated with a DFM, but was also a WOP/AG. The former signified he had, as an NCO, already done a tour of operations, and the latter required some explanation since all the WOP/AG's, with whom we had been associated, had gone elsewhere. It transpired he had indeed done a tour in 105 Squadron on Blenheims with his pilot, Squadron Leader A.R. Oakeshott who, on returning to the Squadron, and having developed a strong liking and respect for his gunner, 'Titch' Trehearne, had recommended him for a commission, and brought him with him.

This was not a unique situation. There were two or three other similar instances and, as a consequence, the WOP/AG's were sent away for a concentrated course of navigation. We, the Observers, who had already been initiated into the world of dots and dashes, rationalised by Mr. Morse in the Code of that name, were to be taught the mysteries of a wireless set and have the Morse Code thrust at us for hours on end, week after week. All this was, as yet, in the near future.

To return to Bylaugh Hall: Up until then I had never resided in the Officers Mess, and although the Hall was in no way the Mess it was entirely taken over by the RAF and therefore was a sort of country annex, fully serviced by Batmen and a staff of administrators. The room I shared with Titch was large with a beautiful roaring coal fire in the open grate. It was attended to exclusively by our Batman, who brought hot water in a china ewer (there was no basin with hot and cold running water) and also tea, coffee, and cocoa last thing at night. He woke us in the mornings, with a cup of tea, cleaned our shoes and polished our buttons.

The Aircrew Sergeants were also billeted in the Hall but the space they occupied was more crowded than ours, and they did not have Batmen to attend to all their comforts.

Transport was laid on at all times between the airfield and the Hall, but I tended to use my bicycle and Pete his car, when he had petrol - which seemed to be most of the time. One day he asked me to drive his car back to the Hall. It was the first time I had driven it and no mention was made of a warning he should have given. Driving down the hill I saw an Airman thumbing a lift, there seemed no reason not to pick him up so I put my foot on the brake and promptly disappeared, with the seat, into the back of the car. The road and the Airman were suddenly no longer there. From my new viewpoint only sky and the tops of trees were to be seen. I retained my hold on the wheel and, hoping the car was still on the road, pulled myself, and the seat, back to where they should have been.

When vision was restored the Airman was some distance behind, getting out of the ditch, and the car was still moving. I brought the car to a stop, by bracing myself against the steering wheel whilst I braked, and the Airman ran up to find out why I had attempted to run him over whilst, at the same time, ducking out of sight. He became subdued when he found the driver was an officer. Instead of demanding he waited for an explanation to be forthcoming, or not, as the case might be. He received one with some fairly fruity opinions concerning the bloke who asks you to drive his car without deeming it necessary to mention that the driver's seat was not fixed down.

There was a very unusual and original plumbing installation to bring hot and cold water to the bathroom(s) at Bylaugh Hall. The taps were enormous polished brass examples of empirical engineering, discharging into a bath representing the best skills of the coppersmith and shaped somewhat like an oversize hip-bath, the bottom being flat and the sides likewise, but curved at the non-tap end. The tap end had a plughole with a great, heavy, column-like thing serving as a plug. The weight and size presumably ensured that it was not stolen by the guests and, at the same time, helped to overcome any discrepancies of fit, whilst making it possible to put the plug in or take it out without either bending over or getting your hands wet. The entire bath was silver-plated, as became such a splendid house, but badly in need of re-plating.

Our stay at Swanton Morley was long enough to discover that sharing a Mess with a Fighter Squadron did not produce many quiet evenings sitting in an armchair enjoying a well earned drink. The armchairs were usually moved to one side to make room for a game of no-rules rugger with a cushion as ball, or employed to crouch behind when a handful of machine-gun ammunition had been thrown on the fire. There always seemed to be plenty of drink, either in the Mess or in East Dereham, where there was a Pub with a heating system in the bar consisting of an enormous open hearth. A sack full of coke was burned in a pile some two feet high whilst the customers gradually retreated to the other end of the room.

On the fifteenth of November 1941 the first Mosquito was delivered. It was officially recorded as 'Another great day in the history of 105 Squadron; even the Spitfire Pilots of 152 Squadron were impressed'. Shortly afterwards we packed our bags and moved the entire Squadron to Horsham St. Faiths, on the northern outskirts of Norwich.

CHAPTER 15.

Horsham St. Faith's

RAF Horsham St. Faiths was a permanent, pre-war station with proper hangers, Mess's and administrative buildings. The Airfield was grass, with no runways and not very large. There were many external attractions, such as the 'Bell' Hotel in the centre of Norwich only a ten minute bicycle ride from the Officers Mess. The villages of Spixworth, Wroxham, Horning and Sprowston, complete with Pubs, were equally accessible though a little further away.

I was now living in an Officer's Mess for the first time. The bedroom, shared with one other officer, had a basin with H & C, and the bathroom was just across the corridor. All this and a Batman too, who would, if you asked politely, even darn socks, provided you had no objection to his method of running a thread around the hole, pulling the ends tight, and then tying a knot. I did not consider myself fussy, but once was enough for me.

The dining room downstairs was adjacent to a large ante room with a superior fire-surround and mantelpiece, framing an open fire, and furnished with a grand piano, radiogram, darts board and lots of comfortable, well upholstered arm chairs. There was a billiards room, a writing room and a guest's sitting room, now used by the WAAF Officers. I began to wonder, perhaps for the first time, if, having come this far, a career in the RAF might be preferable to going back to being a student of architecture!

Although this was an operational station the big snag was that there were no Mosquitoes for us to use. There were various other aircraft to which we had access for training, fetching and carrying, visiting, going on leave and simply for enjoyment. There were a couple of Masters - single engined, two seater fighter-trainers, an Anson, at least two Blenheims, a Tiger Moth, at one time a Puss Moth, and the use of Airspeed Oxfords belonging to the Blind Approach School who also used the airfield. It was to be some time before sufficient Mosquitoes arrived to make operations possible, but in the interim, although there was considerable frustration, there was seldom tedium.

The Anson was used as a general workhorse and on one occasion I was in it on a journey to Hatfield, the birthplace of the Mosquito, to fetch some engine cowlings, either as spares or replacements, for the few Mosquitoes we did have. The opportunity was taken to look over the factory and see the fuselages being molded from Birch plywood and Balsa wood. The ply, about one sixteenth of an inch thick, was laid over the mold, covered with glue upon which was placed close-boarded Balsa, about a half inch thick, then more glue and another layer of ply. The three layers were then pressed down over the mold with metal straps through which an electric current passed, inducing the straps to heat up and the glue to set. Having produced a beautifully streamlined fuselage, large sections were cut away to accommodate the wing and form the cockpit, which gave the appearance of a disaster in the making, but I was assured they had realised this and would compensate for the parts cut away.

At the end of the factory tour, having been told the entire neighbourhood was by now devoid of dog kennels, garden sheds, rabbit hutches and any other timber structure easily removable during the black-out, we returned to face the problem of getting four aluminium engine cowlings into the Anson. Each cowling was some seven or eight feet long by around two feet wide and quite substantial. It was soon apparent that the pilot and navigator (me) would have to get in first and the rest of the crew, two ground crew fitters, would have to get the cowlings in with no assistance from us. I didn't mind this, but with almost no possibility of us at the front ever getting out of the door at the back without the prior removal of the cowlings, this I did mind, but fortunately the necessity did not arise. The Anson rattled noisily into a take-off, even more noisily into the landing at the other end, following a flight of happy rattling heard easily above the noise of the engines.

The Miles Master was an altogether different kettle of fish to the Anson. Single engined, low wing two-seater advanced fighter trainer, it was reputed to be the fastest training aircraft in the world. Being dual control I was able to practice piloting on almost every occasion when I was taken along for the ride. Why I was invited to go is not, at this distance in time, very clear to me. I suppose there were times when the pilot wanted someone along, preferably a navigator, to take the blame for becoming lost, or liked to have company, or, on one occasion, the opportunity to frighten the life out of someone. How this lucky person came to be selected did not appear important, at least I hope this was so, otherwise why pick on me?

I do not recall who it was with the ambition to frighten me. I think it was a senior officer who, having heard the Master, normally well behaved, was quite unpredictable in a stall turn, and not having had the opportunity to experience this personally he decided to put it to the test. He asked me if I would like to come for a 'short trip' in the Master. Sensing the opportunity to practice my piloting I readily agreed. At about six thousand feet I heard in the intercom: "Are you well strapped in? I'm going to do a stall-turn". I admired his concern for my well-being and awaited the manoeuvre. He had not thought to warn me of the Master's reputation but I knew a stall turn was a normal enough procedure whereby the nose of the aircraft was raised until the climbing angle became too steep for the engine to sustain flying speed. The 'plane would stall, the nose dropping rather suddenly, usually controlled to be either to the right or left, and when you pulled out of the dive you had not only regained flying speed in the dive but you were going in the opposite direction.

Most aeroplanes were predictable in how they would behave in a stall. The Master was not. Up came the nose, the speed dropped away, the engine fought a losing battle, everything juddered and suddenly I discovered what it might be like to be a fly on the tip of a stock whip at the moment it cracked. I have no idea whether we went right, left or backwards, and had I been asked in that split second for my opinion it would undoubtedly have been to assume the aircraft had disintegrated. Relative peace returned when we went into a vicious spin, and I had time to realise I did not like being in a spin. It was the first time for me, but not unfortunately the last. The pilot, who I am sure was just as shaken as me, pulled us out of the spin and decided aeroplanes did not do that sort of thing to him and had another couple of go's. The results were exactly the same as the first time, except they were by now predictably unpredictable.

After mastering the rudiments, the flying of an aeroplane once airborne, straight and level, calls for no great skills. Aerobatics require tuition and practice but taking off and landing - particularly landing - present the greatest hazards. I had taken off in a Tiger Moth and therefore considered myself competent at that manoeuvre, but the first time I was allowed to take off the Master it was to find I had a lot to learn. We sped down the runway behind the seven hundred horsepower Rolls-Royce 'Kestrel' engine, (it was the same engine used to win the Schneider Trophy at a world record speed some little time before the war). I pulled back on the stick, we shot into the air like the fighter plane it nearly was and I smartly raised the undercarriage, at least that was the intention. I knew which lever it was but it did not wish to budge, I believe it had some locking device which every one should know about. During my struggles the aeroplane was not receiving the attention it required and our rate of climb began to exceed its capabilities. If the chap in the back seat had not pushed the stick forward we might have been into one of those stall turns from which, at a height of about one thousand feet, there would have been small chance of survival.

Only good luck prevented an unscheduled visit to the house of a girl friend by making our entry through the roof. Undaunted by the near disaster of the take off I was allowed to 'beat-up' her home without appreciating an aircraft of such high performance does not pull up on the instant but tends to squash down a bit. The loss of this critical piece of height, just above the chimney pots, was almost our undoing.

I was never taught to be a pilot, but one way and another and mostly by the generosity, kindness, perhaps even the lack of wisdom on the part of the pilots with whom I flew, usually Pete Rowland, I attained a fair degree of competence. Enough anyway for W/C Hugh Edwards V.C., who was flying in the Master with me on one occasion, to promise me a pilot's course when we finished our present tour of operations. Alas it was never to be, but maybe it was not 'alas'- who can tell?

There were two Blenheims on the Station, one a 'long-nose' with which we were already familiar, and the other a 'short-nose'. The former turned out to be the most useful by taking me down to RAF Thorney Island, from where it was but a short distance to Denmead, home and a spot of leave. The short distance on public transport took somewhat longer to accomplish than the journey from Norwich in the Blenheim. A small disadvantage arose in so far as I had to travel in the gun turret, the front of the aircraft being full of pilot and navigator who had kindly agreed to fly me down and then take the Blenheim back to Horsham St. Faith. The gun turret was noisy, not all that comfortable, and draughty, but with a splendid view, providing you were more interested in where you had been rather than where you were going.

The 'short-nose' version of the Blenheim was fitted with dual control, and being short nosed the pilot and his pupil sat inside a completely glazed cockpit from which a good view was obtained forward, upwards, sideways and downwards between ones feet, which was unusual for most makes of aircraft. I was permitted to land it and I am sure the ground rushing past between my feet had an off-putting effect. It was a good job the under-carriage was of sturdy construction!

The De Havilland Tiger Moth was the best of the lot. It was probably the only one which actually 'flew', instead of being dragged into and through the air by ever more powerful engines. Should the engine fail in a Tiger Moth there was time to look around and glide gently towards a small field, or something, whereas the others, particularly the Mosquito, tended to emulate a brick when losing power, and called upon to glide.

'Jock' Pringle, of whom more a little later, had never managed to achieve a slow-roll in a Tiger Moth, so one day when he was giving me some dual instruction he said he was going to have one more try. During a slow-roll the aircraft rotates on its horizontal axis from being the right way up, to being sideways down, to being upside down, followed by the other side down and back to being the right way up. I do not believe there is much profit to be gained by achieving the manoeuvre, apart, that is, from personal satisfaction, and this Jock was determined to have.

All was well until we were upside down and there we stuck. I clearly recall - I was in the front cockpit - hanging at the full extent of my somewhat loose straps and looking across the top surface of the top wing, (in our attitude at that moment it was, of course, the bottom surface of, what had now become, the bottom wing). We were being buffeted by the slipstream, and not a bit liking the experience of hanging, insecurely, upside down two or three thousand feet above the ground. Suddenly the nose dropped and, with me not yet back in the cockpit, we sped towards the ground. What was happening to Jock at this time I had no idea, he being behind me, but it is to be assumed his straps were tighter than mine and he was still able to reach the controls. He pulled back on the stick, and as the 'plane leveled out I shot back into the aircraft assisted by considerable 'G' force.

I said to Jock that 'I didn't like that.' 'No,' he answered, 'nor did I, its what always happens. I don't know why, I'll try again'. And so he did, and again, and again, and again, until I was completely familiar with the top surface of the upper wing. The experience of completing a slow roll in a Tiger Moth still awaits me. I landed the Moth and was carefully and slowly taxiing back across the aerodrome, swinging the tail from side to side in the approved manner to obtain a view forward to either side of the engine. Jock, impatiently, (and who could blame him after the failures to complete a slow roll?) said 'Well done, I'll take over now'. He opened the throttle and we almost flew across the grass towards the Control Tower - where we stopped rather suddenly, with a broken propeller, amongst the coils of barbed wire, the tail stuck up in the air, and me once again hanging on my straps. The silence was broken by a wail from the back seat – 'I forgot the damn thing doesn't have any brakes!' He was to discover a new propeller was rather expensive.

The tale of the Tiger Moth has to end on a very tragic note. It crashed on the airfield perimeter killing one of the occupants and badly injuring the hands of the other, who would never again play the violin, at which he was so competent. One of them had borrowed my Gosport Tubes (speaking tubes); on another occasion someone borrowed my parachute and never came back. I would never lend anything after that without mentioning these two occurrences and the result was always the same, the would-be borrower went to try elsewhere.

Another aircraft to which we had access was the Airspeed Oxford. Our squadron did not, as it were, own one, but one could be borrowed from the Beam Approach School, who shared our airfield. They had several, which would be made available for matters of emergency, such as going on leave, if it wasn't too far. Portsmouth, though the birthplace of the Oxford, was too far, and that is the reason I was taken in a Blenheim. The Oxford was a very sensitive 'plane and I was not the only one who found it needed great concentration to stay straight and level and at the same height.

On some mornings in East Anglia a mist, about ten or twelve feet thick, covers the flat countryside and when airborne it was like being above cloud with chimney pots and trees poking through. If at the time you happened to be wondering where your aerodrome had got to, you could, with a bit of luck, spot an Oxford going down as if to land through the mist, then pull up, to be followed by another and another. These were the Beam Approach pupils doing their thing. They did not need to see as they were following a radio beam, and thus proved a reliable indicator of where we wanted to be.

CHAPTER 16.

Mosquitoes.

For some time Mosquitoes were very scarce. The concept of a wooden aircraft in an age when every self-respecting aeroplane was made of light alloy metals, was not joyfully received, or approved, by the important people from whom decisions are required before mass production can begin. To cut a long, and fascinating story, short, the prototype demonstrated the remarkable potential of the machine, showing it to be capable of carrying a bomb load of two thousand pounds (later to be four thousand pounds) to Berlin at a speed, equal to, or better than, most fighter planes. From being not really wanted it became the aeroplane everyone wanted. The first Mosquito was, as already noted, delivered to 105 Squadron on November the fifteenth 1941; but, due to the shortage of production, and its increasing popularity, the Squadron did not carry out its first operational sorties until May 1942.

The six months between the delivery of the first Mossie and the first operational sortie were put to good purpose. There was a great deal to be learnt concerning the capabilities and virtues of this new aircraft and the best way for these to be exploited. I recollect no vices. I suppose there must have been some, but from my viewpoint - no vices, only a few inconveniences.

The wireless installation, for example, comprising two large metal boxes, with big brightly coloured knobs, was situated on a shelf behind my head. These impressive and colourful wireless sets - a transmitter and a receiver - not only interrupted the view backwards, but required me to turn and kneel on my seat whenever I plucked up enough courage to try and make them work. They were, in fact, very good sets and had a remarkable range; the only fault was their inability to ensure they had competent operators. Receiving was not too difficult as long as the 'Home Service' or the 'Light Programme' satisfied the needs of the moment. But when highly technical deeds had to be done, like tuning the transmitter to the same frequency as the receiver in order to hear the reply to your transmission, usually a cry for help, hopefully tapped out on the morse key, then all manner of complications arose. Was it the yellow, blue, red or white knobs? Why did the little dial indicating the output power refuse to budge? Oh dear, forgotten to wind out the aerial? Why had the fluctuating green light known as the 'Magic Eye', lost its magic?

You didn't TALK on our wireless, you used the Morse Code, a series of dots and dashes representing the letters of the alphabet and produced by pressing down a key for a very short time if you wanted a 'dot' and rather longer for a 'dash'. If I had invented the Morse Code I would have been a proud man, but I did not invent it, I had to memorize it! Not something I found easy. I received consolation from an Instructor when I asked if there was any explanation as to why I was having such difficulty and others, who, not to put too fine a point upon it, did not seem over bright, fairly lapped it up. It appeared I have a logical mind, (rather pleased about that) whereas the rapid assimilators, of dots and dashes, are quite happy to absorb unrelated symbols without concern for their being completely illogical. He cited parrots as being capable of learning without logic, or even understanding.

This inspiring boost to my ego did nothing for my shortcomings as a wireless operator. It is much easier to 'send' Morse than to receive it, probably because when sending you know in advance what the letter is to be, but when receiving your brain has the choice of twenty-six letters to fit the series of dots and dashes in the earphones. While this process is going on the next letter turns up, thus ensuring the previous letter is forgotten, and likewise, because by now mental panic has set in, the subsequent stream of electronic noise remains incomprehensible. A really competent operator does not hear 'dots and dashes' but recognises the sound of each individual letter. He can easily write down the message, in joined up writing a line at a time, at a rate of eighty or more words per minute. We were required to attain a speed of about twenty-five words per minute. Some did!

At times one was tempted to show off by sending at a speed in excess of one's ability to receive. The chap at the other end, who was there because he really was competent, naturally assumed here was someone who knew the code and came back even faster, just to let you know he was better than you. It sounded like a buzzing in the earphones and could only be ignored. When it stopped I would send dot-dash-dot, being the letter 'R' signifying 'Repeat', and I would keep doing so until he slowed down to my 'Airborne Receiving Speed' of about seven words per minute. It was always my sincere hope never to meet the chap at the other end.

They told us it was a well known fact for confidence to drop by twenty percent on approaching an aircraft and by a further forty percent on entering, or something like that, but it helps to explain why 'Airborne Receiving Speed' is rather less than when not Airborne. The trailing aerial, as distinct from the fixed one, was a long thin wire normally stored, wound on a drum, within the cockpit when not in use. At the bottom, or free end, were a dozen or so lead beads, each some three quarters of an inch in diameter, and as a consequence fairly heavy, designed to keep the aerial trailing below the aircraft. Letting the aerial out was easy, unless it went with a rush and broke free of the drum, in which event, of course, you no longer had an aerial. Winding it back was hard work. It was not only the weights, a slipstream in the region of three hundred and fifty miles an hour made considerable resistance. In anticipation of the retrieval difficulty, it was tempting to let out only a proportion of the full length. But to do this was, so they said, to invite disaster by way of a build up of electric potential in the coils remaining on the drum, resulting in a sudden discharge and a loud spark.

If, as was quite frequently the case, the aerial was forgotten and not wound back before landing, it became a lethal contrivance should it come in contact with any living thing as the aircraft came into land. On these occasions the aerial always finished up a great deal shorter with a nasty ragged end where the weights should have been. We were told how much a new aerial cost, but as we were never called upon to make restitution, the amount has failed to be impressed upon my memory. There was a story that a pig was cut in half by a trailing aerial!

Another inconvenience was the lack of space. It was cosy but left no room for a chart table and the navigator had to work on his lap, or on a 'Bigsworth' board. This was a board about eighteen inches square with an attached parallel motion straight edge. It was an adequate instrument but even eighteen inches square was a bit cumbersome in a Mossie and with maps to a scale of eight miles to the inch it took less than thirty minutes to cross the map area on the board. It had been designed for aeroplanes of a former era.

A great deal of snow fell in the winter of 1942 and the airfield was covered to a considerable depth. Although it was unlikely that we would be called upon to carry out any operational sorties, the Station Commander decided there should be a usable runway just in case someone in dire straits happened to be in the vicinity and needed somewhere to land. Almost no one was spared, shovels, boards and anything capable of shifting snow from the ground into the back of a lorry were issued to everyone, from the highest ranking officer down to the humblest Erk. There is an enormous amount of snow in a strip thirty yards wide, half a mile long and over a foot deep but by dusk the impossible had been achieved. It was done and we had, as a monument to our efforts, a usable runway - never to be used.

Soon after moving to Horsham St. Faiths it was decided by some high authority that Commissioned Navigators should fly with Commissioned Pilots. This resulted in Pete Rowland and I parting company. We had got on well together and it seemed a pity for both of us that we should now have to get used to someone else. My pilot was now to be Pilot Officer 'Jock' Pringle, a thoroughly agreeable Scotsman, some years older than I, married to a charming Scots lady with whom he lived in a nearby house off the station. This arrangement was not usually considered to be a 'good thing', and so, I think, it turned out. When Operations were imminent all those living out were confined to the station. This meant there was no way Jock could disguise from his wife that there was something happening, and certainly he could not divulge anything, even if he knew. She was therefore in an agony of apprehension until he returned. It affected them both and in my opinion was mostly the cause of what eventually transpired. Nothing disastrous, I hasten to add, but certainly rather upsetting.

It is a good tale, possibly true and certainly possible, and concerns one of the early Mosquitoes doing a bit of familiarisation flying. After holding a southerly course a little too long in a strong North wind above ten-tenths cloud, they descended below the cloud and found themselves to be rather South of the Thames. This was quite alarming since aeroplanes were not allowed to flit around London as they pleased. They were meant to stay in corridors where it was less likely the Ack-Ack people would want to shoot at them. The crew of the Mossie, whilst aware of these corridors, had no idea of their whereabouts. Luckily they came across a Spitfire going North, so they drew up alongside, waved in a friendly fashion to the Pilot, who looked somewhat puzzled, never having seen a Mossie before, but being reassured by the friendliness of the greeting, the RAF roundles and the Squadron identification letters, waved back. Having thus indicated his intention to remain friendly he did his duty as the pilot of the finest fighter in the world and opened the throttle to draw ahead of the cheeky twin-engined-two-person interloper who thought to formate on a Spitfire. The increased speed failed to produce the desired effect, the Mossie stayed firmly alongside. The look of puzzlement on the pilot's face changed to complete bewilderment when, being safely North of the Thames, the Mosquito, with waves of thanks and farewell, drew rapidly ahead to disappear in the direction of Norwich.

Dropping bombs was another skill which, although acquired in Battles, at Picton in Canada, and at Upwood in Blenheims, had now to be adapted to the new aeroplane. We used the same bombsight and the general principle remained the same, it really was more a case of keeping ones hand in. A few of the Mossies were equipped with bomb racks to carry the eleven and a half pound practice bombs, which were released by pressing a button on the end of a wire, rather like the bell push one sometimes finds hanging from the ceiling in a bedroom. This button operated a progressive mechanism so that 'press one' dropped a bomb, 'press two' dropped the next bomb and so on. There were racks for eight bombs but we were only to carry four. Why this should have been the case was not explained, and all other things being equal, what did it matter? But on one occasion other things were not equal! The range was in a field near a farm and we flew over at about one hundred feet, dropped a bomb, went round again to come in and drop the next - nothing happened. I repeatedly stabbed my thumb on the button muttering, 'what's wrong with this damn thing?' only to realize seconds later that I had now let go three practice bombs. I knew this because I could see them falling away as we climbed steeply to go around to make another run. I began to take a very close interest in the trajectory and ultimate destination of those errant bombs. The first fell in a field, the second in the farmyard and the third in another field of mildly interested cows. I should, perhaps, explain that 'practice' bombs do not explode and scatter lethal bits in all directions. I was never near one when it went off, but understood there to be a, not very loud, bang, followed by a silent and sustained emission of white smoke.

Someone had put the four, out of the possible eight bombs, on alternate racks so that the second press had dropped a bomb, which wasn't there! and the subsequent infuriated pressing of the button had released one bomb for each two presses. I expected repercussions from the bomb in the farmyard, but nothing further came of the incident. Maybe the farmer was used to having poorly aimed bombs in his back yard! It was on this occasion, whilst waiting our turn to use the range in very bumpy conditions, that I was for the first, and last time in a Mosquito miserably air sick, which may well have been a factor in my unreasonable reaction to the faulty bomb loading.

An officer who was not aircrew was called a Penguin, one of whom had to be flown to Belfast. I was to do the navigating but I cannot recall who the pilot was. The Penguin had to sit on the floor up in the nose, there being no other place for him, and share the limited space with the bombsight. He seemed quite happy about this and thought it was all rather exciting. To ensure he had his fill of excitement it was decided to go low-level, which means that if you are on the floor looking through the bombing clear-vision panel you are about four feet nearer the ground than the crew. To get to Belfast by the proper corridors required flying over Wales, which has some very steep mountains, one of which slightly exceeded the Mosquito's maximum rate of climb. 'I say,' said the Penguin looking round, into the perspiring face of the pilot as we just cleared the mountain top, 'that was jolly exciting, do you know I could see each blade of grass!'

The West side of the part of the Isle of Man where we crossed is a high cliff with a long slope up from the East coast. Here again we went up the slope at low level, but not quite so low as up the Welsh one, and fortunately not so steep. It is an odd feeling, and our Penguin certainly found it so, when one moment you are flying at thirty feet above the ground, then suddenly over the cliff top you are five or six hundred feet above the ground, or in this case, the sea.

Arriving at Belfast our Mossie was left in the admiring care of a ground crew, who re-fuelled it ready for the return journey whilst we were invited back to the Officers Mess for lunch, preceded by a pint or two of draught Guiness. The bottled version was not uncommon on the mainland but, being a bit expensive, neither was it too common. This draught variety was unknown to us. I believe it was a splendid lunch, I know we enjoyed the Guiness and the generosity of our hosts and I am quite sure our confidence on approaching and entering the Mossie did not, for once, reduce by fifty percent, but went up by, possibly, the same amount. Once inside this increase in confidence made up for an apparent inability to focus on figures, let alone do any calculations.

The pilot started the engines, waved away the chocks and careered across the airfield to the end of the runway. He turned to look at me and asked, 'What's the course?'

'Climb up until you can see the Isle of Man, and then aim for it.' I replied.

'Tha's a good idea. You know those blokes were very good to us. I'll give them a chance to see what a Mossie can do.'

Before taking draught Guiness he was a quiet, steady, mature and totally reliable pilot, now he was none of those things. We hurtled into the air in a steep climbing turn and then proceeded to beat-up the Aerodrome in what was vulgarly termed a 'split-arse' fashion, quite ignoring, and fortunately missing, the cables of the balloon barrage floating over Belfast. The balloons were near enough to the airfield to require some of the passes to be between their cables, either when diving into a low-level pass across the field, or in climbing from one. Eventually, with a final waggle of the wings, we went into a spiral climb over Belfast until the Isle of Man was visible some sixty miles away. I clearly remember it was a beautiful day.

'What's the course after the Isle of Man?' was the pilot's next question. I had no intention of telling him, even if I knew it. The method of aiming for some clearly visible point was a lot more peaceful on such a lovely day when I felt so sleepy.

'You'll have to aim a bit to the right of where England bends into Wales, and as that's about ninety miles beyond the Isle of Man we'd better keep climbing.'

He accepted this without question, put us into a gentle climb and said, 'I'm popping.' 'Me too!' I agreed.

The time had come to try out the, hitherto unexplored, toilet facilities of the Mosquito. They, it, consisted of a flexible tube emptying into a tank beneath the pilot's seat. At the free end was a funnel and it was obvious what was meant to happen. Following some interesting contortions, (remember he was strapped-in) he tried first. As you get higher the air becomes less dense and if it happens to be in a small tank beneath your seat, it tries to get out without any consideration for the fact that someone is, at the same time, trying to put something in. The air wanting to get out waited until the tube and funnel were almost full and then erupted, pushing all before. It was easier for me, than for him, to appreciate the amusing side to this. Instantly recognising the scientific implications I suggested we lose height for the next few minutes, which enabled me to successfully complete the operation without any bother, after which the climb was resumed. In due course we were high enough over the Isle of Man to be able to see where Wales joins on to England.

It seemed unlikely we could get high enough to see the Wash from Liverpool, a distance of about one hundred and fifty miles, so I reluctantly abandoned the ultimate in fine weather navigation. Fortunately, reverting to the more normal, and tedious, method of plotting a course by now no longer seemed to me to be impossible.

If you had the afternoon off and the weather was good it was very pleasant to go to the Broads and borrow a sailing dinghy. However, you had to be prepared for the possibility that a colleague might be flying around aware that any sailing dinghy was almost certainly going to be inhabited by aircrew, who might appreciate a little more wind. This was easily within his power to gift, and achieved by making a low pass across the masthead to give the benefit of the slipstream to the mainsail, thus greatly increasing the speed of the dinghy and, with a bit of luck, causing it to capsize.

CHAPTER 17

Contact with the Army.

When we Observers were assumed to be competent as Wireless Operators it was decided to send us off on a longish flight using the radio as the sole navigational aid. To ensure cheating was kept to a minimum the route was planned to be, as far as possible, over water. We set off in the direction of Norway and when well out to sea, and out of sight of land, altered course to fly north. Now was the time to demonstrate the marvels of this miracle of technology, the radio. Out went the aerial, the transmitter was tuned to the wavelength of a station we had been assured was anxious to co-operate and, having made contact, the appropriate 'Q' code signal was sent asking for a 'fix'. In those days the only meaning to be inferred from a 'fix' was the position of the aircraft in terms of latitude and longitude.

Back came the reply - another 'Q' code - asking for the morse key to be held down, thereby giving a continuous radio signal to provide a target for the land based Direction Finding aerials to obtain bearings. These D/F stations were scattered around so that any two, or more, would be in such relationship to the 'target' that their bearings, when plotted, would cross and give the position. When all this had happened and I plotted the position on my map, it was not where I expected it to be.

The object of the exercise was to rely entirely upon the radio so I gave an alteration of course to the pilot and resolved to obtain another 'fix' a little later. After a suitable time lapse I again approached the radio, which knew I was terrified and to show its contempt blew out a little puff of smelly smoke. When radios do that it is not a good thing, and so it turned out. To all intents it was now dead. This was intended to be a radio exercise so on we went as if the fix received had been correct, and mainly because I now had nothing to do except carry on with the flight plan. With the aid of my pen-knife I took the front off the transmitter, removed and looked, without comprehension, at the valves, put it all back together again, and, would you believe, it still didn't work?

All the time we were steadily flying to the north somewhere around a hundred miles off the coast of England. The plan was to reach a completely un-identifiable spot in the middle of the sea and, from there, change course towards the coast of Scotland. Then, having pinpointed our position, set a course for Norwich, home and Horsham St. Faith.

Scotland did not turn up as expected. Indeed nothing turned up, and after a while it became a distinct possibility we had somehow missed the British Isles and were bound for the USA. Then we arrived at some islands - quite a lot of islands -, instantly, though not positively, identified as the Orkneys. It was not possible to be positive because our maps only reached as far north as Dundee, but anyone knows the Orkneys are just off the coast from John o' Groats. So we turned south. Only sea appeared, so, assuming the Orkneys were more to the east than expected, we again flew west and could hardly believe it when more islands turned up. This time they were indeed the Orkneys, the first lot had been the Shetlands! Having at last discovered the coast of Scotland it was not difficult to follow it until we arrived back on our map.

Our reception was mixed, considering we had just been posted as over-due. They were glad to see us, of course, and whilst not believing my theory that the speed of my morse transmission caused the wireless to blow up, they admired, with some reluctance, my persistence and integrity in adhering to the rules of the exercise.

It was arranged for some of us to spend a week to ten days with the Army in Great Yarmouth. We were met by a couple of officer 'brown jobs' and a large covered truck in which we were to make a tour of inspection of the shore defences. I recollect being shown a World War One gun in an emplacement. It was huge but they explained that the gun was not very accurate, owing to the barrel being worn smooth, but if it should hit anything the damage would be frightful on account of the shell going sideways, or even backwards! As far as I remember that was the entire extent of the seaward defences in the Great Yarmouth sector. For the rest of the morning every Pub in the town was closely inspected and after lunch they showed us how to fire genuine Chicago gangster style Tommy Guns, on the beach, using a bucket as a target, which remained almost totally unmarked.

The local Workhouse was an old three or four storey, unused, brick building long since condemned as an unsafe structure - which was now to be used as our sleeping accommodation. This was the only time my camp kit issue was ever used for the purpose it was intended. It proved adequate and comfortable. As no one was allowed into the building after mid-night we were shown how to scale the garden wall at a place where foot holes had been formed in the brickwork. This is when you discover the real reason why the Army wear khaki. It does not show brick-dust and algae stains nearly as badly as air force blue.

If you are told a Bren Gun Carrier can turn in its own length, and reach thirty miles an hour across the golf links it did not seem unreasonable to me that I might put this interesting ability to the test. When the track came off they were not at all pleased and said they had not meant both manoevres at the same time! They also said the Carrier could leap off a bunker and land on the ground after a flight of some ten or twelve feet, which was demonstrated by an Army Sergeant, who lost his nerve at the last moment. The Carrier hesitated on the brink of the jump and nose-dived into the bottom doing horrid damage to the drivers teeth and face when his head hit the, whatever it is that a carrier has, as a dashboard.

A demonstration of street fighting, in which we were persuaded to involve ourselves, in and around a bombed out button factory, proved beyond any possible doubt how sensible we had been to join the Air Force. A box full of buttons emptied over your head from an upstairs landing was a good joke but a thunder-flash going off behind your back in a small room was quite terrifying. Another demonstration, put on for the benefit of other Army units, and to which we were invited to be part of the audience, was very well presented. It involved such things as boring a deep hole in the ground, exploding a charge at the bottom to form a cavity and then filling this cavity with explosive. All then retired a considerable distance, the explosion was very impressive and the resulting hole in the ground, enormous. It was very useful, they explained, if you wished to stop a road being used.

A bridge was built across a ravine in the face of 'enemy' fire and when complete, soldiers with nothing more sophisticated than a bayonet went over and, wriggling along on their stomachs, prodded the ground ahead to discover and remove mines. One of them crawled into a shell hole and for a moment disappeared from view before coming out again on the other side. After going forward about ten feet there was a sharp bang and bits of soldier flew in all directions. A gasp of horror came from the audience, followed by nervous laughter when the soldier in the shell hole stood up with a happy smile at the success of his little trick. He had used a rope, looped around a stake in the hole, to pull a very realistic dummy out over a real mine.

Driving tanks in Thetford Forest was great fun. One of our people became lost, it being somewhat misty, in the middle of a cabbage field. Another, having seen it done on the Newsreels, pushed a tree over. I managed to give a Sergeant the biggest shock of his life. I was driving a Matilda tank, which was very heavy and had a pre-selector gearbox. The Sergeant was sitting outside instructing me through the open hatch. I succeeded in getting into top gear, there were about ten forward gears and six reverse, and we were going at full speed, something like twelve mph. I asked the Sergeant if there was anything difficult in turning a corner. 'No, just change down', he replied, which I did - from top gear to bottom – which was quite easy with a pre-selector gearbox. The tank lurched and virtually stopped, the Sergeant didn't and suddenly appeared on the ground in front of the left side track which was still moving, in bottom gear, towards him. Fortunately, in sheer panic, I did the right thing and pulled back on both steering levers, which stopped the tank. It is a good job I was an officer otherwise I do not think I would have liked to hear the, very pale, Sergeant's opinion of my part in the incident.

Our last adventure with the Army was a visit to Hunstanton, a town on the North East corner of the Wash, where we were to observe an artillery shoot. The guns were placed a mile or so back from the coastline where, on the vast sandy beach at low tide, the targets had been erected. To get the best view of these targets we walked, with an army officer to guide us, to a very attractive empty house built not far above high tide mark, and looking out over the beach. It was a walk of about a mile, from the transport parked near the town, along a sandy path behind the dunes, beyond which was the seashore. The shoot was to begin at mid-day and we were looking, with keen anticipation, out over the beach waiting for the first shell burst. On the dot of twelve there came a muffled bang but nothing to be seen out on the target area. 'Oh dear,' said the army officer, 'I think that was behind us, a ranging shot, I dare say'. We all went to look out the back of the house in time to see the next shell land in the field just behind us, inducing a good turn of speed in the cows, who had been under the impression they had the field to themselves

'Gentlemen,' continued the officer, who had deduced the next ranging shot was likely to be on us, 'I suggest discretion is called for and we run like hell'.

We did as he suggested and were about fifty yards back along the sandy path when there was a strange whoopy/floppy sort of noise in the air, as if some badly designed flying object was coming down on us from a great height. 'DOWN!' yelled the officer, about half a second before the shell exploded some forty feet away. 'RUN!' was his next shouted instruction, and as no one was hurt we did, and then the same thing happened again. This time the blast helped me on my way down and a piece of shrapnel went through the sleeve of my raincoat but, this apart, there was no other hurt, although one chap did lose his silver Identity Tag from his wrist. We went back and found it later about twenty feet from the shell crater.

The Army, some of it anyway, was invited back to spend a little while with us. We did not have exciting things like Tommy guns, Tanks, Bren Gun Carriers or high explosives. We did have Pubs, in near-by Norwich ten minutes from the Mess on a bicycle and rather less in a car, and these were properly exploited. Otherwise it could only be hoped they might find being a passenger in an aeroplane was sufficiently rewarding to make up for the hours of tedium spent sitting around in the Officers Mess. It was obligatory, when taking them for a flight, to get them wound-up by flying dangerously, just above the trees and chimney pots, but in their ignorance they tended to associate the ground with normality and safety. They were not in the least concerned that it was flashing by, just beneath them, at around two hundred mph. One chap literally pleaded with the pilot to go back down again as he did not at all like being up at two thousand feet.

We enjoyed our visit to the Army but were, nevertheless, very glad we had not joined it. I hope the Army found their visit to us not too mundane.

CHAPTER 18

The Navy etc.

Following a week with the Army, a day out with the Navy seemed appropriate. Lowestoft was near to hand with minesweepers, of the very latest type, equipped with the means to detonate magnetic mines, as well as conventional mines, by towing paravanes at the end of long wires. The magnetic mines were set off by a long electric cable towed behind the vessel and energised from a hold full of batteries. So much I remember clearly, as also the perfectly adequate gangplank over which we had to cross the narrow strip of water separating the boat from the quay. The Captain's cabin was small, neat, elegantly paneled in hardwood and very welcome after a chilly, and hasty, look at the hold full of batteries.

'I expect you would like a drink?' the Captain said with no conviction that he might receive a negative reply. 'What would you like?' An entirely rhetorical question because although we expressed a preference for beer it appeared beer was expensive and Gin was very cheap in the Navy, as they paid no Duty, and anyway he only had gin.

Tumblers were produced with measures of Gin that left little room, even in a tumbler, for any kind of dilution by way of soda, water, orange, lime, bitters or whatever. I have no idea how long the session continued, or the pressing reason for its curtailment, but without doubt it was most convivial and had one curious side effect. When the time came to return ashore, the perfectly adequate gangplank had turned into an insecure, bouncy, and exceedingly narrow bridge above an angry, freezing sea at the bottom of a yawning gulf of unimaginable depth.

It was arranged for a return visit of the Navy as the guests, jointly, of ours, No. 105, and No. 139 Squadrons, with whom we shared the Station and the Mess. The invitation was, I am sorry to say, more devious than generous, and had almost nothing to do with any notion of returning hospitality.   Jamaica had adopted 139 Squadron, to the extent it was usually referred to as '139 Jamaica Squadron'.   Consequently the fortunate members of 139 received goodies and comforts from Jamaica, including crates of Rum in bottles. With bad memories of being very ill from too much Rum and Pep, I did not like the stuff and, for whatever reasons, neither did most of the members of the Mess. The crates, therefore, piled up until someone, recalling having heard that sailors liked rum, had the bright idea of getting as many Naval Officers as possible to come and drink it.

The Catering Officer of our Mess was possessed of a great talent and a suspiciously complete knowledge of the workings of the local Black Market. A magnificent buffet was laid in the Ante Room on a long table, covered with unheard of delicacies disposed around the piece de resistance - a great big beautiful cut glass bowl, lit from below, and full of Rum Punch. This was no ordinary Rum Punch, apart from a few lemon and orange slices floating on the surface it was all Rum, undiluted and poured straight out of the bottles.

Our guests arrived and I was allocated a Lieutenant to host throughout the evening. We did not get to know each other very well.

'Do you like Rum Punch?' I asked.

'Yes,' he replied rather doubtfully, presumably with visions of the variety of 'fruit cup' dished out at garden parties. I scooped out a wine glass full, he knocked it back in one, and said: 'That's good I'd like some more. Perhaps in a larger glass?'

I picked up a Pony glass, which evinced: 'Is that all I get?'

So, muttering polite denials, I took a half pint tankard and dipped it full. He downed it, as he would a glass of beer, expressed his approval of the punch, then lowered himself gently to the floor, under a table, and went to sleep. As far as I know, he remained there for the rest of the evening. I have never reckoned myself to be a good host, being a bit on the shy side, but I excelled myself that evening by discharging my duties, to my entire satisfaction, and rendering a guest blissfully happy - at least he appeared to be so under his table.

It was customary, so they told me, for an Officer of the Squadron to visit a group of Army Officers and deliver a lecture on 'Camouflage'. This was, to me, a matter of complete disinterest until someone, who held the power of life and death, confided the alarming information one day that the Officer who normally gave the lecture was unwell and I had been elected to take his place.

At that time the only lecture I had given was to my class at school, when I had discovered that neither the class or the Master were in the least bit interested in the construction of model aeroplanes. At least then I had known something about my subject, but what did I know about 'camouflage'? Nothing! increasing to very little if I concentrated extremely hard. Apparently this was nothing to worry about, because the Army Officers knew even less, and possessed little, or no knowledge, about aeroplanes and the flying of them. So, if one concentrated on the aspect of camouflage as witnessed from the air then they were in no position to know they were not receiving absolute 'Pukka Gen" (undiluted truth). It did not seem to matter that the 'air-view' aspect had to be entirely negative. If something was well camouflaged then it would not be seen and there is, therefore, nothing on which to comment. If it is badly camouflaged then you can say so, but no advice can be offered because you had not seen how the job might have been improved, on account of not having known it was there.

I was handed the sick officer's notes, a bundle of photos, and several maps. After spending the rest of the day and some of the night studying this information, I was collected next morning by a WAAF driver and taken to the disaster area, a barracks in Norwich. The WAAF was familiar with the routine, having taken the officer I was standing-in for on several such occasions, and told me 'not to worry as it only took half an hour'. A lot can happen in half an hour, so I went on worrying.

I was met and taken to a large room where the blinds were drawn and the lights were on. There was going to be a Magic Lantern show and I was going to give it. The room was full of Army Officers consisting, as far as I could establish then and later, of one Second Lieutenant and nothing else below the rank of Major. Colonels abounded and there was a scattering of higher ranks beyond my ability to identify, not having had occasion to study such exotic insignia.

Someone introduced me as 'Pilot Officer Thomas, an Air Force officer of considerable operational experience'. At that time I had never, even by accident, been within a hundred miles of enemy territory! The pictorial content of the lecture was handed to the Epidiascope operator, the lights went out and I watched the screen with as much anticipation as my audience. Improvisation became the order of the day and to my great astonishment I discovered I was actually enjoying myself, to such an extent that an hour went by before someone remembered the galaxy of rank, comprising my audience, was due somewhere else. The WAAF driver was not very pleased either. It seemed they stopped serving lunches in the Airman's Mess some ten minutes before we began our return journey.

I wish to place on record an original gem of information derived entirely from my own observation, and not even hinted at in the briefing. I told my audience that it did not matter how carefully and ingeniously they painted camouflage onto a road, runway, roof or other smooth surface. A shower of rain would nullify their efforts because, from the air, the shine from the now wet surface would highlight whatever it was they were trying to render invisible.

Two things were learnt from this experience. First, that provided I had something to say I did not mind standing up and saying it. And secondly, when next asked to give a talk or lecture I would never again feel sorry for myself for having to do it, but rather for the audience who would have to hear it!

For some, never very clear, reason there was a time when Aircrew, and others, had to turn up on an early morning Parade. One morning it started too early for me and as I peeped round the corner of a hanger, to discover if there was some way I might, even now, do my duty in swelling the ranks, I had the misfortune to catch the eye of the Wing Commander. He recognised who it was and awarded me a week's duty as Orderly Officer. The lesson here is, if to be late is heinous then stay away altogether, you will either not be missed, as I am sure would have been the outcome in my case, or you will have sufficient time to come up with a good excuse.

Orderly Officer was a job only infrequently awarded to Aircrew. There was no formal instruction, only the precious belief that by some miraculous intervention the awarding of a Commission conferred upon the recipient the ability to do the job at a moment's notice. One was, however, accompanied by an Orderly Sergeant, who knew exactly what to do. He never let the Officer out of his sight, thereby ensuring, by the relegation of the Officer to the status of a figurehead, that the job was done properly, that is to say, HIS way. Ignorance in the Officer was, therefore, an asset! It preserved that state of harmony so desirable between an Officer and 'other ranks' by diverting any nasty, 'erk type', thoughts towards the Sergeant, who didn't mind a bit, for had he been so sensitive, he would never have become a Sergeant. Whilst inspecting the Airmen's Mess at lunch time, and arriving at each table, the Sergeant would bark, 'Attention, Orderly Officer, any complaints?' There was one complaint, by a very brave Airman who mentioned the inadequacy of the washing-up arrangements, stressing in particular his belief that the drying-up cloth was rarely, if ever, changed, and had become, quite revolting. We, the Sergeant and I, duly went to inspect the 'arrangements'. This consisted of a large bowl of lukewarm greasy water, (it had, originally, been hot and clean) into which a couple of hundred, or so, airmen had swished their knife, fork and spoon, prior to wiping them dry on the offending cloth. The cloth was greasy, soggy and quite useless for drying anything, even becoming inadequate for wiping off the grease, custard etc., hastened into congealing by the coldness of the water. Indeed, to use the cloth was to risk producing a result greatly inferior to a good lick. The complaint was duly referred to the responsible department. Surprise and horror were followed by assurances that it would never happen again. But I expect it did.

On Sunday there was a Church Parade. The parade ground was full of flight after flight of airmen in neat ranks, and one flight of WAAfs, who were to be the rearguard, and me out in front of them, supposedly in command - certainly not in control - and very conscious of my vast ignorance as to what might happen next. The Sergeant was never too far away with his penetrating whisper when required. All went well; they came to attention, they stood at ease, they open ordered, I inspected them, they closed ranks, right dressed and everything was ready for the parade to leave and march to the church. It is quite a tricky procedure to get half a dozen, or so, squads of people, initially neatly arranged long-ways one behind the other, into a column of march, end-ways one behind the other, and then get them, in step, off the parade ground and onto the road.

I no longer recall the commands, suffice to say I left them in no doubt it was my earnest desire they should get in the correct sequence behind me and we would all go to Church. Each flight commander in turn duly shouted out the commands right back to the WAAFs, where the shout was distinctly squeaky. And so it was each time we came to a corner. If I had not been in command I would have found the situation decidedly comical and I could sense that those behind me, without a care in the world, were on the brink of a snigger each time the final command squeaked out. Something would have to be done, so, looking over my shoulder and catching the eye of the leading N.C.O. I muttered 'Follow me' and thus the short journey to the church, outside the Station, was completed in silence. I did not feel it right to take into Church the unholy thoughts I entertained towards the person who had put me in this predicament, so I found a suitable tombstone on which to sit and awaited, in the sunshine, the return of my flock.

Some poor fellow, not one of ours, flew into a nearby electricity pylon, or it may have been an aerial mast. His funeral was to go from our Station and I, as Orderly Officer, was to be in the Guard of Honour. His Parents were there and I dreaded the moment they would come to me hoping for some word of comfort from a colleague and discover I had never met him. Fortunately for me, and very likely for them too, a messenger came motoring after the cortege to collect '.....P/O Thomas who is to report to the Operations Room immediately'. It might have meant I was going to my own funeral but, oh my, I was so relieved.

'Call the Parade to attention, give the Bugler a 'knowing look', at the first sound the man will start to raise the flag. Call for General salute...', and quite a bit more in this vein. So read the notes handed to me the night before I took the morning flag hoisting parade. I tucked the notes into my right glove in such a way as to enable me to mug up what came next whilst standing at the salute waiting for the flag to get to the top. It must have all gone off well enough because nothing more has left any impression. The most lasting memory will always be the instruction to give a 'knowing look!' I think it was to the bugler, but it could have been the flag-puller-upper.

So much for being Orderly Officer. I have often wondered if all the people whose fate it was to have been lectured, ordered around, criticised or otherwise suffered as a result of my tour of duty, ever realised my qualifications for the job were non-existent and I was doing it as a punishment!

At the end of April 1942, Norwich was the target for a largish attack by the Luftwaffe. There was a deal of damage and all ranks from the Station went into the town to render assistance to the victims. I seem to remember one of our officers was hurt when attempting to rescue someone buried in the rubble of their home. At the time of the raid on Norwich I was listening, from the safe distance of some eight miles, to a raid on Portsmouth. Despite an inauspicious beginning, the return to Horsham St. Faith, on the train, from that leave, was enjoyable and even happy,

The train out of Kings Cross was packed full and having, by some mischance, caught the "daisy picker", which went via Cambridge stopping at every station, and other places when the mood took it, heralded the prospect of a long, uncomfortable journey, seated on a suitcase in the corridor. I met another fellow in the same predicament, with whom to bewail our lot, and while we were doing that I had a brilliant idea. In my suitcase, as a result of meeting a drunk, benevolent, Irishman in a Norwich Pub some time before, was a half pint beer bottle full of Irish Whisky. The beer bottle had been rescued by me from under the bar after having been approached, for no reason I ever discovered, by the Irishman who muttered, as if conveying a State Secret, 'Would yer loike some whisky?' The transaction was performed in a remote corner of the Gents. Irish Whisky has a taste, which I had not then acquired, and no doubt this accounted for it being still untouched in the suitcase. When the train drew into Norwich the bottle was empty, the shortcomings of the corridor accommodation were as nothing and I, together with my new friend, had acquired a taste for Irish Whisky. I had considerable trouble dialing for a taxi, the number was easy to remember, it was all threes, but counting the right number of threes proved difficult.

CHAPTER 19.

My Car.

Heaven on Earth is a rare and unlikely condition, but to a young man of not yet twenty-one the ownership of a motor car must approach such a state of bliss as to be the next best thing. Flight Lieutenant 'Somebody' wanted cash rather more than he wanted his car. Although there were several who would have liked the car, money was in short supply and the asking price out of reach of all but me. Not that I had any supply other than my pay, but I did have a system, arisen from ignorance and inexperience, whereby I had agreed to have a statement from the Bank at six monthly intervals, instead of the usual monthly. This meant the state of my Bank balance was, for most of the time, unknown to me. To avoid the stigma of being overdrawn I was very careful to ensure that cheques drawn in a month were less than the amount the Government were paying me to win the war. The sums involved were roughly; pay £19 a month, drawings £15.

The availability of the car happened to coincide with my first Statement from the Bank. It showed I had saved something like £65, a considerable fortune, and quite sufficient to pay for the car and leave enough over to pay an insurance premium and buy lots of petrol at less than two shillings a gallon, provided coupons could be fiddled from somewhere.

I signed the second largest cheque of my life, the largest had been for my uniform but that did not really count as I was merely passing on the grant. For the sum of £10 I became the owner of PK 8695, a seven horsepower, two cylinder, four-door, wood and fabric saloon, made by Jowett some thirteen years earlier in 1929. It was not perfect, but it went and never once let me down to an extent where I was unable to make the necessary adjustments or repairs. It did, however, require its owner to learn some different techniques, such as double de-clutching to avoid stripping the "crash" gear box (i.e. no synchro-mesh). The accelerator peddle was positioned between the clutch and the brake, instead of to the right of the brake peddle, and a very gentle foot was necessary when letting in the 'cone' clutch. A cone clutch only slips when you don't want it to, that is to say when climbing a hill or trying to accelerate. When you would like it to slip to achieve a smooth transition from stop to go, then it is either in or out, nothing in between. If you were prudent you carried a packet of 'Fullers Earth' to throw into the cone of the clutch when the slipping became too bad, which could be done from inside the car by lifting a floor board.

The dynamo did not work and, being intimately involved with the distributor, could not be removed for repair without immobilizing the car. The remedy was to be found in the Wireless Department (W/T Section) where they had an ample supply of two-volt batteries. Three of these placed in the boot could be linked to give the six volts needed via a miniature grid system of wires brought round to the place on the running board where the battery had been before being taken, to the same W/T Section, for re-charging. This system of electrical supply was ample to run the ignition, and therefore the engine, for quite some time, but to use the starter would cause a burn out of the 'grid system', and the headlights ran down the batteries at an alarming speed. None of this really mattered, headlights were not allowed in the blackout and the starting handle was a permanent fixture in the front of the car.

Speed was not its forte. Fifty mph flat out, maybe sixty downhill with a good tail wind, but I never really knew because the speedometer had given up trying to pass any message long before I became its owner. There was no ignition key, only two identical Bakelite 'turn' switches, one of which would turn on the ignition and the other the side and headlights, if it had been possible to use them. The ammeter did not of course function owing to the lack of a dynamo. The fuel-guage was the only instrument which could be said to work with one hundred percent reliability. It took the form of a length of wood dowling, stored under the bonnet on top of the petrol tank, and could be dipped into the tank, to register against pencil markings, the quantity of fuel remaining; always providing the car was on an even keel. There was also an 'advance and retard' control on the steering wheel, which enabled power to be increased when ascending a hill, by retarding the ignition, and would also send a message to the engine to break your wrist if you had forgotten to retard before using the starting handle.

Jowett published an advertisement picturing an Indian tribesman in the Himalayas pointing the way, to the driver of one of their cars, above the caption 'Try not the pass,' the tribesman said, until he noticed it was a Jowett and then he waved him on! I never found a hill it could not manage, not that there were many hills in East Anglia, but we did get thirteen happy people into, and on, it one night all safely brought home! Which is more than could be said for some others.

There was this chap who owned an Austin Seven saloon who, returning home from a successful Pub-crawl with six passengers, took a corner too quickly and slow-rolled into the ditch. No one was hurt - they were much too drunk to come to any harm - so those who were not thrown out joined those that were, and together they picked up the car and put it back on the road. You could do that with an Austin Seven, if there were six of you. A return to the ditch was then necessary to retrieve the odd bits that had fallen off, such as the passenger side door, the sunshine roof, and the bonnet cover. It was reassuring to find the engine still happy to go on working so they all remounted only to find the steering wheel was, with the exception of one spoke, missing. The single spoke was still attached to the car and the rest of the wheel was discovered under one of the back seat passengers where, to avoid further disturbance, it was allowed to remain being now surplus to requirements. They then drove back to the Mess with a passenger holding the door in position and the driver, managing perfectly well, using the spoke as a tiller in lieu of the wheel.

Next morning essential repairs were made. The bonnet went back quite easily, the door was tied on with wire, (none of your cheap and nasty string) which was not necessary with the driver's door, it being jammed immovably shut. The way in was now through the top where the sunshine roof had been. The steering wheel looked okay when carefully placed in position, but of course it only had one of its spokes attached to the column.

Another Officer who, to the envy of us all, was the owner of an M.G., could not get the car to start on that same next day. Being unaware of the previous night's adventure, he asked if he could be towed to the garage in Norwich by the Austin Seven. Half way into Norwich all seemed to be going well, when the driver of the Austin decided to relieve the tedium by removing the steering wheel from its one spoke and waving it through the hole where the sunshine roof should have been. This caused a quick reaction from the M.G. driver who, sensing a disaster, banged on his brakes, thereby effectively removing the part of the Austin to which the rope was tied. I expect it was the carrier.

I believe it was the owner of the Austin Seven who was overheard to remark that he '....had been doing so much instrument [blind] flying lately that he found he had driven half way to Norwich without looking up from the dashboard!' This was known as shooting a line and duly came to be recorded in the Squadron 'Line Book', as did the remark of the R.C. Padre who replied, when asked if he would like a drink, 'It is very kind of you, but I only drink to be sociable. A double Scotch please'.

About this time, whenever that might have been, there I was drunk and incapable, by any standards, and at least another ten minutes to closing time, when in came the village Bobby, wanting to know if the owner of motor car PK 8695 was in the bar. Well, yes, it was me and my beautiful Jowett was parked outside. No doubt you know, or can guess, the feeling when confronted by an inquisitive policeman, knowing that your driving licence expired in 1939, the Road Fund Licence had run out three weeks ago, and the Insurance Cover Note had been promised for next week? Fortunately I was in far too happy a state, either to know, care or guess how I should have felt. Bursting with pride I admitted it to be my car.

"Oh, then that's all right, Sir," came the surprising reply. "I thought it belonged to George Bloggs, it's just like his, and I would have wanted to know how he came by the petrol. Goodnight Gentlemen." And he cycled off into the night.

Although, weather permitting, we were now flying operational sorties most days, life on the Station proceeded much as before. There were Pubs that had to be visited, there was the Sampson and Hercules Dance Hall in Norwich, at which one's dancing prowess and enthusiasm increased with each visit to the bar, in approximately the same ratio as partners became less enthusiastic, and even difficult to find. There was the time, in the mess. During a splendid sing-song (of very rude songs) around the piano, when my beer induced exuberance led me to address the Wing Commander by his Christian name. I sensed at once that he did not like it and next day all doubt was removed by a summons to his office and a good dressing down. I am sure he was quite right to do so, being a very good W/C and knowing ALL the words to the songs, which was more than I did.

Some time before becoming the proud owner of a motor car, Jock Pringle had been replaced as my pilot by Jim Lang, who owned a motorbike. Now there are times when a motorbike is inadequate if you have more than one passenger. On one such occasion Jim asked if he could borrow my car. I was quite happy for him to do this but there was a difficulty in as much as I had promised to take out a girl friend that evening. He thought for a moment and then came out with the brilliant suggestion that I should borrow his motorbike. There was one minor snag - I had never ridden a motorbike. It was decided to give me instant tuition and practice.

The controls offered no problem so off I went to do a few practice circuits of a hanger. That essential ingredient, confidence, was in short supply and the Wing Commander, on his way from the Control Tower to somewhere via our hanger, was not very amused when he was obliged to leap from the uncertain path of the fearsome machine over which I was supposed to have control. Gaining confidence with every yard, the machine and I came round to the back of the hanger where the Wing Commander, having taken his short cut through the hanger, was just in time to be very nearly the victim of a second nasty accident. This time he was not even slightly amused.

It was generally agreed I was now competent to go out on to the road, where it was probably safer, there being less traffic and almost no Wing Commanders. The girl friend was well brought up and on finding she was expected to ride pillion exclaimed, 'How exciting'. I had not thought it necessary to tell her today was the first time I had driven such a machine, or that she was the first passenger to experience my newly acquired expertise. I have happy recollections that there were only 'near disasters,' such as when I tried to double de-clutch, to change down going up a hill, as was necessary on my Jowett, but apparently not done on a motorbike owing to it being impossible. The attempt resulted in the engine screaming at full revs, and, it seemed, trying frantically to get out from under me, so when I let in the clutch the 'bike shot forward nearly losing my passenger, backwards, off the pillion seat.

If, and when, one should become attached to the RAF Regiment for a week, great care should be taken to appreciate that although the Corporal understands perfectly why an Officer does not wish to attend the roll call at the crack of dawn, the same is not true for the Units'

Commanding Officer. I found this out at breakfast when I lowered my newspaper, to discover him sitting opposite and fully aware of who I was, and where I ought to be. It was embarrassing for both of us but more troublesome for me.

They took us to an airfield to look at, and inspect, captured enemy aircraft, some of which they had flying. We were standing in a group watching the flying display when one of the 'one time Air Gunners' who had done a tour of operations, wore the ribbon of the DFM, and was now a Navigator, remarked on seeing a single engined aeroplane coming head on. 'Ah yes, a Messerschmitt 109. I should know, I've shot down enough of them'.

It turned out to be a Spitfire!

For the second time in my Air Force career I had to visit the dentist. The first time had been in Canada, when a most agreeable dentist told me the offending tooth must come out, and he intended doing this under a local anaesthetic. This was to be a new experience for me as I had, until then, always been given gas. There is very little in dentistry for the potential patient to look forward to, and certainly I never liked gas because there was always the same nightmare. I was falling down a bottomless pit from which someone, or something, was trying to hold me up by a tooth. This was unbearably unpleasant, but since nothing could be done about it the unpleasantness continued until there was a sort of 'electric bang' accompanied by a red and white flash, a glorious, short-lived oblivion, followed by a gradual return to the torture chamber. Realizing, though unconscious, that I was feeling the tooth being drawn did not improve my anticipation of having it happen again. So, without in the least looking forward to trying a local anaesthetic for the first time, I resigned myself to the inevitable. I received the injections, felt virtually nothing, and was happy to accept his explanation of why he found it necessary to put his knee on my chest to obtain the leverage to pull out a tooth 'embedded,' so he remarked, 'in concrete'.

The second time, in England, the dentist - known as 'Tusky' - was, not surprisingly, a brother Officer. Whilst I was waiting in his office, (none of your waiting-room 'wait' among the other ranks,) to pass the time he gave me an interesting account of the methods used by his predecessors of many years ago. One method I remember consisted of using a hammer and chisel to knock the top off the aching tooth, thereby reducing the duration of the agony to a minimum as one sharp blow sufficed. He gave me gas and when I came around he admitted the tooth had defeated him and he had only managed to break the top off! He was never again quite so friendly when I remarked, 'Ah, you must be one of those old fashioned dentists you were telling me about'. It should be recorded, in defence of 'old fashioned dentists' that the tooth never ached from that day on until it was removed, in different circumstances, in Stalag Luft 3.

The Whitley, a heavy bomber, was the mainstay of the bomber force in the early days of the offensive against Germany until the arrival of the four-engined aircraft. It was, in my opinion, not at all an attractive aeroplane to look at, either on the ground where it looked heavy and cumbersome, or in the air where it flew in a nose-down attitude still looking heavy, cumbersome and slightly ridiculous. These are all, of course, aesthetic considerations. I know nothing of its practical virtues, of which no doubt there were many for it certainly was instrumental in carrying the war deep into the Reich when there was nothing else capable of doing so.

A Whitley landed, for some very good reason, with a full load of bombs, on our airfield, stayed the night and departed next morning, or it would have done, had the Gremlins not intervened. It taxied to the down-wind side of the field, where the end of the runway would have been if there had been one, and started to gather speed for the take-off.   The tail rose, and went on rising to well above the horizontal whilst we, the onlookers, marveled at the sight of this large aeroplane tearing across the grass looking more as if it were going to try tunneling instead of flying.   At the halfway point the only part to give any indication of eventual possible flight was the rear turret, its occupant already some thirty feet above the ground.   This had to be the most unusual take-off ever witnessed, and so it might have been but the tail never did come down to allow the nose to go up.   At, maybe, seventy miles per hour, the Whitley, with its crew and a full load of bombs, demolished the perimeter hedge, crossed the road, went through another hedge and fence coming to rest in, rather appropriately, the yard of a car breaker.   The crew, aware that 'safe' bombs and full petrol tanks are a combination best admired from a considerable distance, disembarked with great alacrity.   Nothing blew up, no one died and I don't suppose the incident was ever mentioned, outside official documentation, from that day to this.

CHAPTER 20

Operations.

Up to now, in this account, the nearest 105 Squadron had been to operating its Mosquitoes against the enemy was on the twelfth of February 1942, when the Wing Commander had inquired of his Flight Commanders if any of them felt like going out to 'attack a couple of Battleships'. This produced mixed emotions. They felt they ought to say, 'Yes, Raa-ther,' but were very conscious of the Squadron being considered not yet operational, the weather was lousy, and they were not at all keen on Battleships anyway. The Battleships were real enough. The 'Scharnhorst' and the 'Gneisenau', in company with the 'Prinz Eugen' plus assorted other small ships, were at that moment making their way through the Straits of Dover. They were on their way from the French Atlantic port of Brest to a berth in the Fatherland, further from the bombers of the RAF, and ready to repel the invasion of Norway by the British, as foreseen by Adolf Hitler. A newspaper article reporting a raid on Brest in which hits had been scored on the Battleships, had produced the immortal headline – 'The Scharnhorst doesn't look so Gneise-now!'

Fortunately the Wing Commander was either trying out the metal of his Flight Commanders or his own sense of humour by frightening them out of their wits, or showing off that he had up to the minute information not yet released for general consumption. The ships were attacked by some incredibly brave crews of the Fleet Air Arm in their, surprisingly effective, antiquated 'Swordfish' torpedo carrying Biplanes, resulting in a VC being awarded to Lt. Cmdr. Esmonde. Other attacks were made by Beaufort aircraft of the RAF, also carrying torpedoes. Unfortunately the Battleships succeeded in getting through, even though both ships were severely damaged by mines, laid by the

RAF. Fortunately neither ship ever again became effective units of the German Navy.

The first Mosquito Bomber Squadron to be established was 105, but in mid September 1941, No. 1 Photographic Reconnaissance Unit, was the first to use the aircraft operationally. This first sortie had to be abandoned when a generator packed up. Two days later they were successful. The first Mosquito to be lost through enemy action came ten weeks after, when, on a mission to Norway, it was hit by anti-aircraft fire. The pilot, knowing he had to come down and that the enemy would dearly love to get their hands on a Mosquito, headed out to crash in the sea. Neither he, nor his Navigator survived.

On the night of the thirtieth of May 1942 the first one thousand strong bomber raid on Cologne took place. Everything capable of flying, and carrying bombs, took part to make up that magic total of one thousand and although we did not join the night bomber stream, we were not forgotten. When the heavy bombers had returned the first ever Mosquito bomber sortie, with a load of high explosive, took off at the unearthly hour of four a.m., heading for Cologne to reconnoiter the damage, and cause a little more. This was repeated five more times, at suitable intervals, with the intent of keeping the Air Raid sirens going throughout the day to hinder the fire fighters. It was my first time navigating over enemy territory and I must admit it was not difficult, being reminiscent of the time we came back from Belfast. I did not have to say 'Climb up 'til you can see Cologne' since we were flying at twenty-seven thousand feet and the column of smoke rising from Cologne was some fourteen to fifteen thousand feet high anyway, and could be seen from about eighty miles. Apart from the smoke, it was a pleasant day with good visibility. It was not noticeable that anyone was trying to shoot at us and no fighters put in an appearance, so I carefully aimed the bombs to fall into the middle of the stricken area, with no hope of seeing where they hit, and we went home.

I am sure this is the point at which I should be highly emotive and moralise upon the folly and cruelty of war, of dropping bombs on women and children. On the de-humanising influence of being a participant, in general, or a bomb-aimer in particular, and so on, and so on. But I am not going to, because whilst all these things are not to be dismissed or ignored, they are, as far as I am concerned only recognizable with hindsight, which was denied to us at the time. Had we thought to think about such things we must have concluded, what a wonderful thing it would be to have this hindsight, if only because we should have to survive to have it! And that was rather unlikely owing to the Germans not having had it when they started the whole unfortunate business.

At the time of aiming my first bombs, I was a young man, not yet twenty-one, and as far as I was concerned my country was at war with a tyrannical regime. We should win in the end, there was never any doubt about that, and I was happy, and frequently apprehensive, to be part of the great adventure to make it happen.

I have already told of losing my first flying Log Book, when it was stolen from the taxi in Montreal. My replacement Log Book was also lost, to me, when I failed to apply for its return after the war ended. Attempts to retrieve it forty-five years later, not surprisingly, proved unsuccessful. It would have been very useful to have had a record of my flights and operations thus enabling this account to be both chronologically and factually accurate. Fortunately, I do not believe either of these virtues to be essential, indeed they could well introduce tedium into what I hope is a tale of memorable, and thereby hopefully, interesting memories, uninhibited by too many facts. After all, dates belong in history books and in the context of an event which, if interesting, might be remembered, are only there to be forgotten!

My operational career consisted of some twenty-plus sorties. Many left no memories, so those that have been remembered contain some incident or happening without which they would not have appeared here. When I include a date it may be assumed that it is either firmly glued into my memory, or someone else has recorded it and I have benefited, by whatever circumstances, from their diligence.

Since we were the first to fly this new 'Wooden Wonder' aircraft, as it came to be called, in its role as a bomber, it is not surprising there was no information as to the best way to use it. Would it prove to be most efficient and effective at high or low level? between the two? in daylight? at dawn? at dusk? at night? or some combination of these alternatives? Guinea Pigs may well ask similar questions. In the early days sorties were designed to test these variants; their success, or otherwise, being deduced from the number who failed to came back, and in those early days the casualties were rather high.

Titch Trehearne, who had been my roommate at Bylaugh Hall and a good friend ever since, was the Navigator for Squadron Leader Oakeshott, now the Commanding Officer of No. 139. On the Second of July, on a low-level raid, in an aircraft borrowed from 105 Squadron, they were shot down over the sea. Neither survived. On the same raid the Station Commander, Group Captain MacDonald was also shot down. We were to come across him again in Stalag Luft 3 some months later. There were to be many similar tragedies in the weeks to come. They were names that came and went, none of them as personal to me as the loss of Titch. I expect it was because I had once been with him to London to meet his wife off the train from Llanelli, and spent a lovely day, before leaving them in their hotel, to catch my train home for a spot of leave.

In the same personal category as Titch was Pete Rowlands who had been my first pilot. Fortunately, he was to survive the war, be commissioned, be awarded the DFC and become an airways pilot until his retirement. Sadly he died of Cancer before I was able to visit him after I had become aware of his existence some forty years after the end of the war. I mention him again because I have already told of his love of low flying and there are not many who have returned from a raid with a large hole in the front of the 'plane and his Navigator, Michael Carreck, nursing a Danish chimney pot on his lap! Michael Carreck, with whom I had trained in Canada, was also commissioned, awarded the DFC and survived to live in the Algarve, where he is now and frequently shames me by replying to my letters instantly.

Jock Pringle flew our aeroplane and I was becoming concerned that all was not as it should be. As already mentioned, he lived off the Station with his wife and I remember her asking me at a mess party one evening if there was anything I knew that might be worrying Jock. It seemed to her he had changed and become withdrawn and distant from her when they were on their own. She was anxious as to the cause, and even fearful he might be involved with another lady. I was able to reassure her absolutely with respect to the latter, but only able to confirm my opinion that there was something, not yet identified, producing a change in his manner.

We flew two or three uneventful daylight missions of which one, at least, was intended to be a cloud cover attack on a channel port. When the cloud ran out we returned to base as instructed, and on another occasion the sortie had to be aborted because there appeared to be a fault with the aircraft. Returning from one of these, as we came into land it seemed to me we went very near indeed to the chimney of a house outside the aerodrome perimeter. I mentioned this to Jock who couldn't understand my concern, in his opinion he had allowed an ample margin. His contradiction of what I knew very well to have happened, made me distinctly uneasy.

With a clear conscience, but feeling very much a rotten sneak, I had a word with the Doctor, imploring him to be very tactful and if possible to approach Jock as if he, the Doctor, had noticed something to alert his professional concern. That is how it must have happened and the next thing I knew Jock was grounded. In due time he turned up wearing spectacles with a job in the Control Tower. I know he felt sheepish, and perhaps a little ashamed about this but there were never any recriminations. To clear my conscience I told his wife about going to the Doctor, her only reaction was sincere gratitude. As far as I know they lived happily ever after.

I think it must have been Jock who was pilot when we went on a cloud cover raid to Wilhelmshaven. The idea was to fly over the North Sea, offshore from the Frisian Islands, just above the clouds, forecast as being ten/tenths all the way, pop down through the clouds - with a bit of luck - over Wilhelmshaven, drop our bombs, and nip back into the clouds. Returning as we had come, just above the clouds, so that in the unlikely event of a fighter coming up with us, we would disappear into the clouds. All went well until, still over the sea, and North of where our target should have been, the cloud stopped in a neat line parallel to the coast and about twenty miles from it.

Our orders were clear: 'If the cloud runs out the bombs are to be jettisoned in the sea and then return to base'. We had done that once already and it seemed a great waste of time, effort and bombs to come all this way for nothing. After all, if we came home safely there was unlikely to be too much bother and if we did not get back there would be no bother at all, not with us anyway. So we turned in to the shore and there was Wilhelmshaven. We were not the only ones to be surprised at this masterly feat of navigation. The Germans were certainly not expecting us and not a shot was fired as we cruised across the town and harbour. I noted a large merchant ship alongside the quay with the hold covers off and it seemed to me that if I could put our bomb load in the open hold then it would be congratulations all round for us and great confusion for the enemy.

We went round again to come back to the ship from the East, conscious of being only at two thousand feet, the height, we had been assured, that was the ideal height for light anti-aircraft fire to be positively lethal. I am sorry to say the ship survived our onslaught. They were beginning to shoot at us by now, thus inducing a modicum of panic and causing the bombs to overshoot and knock down some bungalows in the town. At the de-briefing when I sadly admitted missing the ship, a kindly intelligence officer told me it was a good thing I had because the bombs were designed for blast effect to knock down houses and other buildings, and would have been wasted on the ship. I still wished I had proved that for myself.

I needed a new pilot and they found one for me. Not brand new I am happy to say but well experienced and positively ancient, twenty-seven or eight, I think he was, and quite certainly one of the most agreeable things that could have happened to me.

Jim Lang, born on Saltspring Island, British Columbia, was educated in England and in 1937 was a Second Lieutenant in the Bermuda Volunteer Rifle Corps. He learned to fly at a private flying school in Bermuda, and came to England to join the RAF where he earned his wings in September 1941. In the spring of 1942 he was posted to 105 Squadron and flew with one of the Wireless Operator/Navigators, until, for a reason I do not remember and possibly never knew, the partnership ceased at the same time as I had become pilotless. Jim wore a shoulder flash proclaiming his country of origin as 'BERMUDA', which I found complicated matters when he was not present. Mentioning this interesting piece of information caused people to immediately assume he was a West Indian! Which, in those un-enlightened days, would have been something to wonder at.

Munster is a German city some forty miles East of the Dutch border. One day it was decided it should be irritated, by Jim and I, at dusk. The main object of the exercise was, although we were not told this, to assess the merits of a dusk raid when related to a Mosquito. The plan was to fly at our best height of twenty-seven thousand feet, arrive with enough light to see the target, descend to about two thousand feet, aim, drop the bombs, and return in the dark. The outward journey, very high and very fast, made us almost immune to fighter interception and flak would have to be extremely lucky, even if it could reach that height, to score a hit. It had to be sheer misfortune if a night fighter, found, or could match, let alone, exceed the speed of a Mosquito as we fled home in the dark. Light flak, at the lower height, was a hazard if you flew over defended areas. This we tried not to do, but not always with success, as we found on another occasion.

One or two things did not go according to plan. No trouble in arriving at dusk, but the predicted break in the clouds did not materialize at the Estimated Time of Arrival and there was no sign of Munster, so we descended in a large spiral to where it ought to be, still above ten/tenths cloud, and then someone started to shoot at us. Not only could we see the shell bursts, following us around in our descent, but also the muzzle flashes of the guns on the ground, seen through the cloud, which could have been a thick ground mist. There was no future, it seemed, in going through the cloud only to find Munster very adjacent to the underside, so I aimed the bombs for the middle of the greatest cluster of muzzle flashes and we set out for home, hoping it had indeed been Munster and we had made a worthwhile contribution to the war effort.

As we climbed away towards home it became quite dark and the port engine was seen to be giving out a continuous stream of sparks. Had we, without being aware, been hit by flak? Was the engine about to burst into flames? Would a night fighter see our trail of sparks and sneak up behind while we were climbing and vulnerable? All things considered it was decided to stop the engine and see if this stopped the sparks - it did. Fire now seemed unlikely and invisibility desirable, so we stayed on one engine. The Mosquito did not mind a bit, and even maintained a good rate of climb at over one hundred and eighty mph. This was considerably below our planned speed, and taking into account that we also did not know for certain our point of departure (from what might have been Munster), the navigation was becoming more and more tenuous.

We flew on, using the flight plan, modified to acknowledge the lower speed, until it would seem we should be over the sea. Jim then re-started the faulty engine, from which the stream of sparks had diminished owing to the gasket, subsequently found to have been the cause of all the bother, having burnt itself out. I then tried to get a QDM on the wireless, which, had I been successful would have given us a course to steer to arrive back at base. I do not remember if success followed my efforts, knowing my luck with the radio probably not, but I do remember we both became aware of a moaning noise in the earphones, and there was no doubt it was getting louder by the second. One of us suddenly recalled an instructor mentioning Balloon Squeakers. These were radio devices transmitting a continuous undulating signal from the centre of a balloon barrage, with a limited range to warn anyone hearing the signal they were near a barrage. If the signal became stronger you were getting nearer and vice versa. The sound had never been demonstrated but had been described as being like 'the final agonies of a dying cow' and that seemed a fair description of the noise in the earphones. Assuming London was in front, we turned smartly towards the west and the dying cow faded from the earphones.

Now was the time to try for another QDM, but before this could be done the cow came back again, faintly at first but getting louder. The immediate, and sensible, reaction when finding danger lurks ahead is to go in the opposite direction. We were sensible, the cow became fainter, great relief, and then it came back again. That dying cow was determined to have us as its audience. After the same thing happened three or four more times, our twisting and turning seemed to shake it off, but by now, from being unsure of our position, we were totally lost. There was, however, always 'Darkie', another radio aid never before used by us. The pilot had a radio with which to speak with the control tower, nearby aircraft etc., indeed the same radio recently dominated by the dying cow. It had, like the balloon squeaker, a transmitter range of about ten miles, so if anyone heard its transmission, then it followed they were within ten miles of you.

'Hallo Darkie, hallo Darkie, this is 'A' for Apple calling,' said Jim into the microphone. 'Please where are we?'

Almost at once back came the reply. 'Hallo 'A' Apple, you are off the coast of Bradwell Bay, we will light up the aerodrome for you.'

Suddenly about five miles away an enormous cone of searchlights went up, there must have been at least fifty of them, all meeting at a point over the centre of an Aerodrome. We flew towards it and coming into land was like flying through the side of the biggest tent you are ever likely to see. We made a somewhat bumpy landing and stopped as soon as possible, because Mosquitos needed a lot of room and we didn't know how long a strange runway might be. Jim, facetiously, remarked into the radio, 'I have just made an attempt at a landing', at which he was told to go round and try again. On explaining he was actually on the ground he was told to taxi to the end of the runway, which took five or ten minutes. It was the longest runway we could ever have imagined. It transpired that the Aerodrome had been constructed exclusively for the reception of lame ducks, four-engined bombers mostly, coming back from Germany, after having been badly shot up and unable to make it back to their own bases.

We stayed the night and flew back to our own Aerodrome next morning, and were able to see, from the air, the extent of the airfield. There were three runways of incredible length, forming a triangle, with a cluster of the original farm buildings in the centre.

This was not the first time Jim and I had found our nighttime performance left something to be desired. It was not the last time either! Navigating at night, without a sextant, was, for me, a very inexact procedure. To start with it is very dark, some people said you could see railway and coastlines, rivers etc. I never saw a damn thing and Jim had the same trouble. As far as we were concerned a Mosquito at night is the nearest thing to limbo either of us ever hoped to experience.

Circuits and bumps at night were a fairly frequent occurrence. The circuits were fine and the bumps not too bad as long as we did not lose sight of the flare path. On one ambitious circuit we flew away for ten minutes and then came back and landed. On coming to a stop I mentioned to Jim that the Control Tower was over on our right and if we had landed towards the West, as we had, it should have been to the Left. This was a very accurate observation. It wasn't our Aerodrome! It turned out to be Oulton, about fifteen miles North of Horsham St. Faiths. As compensation it was quite an experience to dine in the splendid surroundings of Blickling Hall, at that time being occupied as the Officer's Mess. A small truck came to fetch us back to our own Mess after dinner. I do not recall how the aircraft came back but I am quite sure it did.

There was to be a significant night attack against some industrial centre in mid Germany. The success of the raid would largely depend upon the weather, either it had to be very cloudy, or very clear, whichever it was someone had to go and see if a predicted weather front was where the meteorologists had calculated. So one fine summers day Jim and I set off in our Mosquito, at an altitude of twenty-seven thousand feet, armed only with two or three code words to be transmitted upon reaching the place where the front should have been. Depending on which code word was sent they would know if they had been right. We were somewhat surprised to discover they had been spot on. Usually our weather comes from the West and as the Atlantic was under the control, mostly, of the Allies our forecasters had a big advantage over the enemy, who had to rely on reports from their aircraft, sent out for that purpose, far out into the Atlantic. I believe the reason we were sent was because the front we had to find was coming in from the East. Apart from the surprise of finding the weather forecast so accurate, the flight was completely uneventful, even to me making a successful radio transmission, and being in daylight we even landed on our own airfield!

We were briefed to fly a circuitous route to Denmark, via Holland and Germany, passing over such places as Essen, Munster, Hanover, Breman, Hamburg, Kiel and Flensburg. The return was to be over water, forty or fifty miles offshore from the Frisian Islands, straight back to Norwich. The aircraft carried a full load of bombs, which we were to drop when a city presented itself, such as any of the aforementioned places, or indeed any other likely looking target, but on no account were we to consider the sortie over when the bombs were dropped. The flight plan was to be carried out in full, whether we found a target at the first city, or the last, or at none of them. In fact the bombs were there to please us, rather than to advance the war effort, and provided we completed the 'Cooks Tour' no one would mind if the bombs were brought back.

You would think that the chances of not finding at least one city, on a summers day perched twenty-seven thousand feet up in the sky, would be unlikely, but it was predicted there would be ten/tenths cloud all over the continent. Only by sheer good luck might there be a hole in the cloud coinciding with a target beneath. They told us the object of the exercise was to calibrate new Radio Direction Finding Equipment, which would be monitoring us and plotting the results against our predetermined route. Would we please, therefore, fly very accurately to the times and compass courses of our flight plan. It was peaceful and gloriously sunny, an infinity of blue above, meeting at every horizon, a woolly vastness of cloud tops. Nothing intruded; no flak, no fighters and only twice the ground beneath the clouds. The first time revealed seemingly peaceful, green fields, small roads and a railway line, but before I was able to match any of it with the map, the cloud resumed, and I noted in the log it was somewhere to the North of Hamburg. The second time the cloud cleared shortly after setting course for home when suddenly below was a coastline easily identifiable as being Sylt, a large island off the Danish coast, known to be heavily defended against aircraft as protection for the submarine and naval base at nearby Flensburg. Being well aware of its reputation, and not wishing to give them any target practice, we about-turned and flew North a bit, over the clouds covering Denmark, before turning again for home.

A new course had to be plotted after getting a good pinpoint as we crossed the coast for the second time and discovered we were much further North than intended. Plotting it was one thing, measuring it quite another since I had not brought a protractor with me, but the Gremlins were kind that day, and the course I guessed was spot on, taking us straight home. At the de-briefing they told us the whole exercise had been most satisfactory. Not only had the plot of our 'tour' worked very well but they had also gained an insight into the excitement our uneventful flight had caused the enemy. Air raid warnings had sounded in all the towns flown over and our people had monitored the scrambling of numerous Luftwaffe fighter aircraft sent to intercept us throughout our progress. All this and the bombs brought back into the bargain!

After our bombs on Haarlem

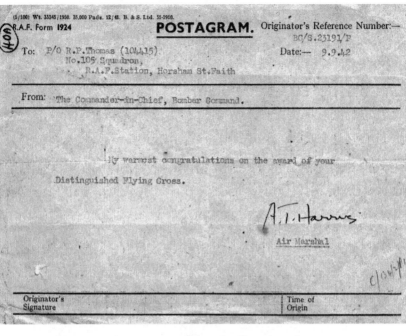

Telegram from Air Marshall ' Bomber' Harris

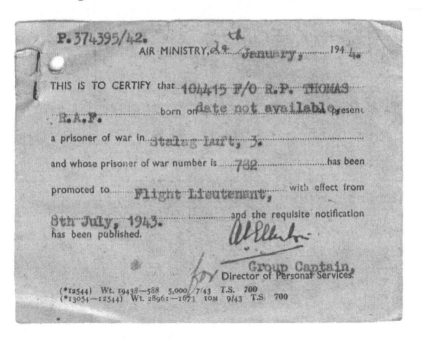

Notice of Promotion 'by survival'

Corporal Gunther Kircher of the 5th Squadron
of Jagdgeschwader 1 (in the side-car)
-who shot us down!

Caterpillar Club membership card

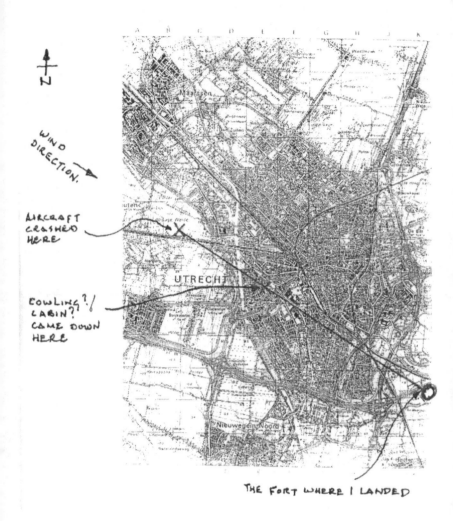

N

WIND
DIRECTION.

AIRCRAFT
CRASHED
HERE

UTRECHT

COWLING?/
CABIN?
CAME DOWN
HERE

Nieuwegein Noord

THE FORT WHERE I LANDED

My parachute glide path

The moat in which I landed

The fort within the moat

Room in the old compound at Stalag Luft 3
-taken by Herr Pieber
L/R - Author, ?, ?, 'Happy', Steele, Bertie Bowler

The new camp at Stalag Luft 3 before the trees
came down
L/R - John Madge, Author, Jim Lang

The then Utrecht Police Station (I think) where I was first taken

The Author and Jim Lang's re-visit to Holland in 1994 - at the monument to the 'Finger in the Dyke' boy

Sergt.

Observer A. Law of Blackburn, Eng. (right), and Sergt. Observer A. Thomas of Portsmouth, Eng., who received the highest marks in bombing and gunnery at the Picton station's second class of air observers.

Portsmouth Pilot Awarded D.F.C.

Pilot Officer Robin Patrick Thomas, R.A.F.V.R., of No. 105 Squadron, has been awarded the Distinguished Flying Cross.

In August, 1942, this officer was the observer of an aircraft detailed to attack an industrial target in Northern France. The operation which demanded a high degree of skill, was successfully carried out in daylight despite the presence of enemy fighters. By his sound judgement and coolness under fire, Pilot Officer Thomas contributed materially to the success achieved.

Pilot Officer Thomas was born in 1921 at Portsmouth, where his home is. He was educated at Portsmouth Grammar School, and Peter Symond School, Winchester. He enlisted in 1940, trained as observer in Canada and was commissioned in 1941.

BRITISH PRISONERS

evening news 9/11/42

Air Officers in German List

Enemy reports to-day name the following airmen as prisoners in Germany:

Flying-Officers T. W. Stewart, 1.9528, Clanricarde-gardens, Bayswater, and R. P. Thomas, 104415, Denmead Farm, Denmead, Hants; Pilot-Officers D. H. Cochran, 122441, Essex-road, Leyton, and John Dowler, 120249, Windmill-lane, Ewell; Sgts. L. H. Dean, 1336968, Shalp (?) Farm-road, Worthing; F. E. Garrett, 1337059, Pine-grove, Maidstone; Harry Levy, 1270422, Langdoncrescent, Ilford.

British prisoners reported captured in North Africa include:

In German hands: Lance-Cpl. Smy, 4750015, Corth(?) - avenue, Harolds Park, Essex; Dvrs. D A Perkins, 10769314, Parkhouse-lane, Walthamstow, L G Brown, T183293, Woodland-drive, Watford; Ptes. J. Steward, 4393244, Wanderton-road (?), North Kensington; Cotterell, 4122925, North Elm-street, Camden Town (Canning Town?); Shepherd, 4120926, Goldington-buildings, Camden Town; Signalman H. J. Thomas, 942835, Cambridge-road, Southall; Trooper R. E. Ormonde, 4271495(?), Fernbank, Ashouse(?) Wood, Suffolk; Gunner

Excerpts from various newspaper cuttings

Some of my home-made artefacts

ESCAPERS STOVE

MUG - made from a tin and large enough to contain the stove

Ventilation slots
Pyjama cord wick on float
FAT is solid until the wick is lit.

A KLIM TIN IS opened by removing the tear-away strip with a key. Inside is a ring forming a spigot on which the lid will now fit, and another KLIM TIN with the bottom removed will fit tightly on this spigot.

KLIM

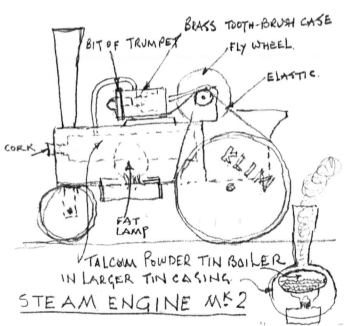

BRASS TOOTH-BRUSH CASE

BIT OF TRUMPET

FLY WHEEL.

ELASTIC.

CORK

KLIM

FAT LAMP

TALCUM POWDER TIN BOILER IN LARGER TIN CASING

STEAM ENGINE Mᵏ 2

Some of my home-made artefacts

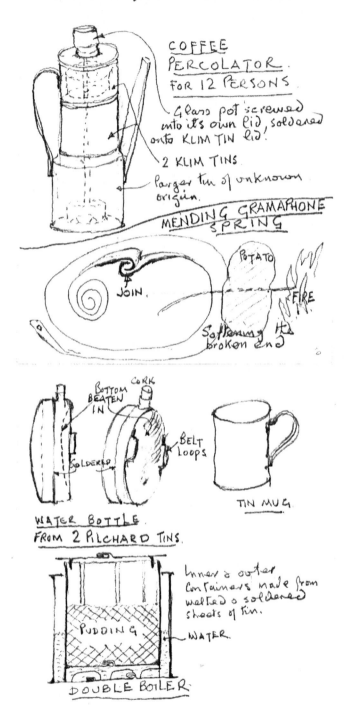

COFFEE
PERCOLATOR.
FOR 12 PERSONS.

Glass pot screwed
into its own lid, soldered
onto KLIM TIN lid!

2 KLIM TINS.

Larger tin of unknown
origin.

MENDING GRAMAPHONE
SPRING

JOIN.

POTATO

FIRE

Softening the
broken end

CORK

BOTTOM
BEATEN
IN

SOLDERED

BELT
LOOPS

TIN MUG

WATER BOTTLE.
FROM 2 PILCHARD TINS.

Inner & outer
containers made from
welted & soldered
sheets of tin.

WATER.

PUDDING

DOUBLE BOILER.

Some of my home-made artefacts

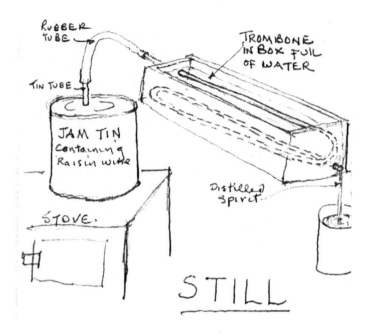

RUBBER TUBE

TIN TUBE

TROMBONE IN BOX FULL OF WATER

JAM TIN Containing Raisin wine

Distilled Spirit.

STOVE.

STILL

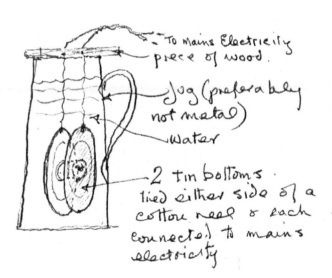

To mains Electricity piece of wood.

Jug (preferably not metal)

Water

2 tin bottoms tied either side of a cotton reel & each connected to mains electricity

ELECTRIC WATER HEATER

(stand well away and switch on)

Some of my home-made artefacts

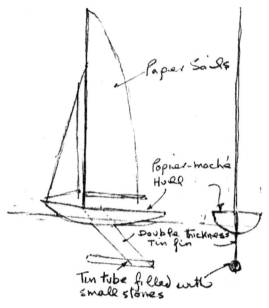

Paper Sails

Papier-maché Hull

Double thickness Tin fin

Tin tube filled with small stones

FIRST BOAT

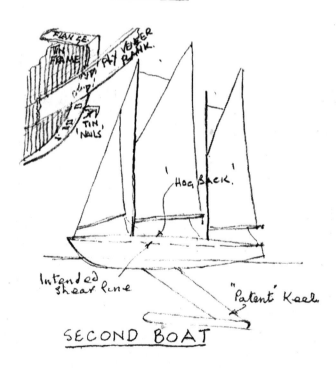

PLAN SE.

TIN FRAME

IN PLY VENEER PLANK.

TIN NAILS

HOG BACK.

Intended shear line

"Patent" Keel.

SECOND BOAT

CHAPTER 21

Attack of Gremlins.

The Gremlins were out to get me and had they been successful – US. One Summers evening when we set out for Frankfurt, or it may have been Wiesbaden, anyhow it was somewhere around that part of the Rhine where it does a kink towards the West before resuming its Northwards journey to the North Sea. We left Horsham St. Faiths' in the late afternoon, the intention being to arrive at dusk and, as on the other occasion, to descend, identify the target, bomb it and return home in the dark. In a straight line it was nearly three hundred and fifty miles but we went the pretty way, about a hundred miles further, over the Somme and the Ardennes avoiding all built up areas where someone might have tried a bit of long range shooting. We were also anxious to avoid giving any hint of our destination, by approaching via Luxembourg rather than from Holland.

In the clear blue sky we were disturbed to see a very noticeable white condensation trail stretching out behind us. Jim tried to stop it by going up a bit and then down, but the only time it really went was rather lower than we wanted to be, so we settled for our best height, twenty-seven thousand feet, and a beautiful white 'con-trail' ornamenting the clear blue sky. Nothing noticeable came to bother us, though we did see what might have been an aerial mine glinting in the sun. (An explosive device hanging from a balloon by a long wire, and very fatal if you became entangled) but it may well have been only a weather balloon. The target, I think a rather special factory, was identified on the bank of the Rhine. We descended to a few hundred feet, taking the defences completely by surprise, it would seem, dropped the bombs with considerable accuracy, at the same time remembering to take a photograph, and then climbing up to about five thousand feet whilst setting course for home. Now if all this sounds too good to be true - it was.

The Gremlins had made sunset in Germany quite a bit sooner than predicted in England, and although we could see well enough the camera could not. Consequently, when, to prove my incredibly accurate bombing, the film was developed, there was nothing there except a jagged streak like a flash of lightening. They assured us it was static, not flak, which would have made a better story.

Rather more significantly, the Gremlins had entered my flight plan and confused the two figures relating to the distance home and the course to steer to get there. This deliberate mischief on the part of the Gremlins was not helped by the poor light and the similarity of the two figures, even to this day I can remember, or I think I can, that both began with a three and ended with a nine. When I came to check the course for home, and having in mind the three and the nine, the figure which jumped out at me, and was given to Jim to steer, was 329 degrees. When a little later it became prudent to re-check, the 329 was discovered to be the distance in miles to the Norfolk coast, and the correct course should have been 309 degrees.

All this was, as yet, unknown to us as, with some satisfaction at having hit our target, we climbed to five thousand feet and set course for home, anticipating a peaceful journey of some one and a half hours, in the dark and over a carefully chosen route to avoid all known anti-aircraft defences. With the darkness came that now familiar feeling of being in limbo. The instruments glowed their luminous green, and that was it, nothing above, nothing below and nothing around the sides, just Jim and I in our comfortable little cabin hurtling home at nearly three hundred miles per hour. And then it was as bright as day, or even brighter. With no warning at least two searchlights snapped on to us, and several others were waiting their turn.

As the searchlights lit us up, from every direction, and in every colour of the rainbow, tracer bullets climbed slowly towards us and then, in the manner of their kind, accelerated horizontally to flash past, (providing they did not hit you) above, below, or to one side. This phenomena was brought about by the bullets being viewed relative to the ground at first and then, in an instant, becoming relative to the aircraft. Tracer is very pretty, more so if aimed at someone else, and considerably less so when you remembered that each visible bullet had between itself and the next in line, six or maybe more mates from the same barrel, and not lit up.

Our most immediate concern was to get out of the glare of the searchlights. Going up would only make it easier for them, so down it had to be, and in no time at all we were among somebody's chimneys and roofs, on which, of the flat variety, we glimpsed machine guns. If they happened to be in front of us, their crews scattered like mad, no doubt thinking we were going to shoot back, which I hope frightened them, as indeed they were certainly frightening us with their lights and bullets. We, of course, had no bullets or even guns, but they did not know this. Because we were so low every gun in the neighbourhood was trying to hit us and the trajectories of their bullets were, at times, horizontal, or even below horizontal. It was very likely that the bullets that missed us, and they all did, caused consternation among the nearby machine gun positions on the other side of the street, or up the road a bit.

Out of all this I recognised four emotions. Amazement that searchlights could flash straight on to us and stay there even at low level, dismay at being lit up for all to see, consternation at the amount of light flak which could be directed towards a solitary aircraft, and sheer fright when chimneys flashed by only inches away, or so it seemed. Jim did a wonderful job of getting us out of the bother the Gremlins, ably abetted by me, had led us into.

When you travel at around three hundred miles an hour, things come and go with great rapidity, and quite suddenly it was dark again and the pretty display of criss-crossing tracer had ended. Jim pulled up the nose, at which time, happily back in Limbo, I studied the circumstances and found we had steered a course which had taken us directly over the Ruhr, somewhere around Cologne, Dusseldorf or Essen, it was never precisely established where, but the neighbourhood was unmistakable! A new course was calculated and when it seemed we should have been over the North Sea, I actually obtained a QDM on the radio, that is a course to steer to bring the aerodrome in front of us. I think we may have flown over Horsham St Faiths but as they were having an Air Raid alert at the time, they did not want, understandably I suppose, to turn on the runway lights. Evidently the Gremlins had not given up. Just think, if there had not been an air-raid we just might have landed on our own aerodrome for the first time at night! As it was, knowing nothing about the air-raid, we could not fathom why it seemed even darker than usual, perhaps we were still over the sea? Then a beacon came in sight. Beacons were mounted on vehicles, in a different position each night and related to the aerodrome with which it was associated. It was identified by a bearing and distance from the aerodrome noted on the flimsy paper, which, it will be remembered, was to be eaten when landing in enemy territory. The beacon manifested itself by flashing initial letters, in Morse Code, with a bright red light. While circling the beacon and trying to read the letters we saw a flare path light up.

To hell with the beacon, and quickly to the runway, who cared where it was? We could find that out after landing. Into the circuit we went, flashing the letters of the day on the downwards light, lower the undercarriage, and into the approach. A green light was aimed at us, we had never had one of those before and decided to land first, before they turned the lights out, and worry about green lights afterwards. A bit of a bump and there we were, without the least idea where we were. A hand held torch directed us off the runway and on to the grass. The headlights of a car came tearing towards us, stopping in front of the Mosquito. From the car a very important Officer signaled Jim to stop the engines. He then walked towards us, obviously with no idea how to get into this strange aircraft, so I opened the floor hatch. A cap, covered all over the peak with gold filigree, (more usually referred to as 'scrambled egg' – which was how we knew he was 'a very important Officer), and beneath it an unfriendly face peering up between my knees. I was about to say; 'Good evening sir, where are we?' But he got in first.

'Where the bloody hell did you come from?' asked the unfriendly face, with a voice to match.

'It's all right sir,' I said smugly, 'they knew we were coming. They gave us a green after we flashed the letter of the day in the circuit.'

'Nobody saw you flashing the letters of the day, and the 'green' was aimed at a Hudson which you overtook as it was coming into land. It had to go round again, and what is this aircraft anyway? We thought it was a German fighter'.

He had never seen a Mosquito before, let alone put his head through the hatch in order to carry on a conversation from between the knees of the Navigator, and interest overcame anger. All was forgiven, and when our recent harrowing experience had been recounted, without laying too much emphasis on how we came to be in such a predicament, he and his colleagues became friendly and even sympathetic.

Missing the Hudson must have been a very near thing. The light from an Aldis lamp has a very narrow beam and for us to have seen the green light directed at the Hudson meant we had been extremely close above him, as we overtook to land in front of him. We had seen nothing except that wonderful, beautiful, lit up runway and the Hudson's 'green' inviting us to land!

Somewhere around this time I became the Squadron Navigation Officer. Not, I hasten to add, as a consequence of any detectable merit, more a matter of survival. There had been a bit of a run on Navigation Officers, they seemed somewhat prone to being shot down, and there was positively no competition for the job. Was there a jinx? You might well ask, and having done so, you would hardly expect a rational answer. I did not know about jinxes any more than I knew what was expected of a Squadron Navigation Officer, and to tell the truth I do not think I ever properly found out about that either.

I had an office of my own at the end of the crew room, in which were two or three chairs, a desk with drawers containing exciting things like paper, string and glue, and the means to brew a pot of tea. The latter made my office a frequent port of call for everyone who could not bear to see me looking lonely.

If you survived a year after being commissioned as a Pilot Officer, without doing anything spectacularly good or bad, they promoted you to Flying Officer. I was now a Flying Officer. So, what to make of this new found rank and status? The Wing Commander had me fix a large wall map of Europe in his office, made up from individual sheets, and, as I recall, not always joining precisely at the edges.

It was suggested a test be made to determine a foolproof method of waterproofing the Very Cartridges carried in each aircraft and stored in the dinghies. Some ingenious person suggested putting the cartridges, which were like those used in shot-guns but bigger, about four to five inches long and one and a quarter inches in diameter, into rubber sheaths such as those made by Mr. Durex.

One cartridge, thus protected, together with another as a control with no additional protection, were placed overnight in a bucket of water. Next day the unprotected cartridge was found to be misshapen, the water having caused the cardboard casing to swell to an extent where it would no longer fit the breech of the pistol. The other looked as good as new. Both would now be tested. The test site was a slit-trench, half above ground, brick lined with banked earth all round. The swollen cardboard, having de-laminated, was peeled until it fitted the breech, aimed at the other end of the trench and fired. There was a quiet bang, only the detonator I expect, the two 'stars' popped out and rolled, unlit to the other end of the trench. The 'good as new' cartridge would also be tested, in true scientific manner, even though it appeared in perfect working order. This, in fact, proved to be the case. The two flaming stars flew down the slit trench, bounced up and over the end wall, bounded away with carefree abandon across tarmac and grass to come to rest, with immaculate perception, blazing in red and green, beneath a Petrol Bowser. Suddenly a large number of people started to take a very close interest in my little experiment. Most of them found that the best view was to be had from a slit trench. It is not often that a hum-drum experiment not only vindicates the perpetrators but also introduces a little excitement in the lives of a good many others.

In a drawer, in the crew room, was a comprehensive selection of Very Cartridges, placed there for crews to be able to help themselves to the colours of the day before going aloft. They were equally available for other less official, but infinitely more interesting, purposes, such as the manufacture of Fireworks. One cartridge contained, not a coloured star, but a capsule of explosive designed to produce a large puff of white smoke, rather like a small cloud. This was jolly useful, although I never really found out what for.

The powder in the capsule was a sort of silver gunpowder and behaved in a completely satisfactory manner when confined in a tube or similar container. A foolscap sheet of Civil Service type embossed and lined writing paper, coated with gum, made an excellent cardboard tube when rolled tightly round a pencil. One end was closed, before the gum dried, with tightly wound string and the tube firmly packed inside with smoke powder. This device would be placed on my desk, closed-end pointing through the door of my office into the adjoining crew room, and the open end projecting a little over the back edge of the desk. The back end was then lit. The resulting rocket would shoot through into the crew room and make about one and a half erratic circuits thereof, bouncing off walls, furniture or people, without discrimination, all the time laying a dense white smoke screen. The ingenuity and consummate simplicity of this elegant device rarely evoked praise from the denizens of the crew room.

The tube, closed at one end and filled with powder, could then be improved by inserting in the open end a much smaller tube, rolled round a pencil lead, also filled with powder, glued in and tied with string. This then became a Banger, which could be drawing-pinned to the back of the only chair in the crew room in which it was possible to take a nap. The selfish devil therin would be frightened out of his wits by the very satisfactory explosion. This was quite popular with nearly everyone.

Since all the ingredients were to hand, either in my desk, or next door, it would seem to have been the intention of the Air Ministry for Navigation Officers to while away any tedium in precisely the manner I had found so interesting.

Whilst on the subject of pyrotechnics, there was the occasion when I took back to the Mess, in my pocket, a couple of Very Light flares, extracted from their cartridge, with the intention of livening up the party to be held that evening. The party was well advanced and in the mood to enjoy a modest diversion when I placed both flares, surreptitiously, in the embers of the fire, and quietly withdrew to await their ignition. Who should come in and stand with his back to the fire, to warm his hands and bottom? No less than the Group Captain! The sudden blaze of red and green flares took everyone, except me, by surprise. The Group Captain, who was the nearest, seemed the most astonished and expressed strong views on the foolishness and un-wisdom of perpetrating such a folly. Everyone, including me, loudly agreed with him, no one owned up, the flares burnt out without requiring any assistance from the Mess Orderly, who stood by with a fire extinguisher, and the event passed into history only to be remembered by me, and maybe the Group Captain.

CHAPTER 22

Shot Down - First time.

Between Lille and Lens at Pont à Verdin was, and probably still is, a power station supplying electricity to the neighbouring factories, at that time engaged in assisting the German war effort. This was not considered a good thing and it seemed desirable to see if the power could be switched off by the only means available to us, by dropping some bombs through the roof of the switch and transformer house, that being the place, so they said, where the least explosive would do the most damage. There was really only one way such a switch-off could be successful. It had to be in daylight at low-level, two Mosquitoes would go in formation led by the Squadron Wing-Commander.

At that time the Squadron was commanded by Wing Commander H.I.('Hughie') Edwards, who had completed a tour on Blenheims and been awarded a well deserved Victoria Cross, a rare distinction. His Navigator was away on leave so he turned to – who-else but the Squadron Navigation Officer? Which was, of course, me. I had never flown with him before and, therefore, knew nothing beyond his reputation which made him, to me, a rather daunting prospect, held much in awe and to be avoided as far as possible.

As we headed towards the coast I was surprised to hear the Wing Commander say he thought we were off course. I was perfectly happy with the way we were going, and said so. 'No,' he insisted, we were off track and getting further off by the moment. I believe he thought he had recognised some feature on the ground over which he knew we should not be passing.

Here was a situation! He thought he was right, and I KNEW I was, but he was rather important and I was not, so I did the bravest thing in my life and with polite deference, oozing humility, I placed the map on his lap. 'Then you'd better get on with it hadn't you?' I said.

I have no idea what I expected, and no recollection of his reaction beyond the fact that the map was not accepted, the course was not altered, the departure point on the coast near Alderburgh came up precisely as planned and there was no more bother, then, later or ever.

There was some eighty miles of sea to cross at low level before reaching our landfall East of Dunkirk. The sea was calm, the sun shone and at about half way we overtook two Bostons going in the same direction but not nearly so quickly. Then suddenly the war took on a very personal guise, and time went into slow motion. The beach in front revealed a Bofors Gun pointing at us, with its crew staring from under their coal scuttle helmets as they aimed and fired their gun and I realised those faces had, at that moment, only one ambition. To bring down our 'plane and kill us. It is not at all agreeable to be shot at, at the best of times, but to look, literally down the barrel of the gun, and into the face of the unknown person bent on your destruction is another dimension altogether. Slow motion stopped, the gun and its crew were behind us, having, I am happy to say failed to score any hits, and we were streaking, some thirty feet above the French countryside towards the next landmark, Armentiers, where the Mademoiselle came from. We made a course alteration to bring us to the target about eight miles away.

With bomb doors open, bombs fused and the camera made ready, the Wing Commander made a shallow dive onto the target and as he pulled up dropped the bombs. We stayed on course for the eleven seconds of time it took for the delayed action fuses to detonate the bombs, and for the camera to take photographs (via a mirror looking backwards underneath the aircraft) before turning away. He closed the bomb doors and, at the same time, looking back over his shoulder to see the bomb bursts. There was another Mosquito with us and as I looked behind I saw to my horror that it was flying over the target and looked as if it might be blown up in the explosion of our bombs. Fortunately our bombs went off about five seconds after they had passed over where we had put them. It appeared the W/C had made a direct hit.

While all this excitement was going on the W/C was shouting at me to give him the new course. I could not hear him, and neither it seemed, could he hear me. A quick look established that his intercom plug had pulled from its socket during the agitations of trying to do so many things at the same time. I wriggled across him, found the plug dangling from his helmet, (somewhat to his surprise as he had not yet realised why I could not hear him,) pushed it into the socket, and once again we could hear each other. I gave him the course and was surprised to hear him say, 'If we get back from this, I'll buy you the biggest pint you've ever seen'. I applauded the sentiment but unless he was clairvoyant and had just received a presentiment, then I could not see what there was to worry about. The job seemed well done, the nasty men on the beach were long past and we were on our way home to tea.

Up to now I had doubted his map reading, wondered at his ability, albeit unwittingly, to detach his inter-com plug from its socket, and admired his skill in putting the bombs in the right place. Very shortly I was to be astonished at his powers of clairvoyance.

The way home was planned to cross the coast near Le Touquet, then over some forty miles of the Channel to the neighbourhood of Folkestone and from thence to Norwich. The French coast faded behind us, the other Mossie was on our starboard side and the sea, thirty feet below, was calm. In about five minutes the sea would become England - and then I saw splashes in the water below.

'Ooh look!' I said, 'bullets in the water'.

'School of porpoises? Where?'

'No, not porpoises, bullets, and there are fighters behind us! turn left, left'.

It is good advice when there is a fighter on your tail to turn towards him thereby increasing the rate of his turn to an extent where he is unable to aim in front of you, which he would like to do so that you may, hopefully, fly into his bullets. This you do not want so, by turning steeply his bullets will go harmlessly behind you. The W/C knew this as well as I did, and since I was the only one who could see behind he would now do as I told him. We were now at full throttle.

'Right, Right!' I cried, almost in the same breath as saying, 'Left, Left.'

'He can't have got across as quickly as that,' said the W/C, suddenly losing faith in his Navigator.

'It's not a 'him' sir. There's about six of them. Focke Wulf 190's.'

No more arguments. He pulled the 'Panic Tit' and we weaved appropriately. Lots more bullets in the water but none in us – until 'BANG' and the Port engine exuded a white stream of vapour. The inflictor of this wound flashed by from in front! He had come at us head on at an approach speed in the region of six hundred mph and put a bullet through the glycol tank. About twenty seconds later the engine, kept at full throttle and boost, and having lost the coolant from the radiator, seized up and was feathered. All the fighters had gone home, I daresay in the belief that the plume of white 'smoke' meant we were done for. We flew on with one good engine and looked around to see how the other Mossie had fared, but it was nowhere to be seen, either then, or ever after.

The Wing Commander decided we should land at the earliest opportunity. Lympne aerodrome was nearest. The control tower was informed of our plight and of our intention to land, a tricky business on one engine but, I had no doubt, well within the capabilities of my pilot. Then there was a snag. The undercarriage would not go down owing to the hydraulic power for this operation being generated from the port engine, which we no longer had.

'You'll have to pump it down,' he said and, reluctantly, I agreed.

This was a totally new experience, only vaguely remembered as something that could be done in such a predicament. Undoing my seat belt I searched for, and found, the pump handle, put it into its socket and started to pump. This had to be done by kneeling on the floor, facing backwards, and was going to take some time. So there I was on the floor, unable to see anything, pumping like mad, the wheels half down, when the 'plane lurched into a shallow dive.

'What's happening, Sir,' I said getting up from the floor and seeing the aerodrome right ahead.

'The wheels are causing too much drag and it is becoming difficult to hold flying speed, so I am going in to make a belly landing.'

'Well you might have told me,' I retorted, forgetting the 'Sir' as I quickly regained my seat and fastened the seat belt.

Lympne was a small grass aerodrome and we made its acquaintance in a surprisingly gentle fashion. The wheels being half down absorbed any initial shock as they were pushed back up into their housings. The good engine stopped very suddenly and the momentary silence was followed by a sustained crumpling/scraping noise from underneath, as the poor Mossie skidded and slithered over the grass, leaving a forlorn trail of bits and pieces, bomb doors, engine nacelle covers, undercarriage doors etc. Then, silence, very nearly complete, except for the dying-down whine of various Gyros, as the depleted aeroplane came to rest not more than twenty feet from the boundary hedge.

The Wing/Co and I came out through the top hatch, observed by an apprehensive crowd of assorted airmen, standing well back, who, it turned out, had never before seen a Mosquito and had no intention of finding out the hard way whether it was carrying bombs or loaded machine guns. Or was it prone to catching fire when belly landing on strange airfields?

It was a little early for tea so they opened the bar and he bought me my large pint, or two, while we waited for the Anson to come and fetch us.

I have made mention of pulling the 'panic tit'. I am reasonably certain this was not the official name, but I never recall it being given a more technical description. It was there to give maximum, instantaneous, boost (that is, supercharged fuel admission) to both engines when it appeared prudent to retreat rapidly. Some time before, a Rolls Royce engineer had given a most interesting talk on 'how to care for the engine'. After explaining how, when set for economical cruising, the throttles would encounter and be stopped at the 'gate', but when more power was required, for take off or going a bit faster, the levers could be pushed progressively past the gate, thereby increasing the boost. 'But, on no account', said the Rolls Royce man, 'should the panic tit be pulled when the throttles are through the gate, as this is very bad for the engine and will shorten its life!'

Certainly this showed his very proper dedication to the product but his priorities seemed a trifle muddled. There is little doubt that had we not ignored his advice and thus managed to equal or exceed the speed of the F/W 190s chasing us, then although the engine may have been unspoiled it would very likely have been on the sea bed. With us to keep it company.

One of the strangest aspects of conducting warfare on the Continent from an RAF Station in England was the complete contrast between a hostile, and a civilised environment, both within minutes of each other. This contrast was, to a small extent, diminished by manufactured excitement, and sometimes anything but civilised behaviour, in the civilised environment.

A few samples:-

If you pile enough arm-chairs on suitable tables and then with the, not very reliable, assistance of your colleagues stand on the top, it is possible, when properly equipped, to stick a stamp on the ceiling and sign your name over it. Thus adding your name to the many before you, for posterity, or the coming of the decorators.

A more impressive effect could be obtained by finding a willing victim, strangely he always appeared happily sloshed, removing his shoes and socks and then anointing the soles of his feet, liberally, with black boot polish. Thus prepared the willing victim was held, by many helpers - also well in their cups - first horizontal, to enable him to walk up the wall, and then vertically upside-down, to walk across the ceiling, leaving behind a splendid trail of footprints. Sometimes, at mid-way, the polish required replenishment and this gave the victim the opportunity to say he was no longer willing. This was attributed to a modest desire to retreat from the limelight and was ignored.

When the owner of the Austin 7 discovered his car in the entrance foyer of the mess he agreed it was a good joke to have a car IN the Mess, and to drive it around the Dining Room. He assumed the trick had been accomplished by driving the vehicle up the external steps and through the double swing doors. He was not quite right and had to discover for himself, as he was by now on his own, that the only way the car would go through the swing doors was by removing the hubcaps. These hubcaps protruded beyond the mudguards, no doubt to protect the paintwork from contact with a wall or something.

A nastier trick, (as far as I am concerned this is entirely hearsay), was to await the departure of the victim - who, no doubt, thoroughly deserved all that was coming to him - on a week-end leave, and then to stable in his room - a horse! The room was on the ground floor and the window afforded entry for a regular supply of food and water, and that was it!

And on the subject of animals, there was a cat, there is nearly always a cat with no apparent owner or home and only too ready to take up with anyone prepared to feed it.

This cat had been provided with a parachute and harness, and was then carried up on to the roof of the hanger and thrown into space. It worked too well, the cat enjoyed the experience, possibly anticipating it could now get on terms with the birds and catch them in their own element. But there came a time when, not appreciating the importance of the parachute, but remembering the way to the roof of the hanger, it cast itself off and, I am sad to tell, used up all its nine lives in one go.

Jim had a golden brown Cocker Spaniel puppy called Smoogie, who, it was automatically assumed, would wish to go flying with him. A chamois leather helmet was made for him, into which his ears were rolled to protect them from the noise, before tying the tapes under his chin.   He, Smoogie that is, really seemed to enjoy flying, although he never entirely mastered the technique of take-off. He would stand at his favourite place in the nose, alongside the bomb-sight, looking through the clear vision panel until the acceleration caused him to start slipping backwards. He would start to walk forwards, and then run as his paws slipped on the shiny surface, until giving up he would about turn, leap into my lap and stay there until he could return to keep an eye on where we were going, and to surprise anyone coming to the aircraft who had never before seen a dog wearing a flying helmet looking out through the front window of a Mosquito. I hope it goes without saying that he was never taken on Operational flights.

If it sometimes appears that the more amusing, and therefore more memorable, events in the mess were associated with a modicum of inebriation, then no doubt this did have something to do with it. This conversation was associated with rather more than a modicum:

A very drunk officer entered one of the two booths in the entrance foyer and spoke into the telephone. 'I wansh to speak to Fli' Letenent Smiff in the Ofishers Mess'.

'Yes Sir, you are already in the Officers mess.'

Pokes his head out of the booth and says to anyone who might be listening,

'Thish shilly Waff shez I'm already in the Offishers Mesh'.

Someone assured him this was so, and he spoke again to the operator. 'Yesh so I am, but thish ish a big joke and I wan' the ovver 'phone. You know the one I can shee over there, now you be a good popsie and make it ring and ashk for Johnnie Smiff.'

The bell in the other booth rang, a Mess Orderly answered, and duly went to fetch F/Lt. J Smith to the 'phone. He was only modestly intoxicated.

'Hello, Smith speaking.'

'I have a call for you, Sir, from the Officers Mess, the caller has not given his name.'

'But I am already in the Officers Mess.'

'Yes I know Sir, I'll put him on the line.'

All this was being watched with drunken ecstasy by the caller, who in the excitement of witnessing his clever plan coming to fruition, and in trying to listen both to his phone and, via the held open door of the booth, the conversation across the hall, had unknowingly cut himself off.

'Hello, Hello!' said Smith.

'Hello, Hello, thersh shomthin' wrong with thish bloody thing,' says the drunk, leaving the booth but still holding the telephone. At the same time Smith, noticing this, leaves his booth and asks:

'Having trouble old man? Me too I think I've been cut off.'

'Yesh, bloody awful shervice, musht be the war, letsh go and have a drink.'

CHAPTER 23.

Gas Holder and Gas Masks.

If I jump forward in time nearly fifty years, it will not, as might be supposed, have any effect upon the overall chronological order, hitherto (not too) strictly observed.

I was called to the telephone in February 1989, by my wife, who said that a foreigner would like to speak to me. A Dutch accent in almost perfect English said:

'You are Robin Thomas?' 'Yes', I replied. 'And on the twenty-second of September 1942 you ver in a Mosquito and you dropped bombs on Haarlem in Holland, and they should have been dropped on IJmuiden. I vould like to know vy you did that?'

'Ye-es, how did you know, and how did you find me?'

'Ah, vell, I haf just been talking to your pilot, Jim Lang, and he tells me how to get hold of you, and he says you can tell me better than him because you vas the Navigator and you drop der bombs'.

'But Jim is on Vancouver Island,' I protested.

'Yes I know that, I haf just been talking to him. I am writing a history of Haarlem in de vor, and I vould like to know all about vy you drop bombs on Haarlem and not IJmuiden?'

This was all intensely interesting, even a little alarming, as my safely dead and buried reputation of long ago appeared to be on the point of unfavourable resurrection. He explained how the RAF Records Office had provided him with copies of the operational sorties for that day, containing all the details he needed to trace Jim, and through him, me. He sent me copies of all the documents he had obtained from the British, Dutch and even German sources. I found these quite fascinating as I now had, for this one raid, not only my own memories but also the reports from the receiving end.

I promised to send him my account of the raid, with a reasoned explanation of why the error was not my fault! This reply had to be delayed somewhat as I had only just retired and, having for the first time obtained a Passport, my wife and I were celebrating with a five months holiday, flying round the world, visiting friends and relations. The highlight of the trip was staying with Jim and Helen on Vancouver Island.

Here is what happened forty-seven years before the 'phone call from Aad Neeven in Holland.

The twenty-second of September 1942 was a fine day, the sea calm and we were briefed to drop bombs on a steelworks opposite the fishing boat harbour of IJmuiden, a sea-port on the west coast of Holland about twenty-five miles up the coast from The Hague. Three Mosquitoes were to fly in 'V' formation at very low level to avoid Radar. Leading the formation was F/Lt. Ralston, an already well decorated and very competent officer on his second operational tour, we were flying on his right. It was planned to make a landfall South of IJmuiden, but North of Haarlem, so that when we crossed the coast we would know the target was to our left and after turning North the first place we would come to should be Ijmuiden.

At very low level the area of visible ground is very limited so when crossing the coast, unless some easily identifiable feature is, fortuitously, immediately beneath, it is not possible to know ones precise position. In our case nothing was seen to identify whether we were indeed a little South of Ijmuiden as intended, or maybe even North! or perhaps further South than could possibly have been imagined and beyond the next town down the coast, which happened to be Haarlem? We knew the period from crossing the coast and arriving at the target would be rather brief so the bomb doors were opened and the camera made ready whilst still over the water.

Shortly after crossing the coast and turning North a substantial town appeared and I remember thinking that we must have been further North than intended and here, already, was IJmuiden, in seconds rather than the minutes expected. Right ahead was a great big gas holder. It is true a gas holder was not mentioned in the briefing, but things were happening with great rapidity, and a gas holder could be an important part of a steel works, couldn't it? So we flew close over the top and I dropped the bombs, it didn't seem possible to miss.

After dropping the bombs and closing the bomb doors, we turned out to sea to take the shortest way home, without at that time, realizing IJmuiden was still some miles up the coast in front of us. Although by then I was beginning to suspect all had not quite gone to plan, the fleeting glimpses I had obtained of the town we had bombed, did not look at all like the configuration depicted on my map. It transpired that only F/Lt Ralston, who led the formation, did not mistake Haarlem for Ijmuiden. Perhaps as he was doing the navigation he had realised he was further South than intended but did not have the opportunity to warn the other two aircraft. No doubt we discussed it at the time, back at base, but I do not remember the outcome.

When, on our return, I saw the photographs it appeared the bomb bursts were alongside the holder, not within. It did not seem possible to have missed. Maybe the bombs had gone right through the holder and burst on the other side? It is now possible, thanks to Aad Neeven, to relate some of the consequences brought about by this fleeting visit to his town fifty years ago.

The incident is summarised in the local Air Warden's report for 22 September 1942. The document is headed:
'GEMEENTELIJKE LUCHTBESCHERMINGSDIENST
HAARLEM'
and is concerned with '..drie Engelsche (three English) aircraft who threw 'bommen' (bombs) on the 'Gaasfabriek and Centrale Werkplaats'...'

The following chronological order of events is as translated, and précied, by Aad Neeven:-

12.01   Air raid alarm.

12.09   Fire brigade (at) Spiegelstraat, at work.

12.10   Big Firetruck to Gasfactory, where gasholder and oiltanks are on fire.

12.12   First Aid Post at work.

12.22   End of Air Raid Alarm.

13.18   Evacuation because of danger of explosion of Gasholder.

13.20   Dud bombs found at Railroad works.

The Air Raid Warden's report goes on to give an account of the damage, listing every property, including its occupants, in the neighbouring streets where damage - mostly broken glass - was sustained. It is most gratifying to learn only one person was wounded. Aad Neeven has not translated this part of the report but I have attempted to understand a part of the text and deduced the unfortunate chap to be wounded was a forty year old crane driver, one Christian Cornelis van der Voort living at 57 Pleiadenstraat Haarlem. I thought he deserved a mention!

Another account comes from the Year Book for Haarlem 1942, translated as follows:-

'On 22 September two bombs were dropped on the factory. The big gasholder was hit, and 110 litres of oil goes up in flames. The tank was destroyed. When also the big gasholder was not usable anymore due to bomb fragments, the delivery of gas to Haarlem and surrounding area's had to be carried out without gas storing facilities. It was not easy but could be done without problems. On the 5th October both gasholders were in use again.'

Interesting - to me at any rate - are the records obtained by Aad Neeven from the British authorities: From Headquarters, Bomber Command, part of the report for the 22nd September:

'1 Mosquito attacked IJmuiden Steel Works at 1057 hrs. from 100 ft. the bombs being thought to have hit the coke ovens. 2 others which failed to locate IJmuiden dropped their bombs on a gas-works believed to be in Haarlem.'

From the 'OPERATIONS RECORD BOOK.of 105 SQUADRON' the 'Summary of Events' notes:

'22.9.42. Three MOSQUITO aircraft took off in morning for low-level attack on IJMUIDEN Steel Works.

1. F/L RALSTON and F/Sgt ARMITAGE - attacked coke ovens which were believed hit, but bursts not observed.

2.W/O NOSEDA and SERGEANT, URQUEHART - unable to identify target. Large factory at HAARLEM was attacked as alternative.

3.P/O LANG and F/O THOMAS. Primary target not attacked. Gasworks at HAARLEM attacked as alternative.

There are two further record documents saying much about the same thing, although one refers to the bombing of the gasholder as 'an error' instead of as an 'alternative'. The former is nearer the truth, but I prefer the latter. For the record our Mosquito was a MK.IV Serial No.DK296, carrying four 500lbs. Bombs. Our time 'up' was 10.16 and 'down' 11.38, which was 2 minutes before F/L Ralston and 4 minutes before W/O Noseda. I suppose if I really made the effort I could tap this mine of information for myself and fill this story with details, but as mentioned before, I am putting down memories, not writing History. It is a terrible thing to become confused with facts and inhibited by knowledge.

One morning, four days after not finding IJmuiden, with no operation or other excitement in prospect, I was given a summons from the Mess Secretary to attend upon the Station Adjutant at 10.30 a.m. prior, I was told, to appearing before the Group Captain who wanted to see me. No reason was given, but it was suggested I should appear in my best uniform, as distinct from the Battle Dress usually worn. I was smitten with terror! What on earth had he found out? Was it the time I had answered the telephone during a gas alert exercise not wearing a Gas Mask? and a cross sounding voice at the other end had said:

'You are not wearing your gas mask, do you know who this is?' I confessed I had no idea. 'I am the Station Commander,' the voice announced.

'Oh dear!' said I. 'I was passing by and answered the 'phone because it was ringing. Do you know who I am?'

'No of course not.'

'Oh good!' I said and hung up.

Was it possible he had found out it was me? Or had the serious crime of being late for the early morning flight at Upwood at last caught up?

In my best uniform I came trembling before the Adjutant who, somewhat to my surprise, stood up and said. 'Ah Thomas, many happy returns of the day. I told my wife it was going to be your twenty-first birthday and she has made you this cake.'

Now wasn't that the very nicest thing anyone could have done? All the better really for its contrast with the previous state of panic, although it took a moment or two to forgive those who had set me up. If it had not been for the cake there would have been nothing to have marked the day of my coming of age. There were, naturally enough, cards and presents from friends and family, including a pair of gold cuff-links (I still have them) engraved with my name and the wrong date! But the cake was enormously appreciated, then and now.

John Paget and Paul Adinsell were, respectively, pilot and navigator who had remained together from OTU days on Blenheims right through until they became Prisoners of War after being brought down in a Mosquito. I think it is fair to describe them as characters. John was undoubtedly of the aristocracy, as the name Paget would lead one to suppose, and at times maybe just a little absent-minded. Paul had been with me right through my training and, being incredibly old, rich, and perhaps a little pedantic, as became an elderly worldly wise person of his wealth, was a personality not to be overlooked in a company where the average age was at most twenty-one. He must have been thirty'ish. He had an almost new car and received an income from the firm where he had worked, and for all I knew might have owned. They were a charming and, to us, an eccentric couple, well suited to each other.

All this to introduce just one anecdote. John Paget, as might be expected, wore a very expensively tailored uniform. His greatcoat had a most distinctive, illegal, scarlet lining! His uniform jacket sleeves were full cut and the cuffs tended to hang well below his wrists when his forearms were horizontal, as was the case when sitting and piloting an aeroplane. This explained, so they said, why his radio was always on 'send', i.e. transmitting, when it should have been receiving, his drooping cuff having caught in the 'send/receive' lever whilst he was operating the throttle/pitch/boost controls. This caused much amusement to those privileged to eavesdrop, and great annoyance to those who might want to call them up, or indeed use their own radio when the frequency was thus monopolized. This was the case at the time when, without a map, and whilst following them to the bombing range, one of our engines failed and there was no way of asking them to slow down. We just had to listen to their chatter fade away into the distance. The following conversation, or something rather like it, was overheard as they left dispersal. To start with, a general discussion concerning the cockpit check, course, height, destination etc. and then:

'I'll call up Control for permission to take off - - Oh dear, the radio is already on transmit.' Silence for a moment or two as he switched belatedly to 'receive', shortly followed by transmit again.

'Hello control, this is 'W' for Yellow calling, 'W' for...'

Paul interrupted. 'John 'W' does not sta...'

'Be quiet Paul, you must not interrupt when I am calling control. Hello control, this is 'W' for Yell..'

'But John...'

'What is it Paul? You really must not speak when I am using the wireless.'

'John, 'W' does not stand for Yellow.'

A short pause. 'Oh, no, neither it does, you are quite right Paul,....Hello control this is 'Y' for Yellow calling, 'Y' for Yel....,'

Again an interruption. 'John, we are 'W' not 'Y'.'

'Oh! Very well, Paul, thank you, what does 'W' stand for?.'

If the cuffs were to blame then John must have worn his Best Blues and not his Battle Dress. And if this is the case then I can quite understand he might not have approved Battle Dress as sartorially acceptable in an aeroplane, or anywhere else for that matter.

In my opinion, and many disagreed, the food was, mostly, good, and where it lacked perfection there was the remedy offered by the always present sauces, tomato, H.P. and Worcester. These gave one the opportunity of choosing the taste of the soup since this was rarely evident in the coloured hot water served up in the soup plate. Sometimes there were splendid occasions when dinner in the mess became a formal event and the maximum paraphernalia of Service custom, tradition and ceremonial was observed, well, nearly. When the Port was passed, and I had discovered it was charged to my mess bill whether I took it or not, I would sit on the 'down' side, fill my glass as the decanter passed to the left, empty it rapidly and push it to the 'up' side of the table for a refill. I had also discovered my mess bill always assumed only one glass of port.

It was very likely during the jollifications subsequent to such a dinner that, on returning from the Gents, I came across the instruments belonging to the dance band in the corridor. The band had provided music, before, during, and after the dinner, and were now on the point of leaving us to our own devices. Having always had an ambition to play a musical instrument, and being at that time full of uninhibited confidence - or something that gave me that impression - I picked up a saxophone, clasped it to my stomach and blew into the reed, achieving a very satisfactory noise. No tune, but a good noise as I marched into the Ante Room to the amusement of all except the owner, who rushed to me looking quite upset and, without the proper respect due to an officer, grabbed it away with much unfriendly mutterings.

Horsham St. Faiths was to be taken over by the Americans, with their Flying Fortresses, and 105 Squadron would move to Marham, an RAF Station, thirty-five miles West of Horsham, roughly in the middle of a triangle formed by, Swaffham, Downham Market and Kings Lynn. A day or two before the move W/C Edwards invited me to go with him in a Master and fly to Marham to see what it looked like from the air. If there was another reason it was never discovered by me. Marham was found without difficulty and on the way back the Wing/Co. asked if I had ever piloted an aircraft, and if so would I like to take over. The Master, being a training aircraft, was dual-control so I took over from then on. I had, as already mentioned, frequently been at the controls and had read a bit about the theory of flight. I had also spent many happy hours in the Link Trainer, a contraption of extreme ingenuity requiring, in my opinion, a good deal more expertise than flying the real thing. The outcome was most gratifying as he was sufficiently impressed to say he would recommend I should be re-trained as a pilot at the end of my present tour. I was hugely delighted, not anticipating the tour was to end prematurely, in less than a fortnight. The RAF was never to find what a splendid pilot it already had in its midst. In the meantime, on the third of October 1942, the Squadron moved to Marham.

I, naturally, drove over in the Jowett, and during the next week used it to explore the surrounding places of entertainment, including a dance in Kings Lynn, which added nothing to my knowledge of that interesting town.

At the time it was dark beyond the masses of available parking spaces in a large square outside the dance hall and a hotel, in the lounge of which we had passed the time between arriving in the town and going to the dance. It might have been in that hotel where I tried to become a Cardinal Puff, a distinction only to be achieved by successfully completing a complicated ritual of progressive words and movements, each progression being marked by one, two, three etc. etc. swigs of beer. Failure in being immaculate in the ritual required one to start again at the beginning. I know I failed, barely qualifying as a Choir Boy, let alone, a Cardinal.

During my very short time at Marham I saw the ferocious beak and head of a large seabird, tenuously attached to its squashed and bloody body, the result of hitching a lift from the middle of the North Sea via the windscreen of a Mosquito. The bird was a Curlew and it had come through the windscreen and hit the pilot, F/O A N Bristow, in the face leaving him temporarily unconscious and blind. The fast reaction of his navigator, F/O B W Marshall, prevented the machine from crashing. The subsequent co-operation between them enabled a landing to be made back at Marham.

CHAPTER 24.

UTRECHT. October 11th 1942.

A reconnaissance flight over Germany had been planned but this was called off and the Squadron was put on Stand Down. Jim was well pleased, having promised his fiancée, in Reading, they would get married the next time he had some leave. This was his opportunity and he phoned to tell her to leave the key in the lock as he would be home that evening. I had no such plans and with time to spare arranged to play squash after lunch. Squash and fives, played at school, were games at which I was reasonably proficient and therefore found enjoyable, unlike most other games where a ball, of whatever size and shape, would always manage to make me appear stupid.

The Stand Down was short lived, my game of squash had barely begun, and Jim was still preparing to go off to get married, when the Tannoy announced that certain aircrew, including us, were to report to the Operations Room at once. The announcement did not penetrate to the squash court and a search party was sent to find me. This they did but, as it turned out, by the time I was changed and arrived in the Operations Room a momentous decision had been made.

Six aircraft, in pairs were to go to Hanover by three different routes, planning to arrive at dusk from three different directions to keep the defences confused for as long as possible as to the final destination. It had been decided that Jim and I would go by, arguably, the most hazardous, albeit shortest and direct route. We would be flying in number two position behind a Squadron Leader, decorated with the DFC after a tour on Blenheims, but virtually unknown to us. Not for one moment would I wish to give the impression that my earlier presence at the briefing would have made the slightest difference to these arrangements. On the face of it they were as normal as would be expected, Pilot Officers and Flying Officers expect to be led by Squadron Leaders, but this one, I repeat, of vast operational experience, had only just joined 105 Squadron. He had no operational experience of the Mosquito, whereas Jim and I had survived several missions before we met, plus some sixteen whilst being crewed together. Indeed we were one of the last five crews surviving from the original twenty.

We became airborne from Mareham in the afternoon of Sunday 11th October 1942, at 16.41 hours, in Mosquito GB-A (serial No.DZ 341) and formed up on the right of, and a bit behind, the other aircraft. It soon became apparent we were losing time and gaining insufficient height. We had to maintain radio silence and Jim was obliged to stifle his desire to get on and up and, very reluctantly, held position on the Sqdn. /Ldr. who, presumably through lack of experience with the Mossie, seemed unfamiliar with its exceptional performance. Whereas we should have been at our operational height of twenty-seven thousand feet five minutes before crossing the Dutch coast and then going like two bats out of hell as the coast was crossed, we were, in fact, still climbing over the coast and five hundred feet below operational height. Our speed while climbing was such as to make us a sitting duck for any fighter patrol, warned by radar of our arrival, and able to be in the vicinity.

There was, without any preliminaries or warning, a very loud BANG, maybe it was more than one. However many it was sufficient to turn our beautiful Mosquito into a very badly mannered aeroplane. I thought that the tail unit was hit but Jim reckons it was the ailerons and since he was driving no doubt that is what it was, at any rate he was by now fighting a losing battle trying to keep control. He shouted that we would have to get out which, in the circumstances, seemed a good idea. I clambered down into the nose, by the bombsight, to collect my parachute from its storage place behind the pilots control panel. By this time another attack had set the starboard engine alight, and as I came back to my seat, prior to opening the floor hatch, I noticed cannon shell bursts all around, and seemingly hitting, the Squadron Leader's 'plane out in front of, and a little higher on our left. Meantime Jim was struggling madly to prevent us turning over on our back. He had, at the same time, managed to jettison the roof hatch, which was the only exit available to him. Getting to the floor exit, past the control column, and down to the floor in an aeroplane with a single-minded ambition to be up-side-down, was clearly not an alternative.

I am sometimes asked if we were required to practice parachute jumping. The short answer is 'No', and quite properly so, for it is not the least hazardous of experiences and no safer for being 'only a practice'. A good time for the first jump is when your aeroplane is out of control and on fire, which provides a real incentive to get out and try the hitherto untried parachute device. There was no need to have to screw up sufficient courage before making the foolhardy leap into space. On the contrary, considerable anxiety existed to try it out as quickly as possible and before the aeroplane did something really unforgivable, like exploding. And anyway there was no alternative.

Instruction had been given, however, on how to leave the aeroplane. A Mosquito in a hanger with a mattress on the concrete below the floor hatch was used to demonstrate the method. Explanation and instruction was entrusted to a Flight Sergeant, who had certainly never used the procedure himself being an expert in the practical matters pertaining to the structure of the airframe, and not the vagaries of flying the thing. The idea, he explained, was to come out headfirst performing a somersault in order to hit the slipstream with your back and fall clear. To do this the hatch had first to be opened. There were two hatch covers, one opening inwards and forming, when closed, the floor immediately in front of my seat, and the other opening outwards and forming the outer skin when closed. The inner cover lifted and clipped back to the side, whilst the outer cover could either be opened by releasing the catch to permit it to open out on its hinges, or it could, in an emergency, be jettisoned. This was done by stamping on a lever that withdrew the pin from the hinge and allowed the cover to fall away in its entirety.

'Please,' pleaded the Flt/Sgt. 'don't jettison the hatch, it takes me half an hour to get the bloody thing back again.'

With this firmly in mind when the emergency arrived I did not 'stamp on the bloody thing', I carefully, and foolishly, opened it!

The parachute used by the navigator was the 'chest' type. It was not attached to the harness, as was the pilot's, (he sat on his) but was stored somewhere nearby and clipped on to his harness, (worn at all times) when required. This allowed the navigator to move around unencumbered. I retrieved, and clipped the parachute on to the harness hooks, situated one on either side of my chest, (they were rather like those on a dogs lead, but a great deal bigger). I then removed my helmet and oxygen mask, having remembered being told the omission of this precaution could result in a premature hanging, and dived head first through the opening in the floor.

It is an odd feeling falling through space and slightly odder when the somersault, done on purpose to get out, initiates the subsequent unending series of possibly elegant, but certainly very high, somersaults. During the first of these I was conscious of the flaming red glare from the burning starboard engine, and then during the next several, of the need to find and pull the ripcord as quickly as possible. Certainly it never occurred to me to do a delayed drop to get down to where there would be more oxygen. My overriding anxiety was to see if the parachute worked. I reached for the ripcord only to discover there was no ripcord and, for that matter, no parachute clipped to my chest!

By forgetting to jettison the outer hatch cover the size of the aperture had been reduced, my 'chute had snagged, and the fine lashings tacking the hooks to the harness, had broken. This was intended to happen only when the parachute opened, not before the ripcord was pulled. After a few more somersaults I was conscious of not being alone, there was some bulky thing floating near me. I grabbed it, recognised it as being my parachute pack and without checking to make sure the hooks and eyes were attached to each other, pulled the ripcord.

There came the happiest jolt of my life as the 'chute opened, proving the hooks had done their job. The fur-lined boot on my left foot, unable to stand the jerk, went sailing all alone, on its way to Utrecht five miles below, while I floated serenely above, hoping that the bits of Mosquito littering the sky, and also bound for Utrecht, would not come too close. My watch indicated it was 5.35 p.m. and Jim was in the distance, way above me, dangling from his parachute. It went through my mind, in a drowsy sort of way, that although I could not know what the future had in store, at least there was still a future. And then I believe I must have lost consciousness through lack of oxygen because the next time, a few moments later so it seemed, I looked at my watch it was 5.45 p.m. All was unbelievably quiet and it was very cold, particularly for my left foot. A few thousand feet below was an unbroken sheet of unfriendly looking clouds.

I came down through the layer of cloud and can assure anyone, who might have doubts on the matter, that when dangling from a parachute at a height of about two thousand feet, the city of Utrecht appears to have more sharply pointed spires to the square foot than any city in Europe!

An entry in the German Daily Report, discovered by Aad Neevens, is translated thus:-

on 11.10 [42]. 18.34 hours a Mosquito was shot down
in Ouden-Rijn (about 2 km. west of Utrecht) by a fighter;
of the crew 1 man is taken prisoner

There is little doubt the prisoner was me. The time, making allowance for the difference of one hour, is correct, likewise the location. I know we were just coming up to Utrecht when we were hit, there was a west wind at the time, now, carrying me with it over the city and fortunately, as I did not like those spires, some distance beyond the built up area. The silence was broken by voices, still well below me, loudly and excitedly announcing my arrival to anyone within earshot. A large lake appeared beneath me and, being concerned it might become my landing place, I inflated my Mae West, a thing I had always wanted to do but, 'till then, never had either the opportunity or the excuse. In an instant it exploded from a flabby yellow inelegant waistcoat to the tightly fitting pneumatic bosom, said to be the equal of that possessed by the film star after whom it was named. Be that as it may, it hugged me tightly and I found this strangely comforting.

The wind blew me clear of the lake and I came down through the branches of a tree projecting out over the water-filled moat of a circular ancient earthwork, one of two noticed on a previous occasion when they had proved a to be a useful pin-point. I grabbed one of the springy overhanging branches and came to a stop with no more shock than as if landing on a spring mattress. But I was now suspended by the harness, caught in the higher branches, with one stockinged foot and one booted foot, a few inches below the surface of the water. Releasing the harness I dropped into less than two feet of water and at the same time became aware I had an audience.

Standing awkwardly on the steep bank was an extremely nervous German soldier - it takes a nervous person to recognise one! He was looking from beneath his coal-scuttle, and pointing a gun in my direction at a range of about ten feet.

'Good evening,' I said hoping to put him at his ease, at the same time raising my hands within the limitations of the inflated life jacket and the branches. 'I do not have a pistol or any other weapon.'

'Comm mit,' he said, gesturing with his rifle. So I did.

It soon became apparent that this ancient fortification was now some sort of camp or barracks inhabited by a large number of soldiers. So much for all the instruction and equipment designed to enable the newly shot down airman to evade capture and escape. Landing in a Barracks has to be the quickest way, ever, of getting to a prisoner of war camp, short of landing in the camp.

I was taken to a sort of Nissen hut and allowed to sit down whilst a small crowd of soldiers gathered round to admire their catch. I took out my cigarette case and, as one would in company, offered it around. Only one accepted, fortunately for me, as it was going to be some time before a re-fill would be available.

'Good flak,' I said hoping 'flak' was a German word, and at the same time thinking they might be happy to believe it was the army, not the Luftwaffe, who should get the credit. At that time I was not sure either way. There then followed one of those conversations, of which there were to be many more, where none of the participants understood a word of the other's language and yet came to understand quite a bit of what they were talking about. They were amazed I had come down from eight thousand metres, (I had made a mental conversion from feet), and they seemed delighted and a little envious that 'for you the war is over.' I gathered an officer would be coming to collect me. He turned up before the soldier smoking my cigarette had finished, which caused him considerable alarm and for the first time I witnessed the terror and trepidation of a guilty German conscience in the presence of a superior authority. The cigarette was smashed out and pushed from sight. Such a waste! Bidding my new friends farewell I was taken by car into Utrecht, after being cautioned by the officer, in English that, 'If you try to run avay you vill be shot!'

Jim had an altogether different experience. He suffered a hard landing in countryside beyond Utrecht and was able to hide his 'chute and dinghy in a ditch before approaching an old Dutchman, who understood no English, at a nearby farm. Jim hid in the barn until other Dutch people, after satisfying themselves he was genuine, gave him a raincoat and a bicycle and he followed them into the town where he spent some time with a Dutch family living next door to a German Officers Mess. He was then taken to a cottage outside the city while attempts were made by an underground agent to find a way of getting him back to England. The agent was caught, and so as not to further endanger his Dutch friends Jim gave himself up to the Police who, reluctantly but with no alternative, handed him to the Germans. Because he had been on the loose for some ten days he was extensively interrogated, including at an airfield where he was told about my capture. He spent the night in the airfield jail in the company of detained German airmen.

Jim was taken to Amsterdam and then Rotterdam undergoing more interrogation before being put on a train, with other Allied prisoners, bound for the main Luftwaffe interrogation centre at Dulag-Luft near Wiesbaden. It was here he learnt we had been shot down by a Focke-Wulf 190, as had the Squadron Leader who, together with his Navigator, had lost their lives.

Dulag-Luft was a collecting point for Allied Prisoners of War before sending them on to the permanent compounds. It was here that Jim and I were again reunited. It was good to find we were both none the worse for our experience.

I was taken in the back of an open car to a Military H/Q in Utrecht. In a room at the back of the building they sat me down at a table to share, with four or five soldiers, a 'help-yourself' meal of cold sausage, dark brown bread with margarine, and ersatz coffee. No one took much notice of me and conversation, understandably, was minimal, consisting only of the standard 'for you the war is over'. My waterlogged flying boot had been left behind at the earthwork and I had discovered a 'war-wound', consisting of a slight scratch on my bottom caused by the tree, tearing my trousers and me, when landing in its branches. More uncomfortable than the war wound was the very slow drying out process of socks and trouser legs.

After supper and a visit to the 'toileten', as I now discovered it was to be called, they took me back to the original room while arrangements were made for the next move. Some of the discussion was conducted over the wall type telephone by an NCO who stood in front of the instrument talking to a officer at the other end, and behaving as if the telephone was the officer. He came smartly to attention with a thunderous clicking of heels, and throughout his conversation every time it became necessary, which was every ten seconds or so, to shout 'Jawohl Herr Hauptmann' he would snap upright and savagely click his heels. The performance ended with a shouted 'Heil Hitler', another heel click, this time accompanied by an immaculate Nazi salute, to the telephone. Up to then, my experience of such goings-on had been confined to cartoon caricatures and burlesque on film and stage, and here it was, quite real, happening within a few feet of me. I quite forgot my cold, damp, and soggy nether regions.

I was taken out and across the street to a large open Mercedes motor car which, I am happy to say, refused to start when we were all sat in. There ensued a bit of Germanic excitement and shame-faced consternation. We were ordered out and into a rather less superior motor car, which took us to a city jail where they handed me over to whoever was running it, certainly not policemen, not Dutch ones anyway. They could have been German Military Police, or even Wermacht soldiers doing police duties. They looked to me like soldiers, but at that time I knew very little about the German forces in general or their insignia in particular.

An officer had me turn out my pockets, relieving me, not unkindly, of the 'escape pack' containing, money, silk maps, Horlicks tablets, fish hooks etc. etc. He also found and took away a small slim knife I had made from the spoke of a car wheel hammered flat, at great personal exertion, and carried in my wallet where it fitted neatly. I explained this to him and he was suitably upset at having to take it from me.

A perfectly charming middle-aged German officer (he must have been German since he had considerable authority) came and decided I would have to spend the night at the Police Station. He conducted me to a cell, took a distasteful look inside, turned to me and said:

"Iss not goot enough for an officer, I am very sorry." There seemed nothing could be done about this sad state of affairs, so persuading me to part with my socks and trousers in order to get them dried, he saw me into bed. I was more than ready for it by then. I wrapped a blanket round myself, saw the door close, and was instantly asleep.

Almost immediately, so it seemed, the door was opened, the light switched on and the benevolent officer was back with a huge smile beckoning 'Comm, comm.' Wrapping the blanket around myself, (I had no trousers) I followed him down the corridor, more asleep than awake, to another cell of splendid proportions. It contained three beds, one of which was not only provided with sheets but was made-up and turned down, as it might have been in an hotel, ready to receive the honoured guest.

'Ziss iss besser for an officer,' said my host, he was no less by this time, as he tucked me into bed, (he really did). Just before he closed the door and turned out the light, he said: "If you have vishes, ze bell', pointing to the button. 'Guten Nacht'.

And so ended the 11th October 1942. A year to the day since joining a Squadron, and likewise, two years to the day since donning a uniform.

As welcomes go, it could have been a great deal worse.

I never thought to have anything even remotely in common with Joe Louis. He was known as the 'Brown Bomber', heavyweight champion of the world, and we were 'Mosquito Bombers'! You cannot get much remoter than that, but "The Chronicle of the 20th Centuary", quotes him as saying, appropriately for both of us, on the 11th October '42:

"My fighting days are over!"

CHAPTER 25.

Now a Kreigi. Preliminaries.

Next morning, after sleeping well, a tray with breakfast was carried in by a rather superior looking NCO, probably a Feldwebel. He did not appear too pleased when I practiced the latest addition to my German vocabulary, obtained from the taps in the washroom, one of which proclaimed 'Kalt', and the other 'Heis'. Pointing to the cold mug of black ersatz coffee I said, 'Heis, please', not yet having discovered 'please' should have been 'Bitte', pronounced as in Beer or Angostura. He explained, and I comprehended, without understanding a word, that they always had cold coffee for breakfast. I went on repeating 'Heis, please', until he seemed to find it unprofitable to argue with an officer who could only say 'heis' and took away the offending mug. He returned it a little later full of hot coffee. I thanked him and both of us smiled broadly, he at having beaten the system, and me at getting a hot mug of lousy coffee. We parted the best of friends. I made do with a slice or two of dark brown bread and margarine with jam (or honey) both saccharin based and, I was subsequently to discover, going to become very familiar during the next two and a half years. Likewise the rye bread with its, not unpleasant, slightly sour taste, reputed to have a large content of sawdust. The margarine, then and for the duration, was a pleasant surprise.

My trousers and socks, now dry, were returned, together with, to my great delight, my uniform cap. It had been found in the wreckage of the aeroplane, a bit bashed about and peppered with broken perspex, but wonderful to have again. And if it should be wondered why my best peaked cap came to be in the 'plane, the answer is simple and logical, it was to have been a dusk raid, that meant coming back in the dark and I felt undressed wandering around strange RAF stations without any headgear. There was no reason to suppose this might have been the only time we were to land at our own airfield at night!

The pleasant, elderly officer, who had tucked me into bed the night before, put in an appearance as it was time for me to leave this agreeably memorable Police Station. He noticed I had no footwear and instructed someone to produce a pair of boots, which turned out to be the right size and also comfortable. Whilst trying on the boots he noticed my war wound, now healed, and more particularly, the right-angular rent in my trousers through which the wound had been inflicted. It would seem there was an ex-tailor now a soldier, on the premises, who, on being instructed to do so, made a professional job of the mend. I detected a certain reluctance on his part, with me remaining in the trousers.

I put my cap on at a rakish angle and wrapped my long white silk scarf around my neck, thereby being fully equipped with all my worldly possessions, not forgetting the borrowed boots. We said our 'Auf Wiedersehens' and set off, by car, for a short journey to the station to catch a train to Rotterdam, in the company of the agreeable officer and a soldier with a gun. The Dutch people, in the streets and on the station platform, smiled sympathetically and made surreptitious 'V' signs when they thought the escort was not looking. On the train, when it had been decided where we should sit, other passengers who had also decided it was a good place to sit, were moved elsewhere to enable us to be in glorious isolation.

The officer had only a limited command of English, and my 'Ja, nein, kalt and heis' contributed little to the communication problem. I must give him full marks for trying to be interested. He pointed, interrogatively, at my Observer Brevet and I hoped that either 'Navigator, Bomb Aimer or Wireless Operator' might have a near enough sounding German equivalent for him to get the general idea. Then he pointed to my medal ribbon, which he decided was the 'British' Flying Cross, being quite unable to pronounce

'Distinguished'. We parted when he left me at a large barrack type building, of fairly recent construction, where I was conducted to a large, clean and well decorated cell containing a bed, a small table and a chair. A notice proclaimed, in several languages, that it was 'Forbidden to write on the walls' - which had not been taken very seriously by some former occupant(s).

The atmosphere of this place was very different. Kindliness was replaced by undisguised, but controlled, hostility. Although nothing untoward happened to me I did hear, at a later time, of some cruel treatment, including a wounded and partly incapacitated prisoner being knocked down the concrete stairs by an impatient guard after a visit to the lavatory on the upper floor. They did manage to find me some magazines, for which I was grateful, even if the written contents were to remain mostly a mystery, otherwise there was nothing to do beyond deciphering the meager amount of graffiti. The cell had no window and my only view of the outside was when allowed to exercise on the parade ground. A canal ran parallel to the perimeter railings along one side of the parade ground and on the opposite side, precisely as in the picture on the jigsaw puzzle at home, was a typical Dutch scene. Tall gabled terraced houses faced the canal, with barges in, and lift-up bridges over the water to connect the roads on either side. After two or three days a windowless cell loses what little appeal it might never have had, and to my relief I was collected by an Unteroffizier (Corporal) and his mate, a Gefreiter (some kind of Private) - maybe they had run out of officers?

Once again a warning was given that I would be shot if I attempted to escape, for which eventuality the Unteroffizier had a pistol and a rifle, and the Gefreiter a rifle and bayonet. Between them they also had three suitcases, whilst I still had only the clothes I wore. We walked a little, and then caught a tram to take us to the station. On alighting from the tram the Unteroffizier ordered me to carry one of the smaller suitcases. It was quite clear what he meant, but I decided not to understand, which made him cross, so he picked it up and thrust it into my hand. I shook my head and put it back down on the pavement. This made him even angrier, but I was eventually persuaded to do as he wanted when he demonstrated that it contained our rations for the journey. Dignity, pig headedness, rank, self-importance, even honour, paled into insignificance at the prospect of going hungry.

At the Station our number increased by one, when P/O John Dowler, having abandoned his Spitfire, came to join us on our journey to Frankfurt. His guards handed him over to mine, and now we were four. Almost the first words he said concerned the suitcase, telling me that he had refused to carry a case his guards had tried to give him, and he thought I should do the same. It eventually turned out that his philosophy in the matter of dignity etc. versus hunger, coincided with mine. If, in the German army, you had the misfortune to be a Gefreiter, you would be the lowest of the low, at the beck and call of everyone who was not a Gefreiter, and we became quite sorry for ours. He was made to carry, in addition to his rifle and bayonet, the Unteroffizier's rifle and two suitcases containing, possibly, the worldly possessions of them both. John and I went in front with the small case of food, followed by the Unteroffizier with his pistol. Bringing up the rear was the poor fellow with two rifles, two suitcases, a bayonet, and (I almost forgot) a gas mask plus his helmet, which he would no doubt put on if either of us looked as though we might be going to knock him on the head.

A compartment was cleared of its protesting occupants, who thought they had been lucky to find a seat, and the four of us settled down for a long journey. After a while one of the guards started to whistle 'The Penny Serenade', a tune popular at home at that time. 'Pfennig Seranade?' I suggested, at which he looked utterly blank. This attempt at communication having been less than successful, John and I thenceforth spoke to one another, and the Unteroffizier occasionally condescended to address a grateful Gefreiter; until, whilst passing through a large built-up area, the Unteroffizier said 'Essen'. Assuming he had decided to fraternize and become our guide, and was referring to the city outside, I put together my longest German sentence to date.

'Ah! Ich have bomben Essen.' He did not seem very pleased about this so it could be assumed he had understood.

'Nein, nein, essen, essen,' he repeated, pointing at our little suitcase, from which it transpired 'essen' meant food, eating etc, as well as the city in the Ruhr at which I had aimed some bombs.

Quite a bit later we changed trains in the dark, I have no idea where, and had to wait some time for the connection. They took us into the station buffet and bought for us - we had no money - ersatze coffee and a bowl of soup, these being the only refreshments obtainable without coupons. Early next morning the train arrived at Wiesbaden, near Frankfurt, and since it appeared we no longer had need of the case, now only containing food for the guards return journey, I left it in the carriage, much to the annoyance of the Unteroffizier who, failing to persuade me to pick it up, made the Gefrieter add it to his load of guns, suitcases etc. And so, two British RAF officers, carrying nothing and a German Corporal, strode down the platform and out into the street to catch a tram, followed at an ever-increasing distance by the now grossly over-burdened Private giving a brave imitation of a perambulating German Christmas Tree.

Dulag Luft, our destination, was the main Luftwaffe interrogation centre. Our guards took us to the reception block, a wooden bungalow structure, like all the other buildings, where they took away my boots, on loan from the Police Station in Utrecht. As our guards prepared to leave I managed to say in immaculate German, 'Auf Wiedersehen'.

The result was unbelievable, the hitherto mask-like features of the Unteroffizier broke into a splendid smile, all was forgiven and forgotten. He shook my hand and delivered the only English I had heard him utter – 'For you der varr is over, auf wiedersehen'. Still smiling and followed by the Gefreiter, with a less enthusiastic smile and now additionally laden with my boots, they passed out of my life forever.

In place of the boots, I was given wooden soled footwear with a leather toecap, and another piece of leather at the heel to stop you falling out at the back. They placed me in a cell, provided a blanket, and took all my clothes away to be searched. The clothes were returned minus many of the buttons, because they had long been aware of the ploy to conceal compasses within brass buttons, and also of certain other ordinary buttons which when placed one on top of the other also became a compass. Some of my buttons had indeed been of this type. The cell was about ten feet by six feet, with a bed, a table, and a stool. On the bed was a mattress, which looked like a hessian bag stuffed with stranded wood shavings and seemingly manufactured for that purpose, a pillow, sheets, blankets etc..

We had been warned to expect, during interrogation, a bogus Red Cross Officer who would produce an equally bogus form containing questions, supposedly required by the Red Cross, to enable them to care for our well being, and to advise our parents of our survival – and so it transpired. He was a rather splendidly attired individual, in a bluish uniform, with lots of silver braid - I think I am correct in saying that it bore no insignia of rank, (someone told me much later he was a 'Sonderführer', whatever that might be, 'sonder' I believe means 'Special'). He most certainly was not of the Red Cross, and neither was the very official-looking form bearing the forged letterhead of that admirable organisation. He spoke perfect English and the conversation went something like this:

'Hello, Flying Officer Thomas. I am from the Red Cross and I have come to help you (?); I would like you to help me fill in this form, so I can tell your parents you are well, and how they can write to you, and send parcels'.

This seemed almost convincing and I could see no harm in giving him, in addition to, Name, Rank and Number, (as I was obliged to do by the Geneva Convention) the name and address of my parents. If I was to write to them sometime in the future, these particulars must become known to the censors anyway.

'Good now what is your Squadron?'

'I am not allowed to tell you that. Why should the Red Cross want to know such information? If it is necessary then I am sure the Air Ministry in London will be pleased to tell you. I have told you my name, rank and number and that is the only information I can give you'.

'I have to fill in this form and you must give me the information. If you don't you will have to stay in solitary confinement until you do, I shall say it is for your own good, because you are not well'.

'But I am perfectly well'.

'Ah, I see you have a spot on your chin', he said, pointing. 'That could be very serious, it might take weeks to get better. I will go now, and when I come back maybe you will give me what I want?'

So much for the Red Cross fiction! It was no more convincing than our compass buttons. Inevitably he returned.

'Now we know your Squadron is Number 105, after all it was written on the side of your Mosquito, 'GB' in letters a meter high, and we know 'GB' is 105 Squadron as indeed we know all the Squadron Code letters, since they are published by your Air Ministry'. This could not be denied so I agreed and he went on talking. 'We know all about you so you might as well co-operate and then we can let you go and join your friends. Now, you are based at Horsham St. Faiths? Yes?'

Well, we had been, before moving to Marham a couple of weeks ago, but if he preferred to think we were still at Horsham, who was I to disappoint him?

'Why yes', I agreed, in a contrived tone of wonderment, tinged with, I hoped, a note of reluctant admiration for their clever intelligence.

'There now, you see it is no good denying it, we know all about 105 squadron at Horsham St. Faith. Your Wing Commander is Peter Simmonds, and we know you were going to bomb Hanover after picking up a camera from the Photographic Unit at Marham'.

'"How do you know all that?' I replied, gasping with astonishment at this wealth of secret information. His delight had to be seen to be believed, he positively smirked as he busily wrote it all down on his form.

Our W/Cmdr. was, of course, Hughie Edwards VC, not Simmonds, who had left a long time before. Jim and I had been going to bomb Hanover, a fact not difficult to deduce as they had, no doubt, found my maps and flight plan in the wreck of our Mosquito. They would also have seen, from the maps etc. that we had set out from Marham. It is interesting to note that they were so reluctant to abandon the idea of 105 being stationed at Horsham, that a theory was produced to explain why we had to call in at Marham to pick up a camera from the Photographic Unit, which may, or may not, have been there. Certainly I had no knowledge of such a Unit.

Up to now, in this interrogation, everything he 'knew', except the target and the squadron number, was wrong, and naturally I had been happy to confirm he was right! The rest of the interview concerned technical details about the Mosquito, and proceeded along the same lines. Sometimes he was right but mostly he was wrong. I agreed with everything he 'knew' and sometimes professed ignorance on a matter not likely to be within the knowledge of a Navigator. I am sure it was more important for him to get his form filled in than it was to run the risk of having his 'facts' confused by the truth. If I was running an interrogation unit I would not want him on my pay roll!

He left me some English cigarettes, hoping, no doubt this might compensate the gloomy look I had tried to cultivate, as being appropriate to someone who had just divulged his country's best kept secrets. I, of course, was fervently hoping he would not 'smell a rat' and wonder why it had all been so easy. Next day, after only two or three nights in solitary, they sent me into the main compound. I had not even had a proper opportunity to explore the details of my cell beyond the device for summoning a guard if it became necessary to visit the 'Toilette'. There was a knob in the cell which, when pushed, unbalanced a vertical hinged iron bar, about fifteen inches long, outside in the corridor, causing it to fall to the horizontal, where it remained having caused considerable clatter bouncing up and down on the stop. If the clatter did not bring a guard hurrying to your aid, and it never did, then he might notice the sticking out iron bar the next time he was passing. It helped if one's visit was anticipated by half an hour or so, or even longer. Some prisoners spent a much greater length of time in the cells and received quite unpleasant treatment. I was glad to leave solitary confinement and to realize the worst ought now to be over and I had been extremely fortunate.

The compound consisted of three or four wooden barrack blocks surrounded by a barbed wire entanglement with a 'Goon Box' - a little house on stilts containing a guard with guns and a searchlight, - at each corner. I retain no impressions of the camp as to its comfort, or otherwise, or even the manner of the sleeping and eating arrangements. I was informed of a few basics concerning my new status, and the few rules dictated by prudence, or by our captors.

All Germans were known as 'Goons'! I believe they were considerably upset when they found that this strange British diminutive of affection and respect, like 'Jerry', to have been derived from a Newspaper Cartoon Strip character, of pre-war days. A sort of large humanised hairy ape of no brain but considerable stupidity, a figure of fun, but not necessarily a target for malice, or dislike. The name was subsequently used in 'The Goon Show', of BBC Radio fame, where these same characteristics were essential to the success of the very funny, utterly good-natured, long running series. All Prisoners of War (POW's) were known as 'Kreigies', this being simply an essential shortening of the German for the same thing 'Kreigsgefangener'. The camp was called a 'Stalag' for the same reason being a shortening of 'Stammelager', the sub-fix 'Luft' signifying it was administered by the 'Luftwaffe'(Air Force). The present camp was called a 'Dulag' of which the 'Du' is no doubt a shortening of some enormous German word meaning, interrogation or collecting? To check the number of prisoners in residence coincided with the number supposed to be there, a roll call, known as an 'Appel' was held, two or three times a day preceded by its own short, shouted, vocabulary of 'Raus, raus! Schnell, schnell,' indicating you were to come out quickly. Followed by the painful process of counting in German, by Germans. Why this should have been so difficult for them was never properly understood. They even had us line up in five ranks, instead of the more usual three, the five-times table being thought easier than the three-times. Five ranks allowed great scope for unseen manoeuverings in the centre ranks, thereby enabling the count to be fiddled to show the correct number, even when two or three had managed to escape.

After, even as in my case, only a short time in 'solitary, there came a great desire to talk to my fellow countrymen, particularly as their experiences would have been similar, and it seemed very important they should be told of mine. But, there were hidden microphones, and great care had be taken to say nothing of interest to our captors. When standing beneath a known microphone position, it was permitted, even encouraged, to discuss the latest ten engined bombers now coming into operation! One other essential piece of information concerned the wire running around inside the main fence at a distance of some ten feet. To step over this was to invite a guard in a Goon Box, or anywhere else, to use you as a target.

Jim turned up after a week or so. It was a happy reunion and there was a great deal to talk about, including the sad news, from Jim, that the Squadron Leader and his Observer, who had been leading us, had been killed.

Soon, after the requisite number had been accumulated, we left on the journey to Stalag Luft 3 in Silesia.

CHAPTER 26.

By Train - 4th. Class.

I was given a pair of RAF airman's boots and a greatcoat before being marched from the camp to board a train. I was delighted to discover as they counted us in, that I was number fifty-five, or as said in German – 'foomph und foomphzig'. When, in our situation and hoping for anything at which to laugh, 'Foomph' sounded funny to English ears, more particularly as there was a radio programme at home containing the immortal catch phrase – 'This is Foomph speaking'. There was, however, nothing even remotely funny about our home for the next two days. The carriage of the train had been very efficiently, and crudely, adapted for the transport of Prisoners of War.

To prevent escape through the windows, all were fixed down with six-inch nails. To prevent the 'Toilette' affording privacy to some dedicated escaper as he forced the window open, the door had been taken away. As time went by these two measures combined to produce an atmosphere unlikely to be tolerated by any self-respecting sewage farm. The seats, I suppose we should have been grateful these had not been removed, were of the type found in pre-war tram cars. The unyielding narrow wood slats, shaped to fit the bottom and back, were quite adequate for a five or ten minute tram journey, but most uncomfortable in a train bumping over a bad track for two days. When these seats came to be used as a place to sleep, only sheer exhaustion made such an ambition even remotely possible. I made a large loop of my silk scarf, long enough for it to hang from the luggage rack above and allow me to rest my head in the bottom of the loop, thus giving an illusion of comfort from a mid-air pillow. It was better than nothing, a great deal better than most others managed, and although it made sleep possible it was at the expense of a seriously stiff neck.

The guards, working in shifts, shared the disagreeable atmosphere with us, but they had a carriage to themselves where they slept, ate and rested. It is difficult to imagine, happily, the sheer disgust they must have experienced at the contrast each time they came from the fresh air outside. There was no corridor and the train had to be stopped to allow the shifts to change, by walking along the track, to the horrid place of their next tour of duty. The momentary ventilation brought about by the doors opening every two hours, or so, was completely unnoticeable and ineffective. As train journeys go, we were glad when it had went.

New batches of prisoners were commonplace at Stalag Luft 3 East Compound, and there were clearly defined procedures for their welcome. The Germans searched us, as they always did when prisoners went in or out of anywhere, but this time they took our photographs and fingerprints. Inside the gates of the compound a small crowd of prisoners were gathered to welcome friends who might be, reluctantly, coming to join them, and others who were interested in discovering the latest news. Others were, most importantly, responsible for setting in motion the administrative details concerning the allocation of a Billet. They also conducted a very thorough investigation to ensure each new prisoner was as he claimed, and not an agent passing himself off as a prisoner with the intention of getting information relating to matters not deemed to be suitable for the ears of the third Reich. This ploy was tried many times by the Germans, and only very rarely did it enjoy any success.

The dreadful train journey had the effect of making the accommodation afforded by the wooden barrack blocks seem almost luxurious. There were double-decker wooden bunks complete with the, by now familiar, woven-paper-string hessian type wood wool stuffed mattresses, gingham or white sheets, and dark colour blankets. A rug, courtesy I believe of the Red Cross, also appeared. The mattress was supported by a continuous layer of bed-boards loosely laid across the short way of the bunk. Or it would have been continuous had the boards not afforded an invaluable source of raw-material for shoring up tunnels, and making all those useful things where a piece of wood six inches x one inch x two feet long was essential. The mattress therefore sagged in the gaps between the remaining bed-boards to a greater or lesser extent depending on the prevailing tunnel and artifacts situation. It was possible, some thought even desirable, and certainly very noble, to give all your boards away and construct, from Red Cross string, a sort of four-ways supported hammock. This was usually restricted to the lower bunk, due to Red Cross string giving little or no warning when it was about to break.

The sheets, as issued, consisted of a bag into which, in the continental manner, the folded blankets should be placed to form a duvet, and also a single sheet to lay over, and tuck under the mattress. A sheet-sized piece of material, white for preference, but blue and white check at a pinch, was just what the producers of theatrical extravaganza were looking for. It was therefore the custom to use the duvet cover as a sleeping bag with the blankets laid over, and forget about these fancy continental sleeping habits. Otherwise there was, in addition, a wooden locker for each person, a table, some well made four-legged stools, a chair or two and some homemade furniture constructed from the plywood boxes in which the Red Cross bulk deliveries of parcels were made. There was also a large tiled stove but never sufficient fuel to get it to the desired temperature.

I was taken to a room in which I was the only 'new boy', there being only the one vacancy. Jim went to another room further up the corridor in the same block. Because the occupants had been there for some time the room had lost its bleak new institutional look, with pictures on the walls and other decorations such as an Austrian Beer Stein with a hinged lid and a long stemmed pipe, also with a lid. The war had been in progress for some years by the time of my arrival, and some of the prisoners had been there, one, two, and a few even three years. In the early days it had been possible for the prisoners to buy such things as Beer Steins and pipes and other objects, which had enabled them to bring some homely comforts into the bare wood-lined rooms. Once again I could count it as my good fortune to be in an established room of, mostly, long-term inmates in which, as a new arrival, I was the centre of attraction, and I didn't mind that either.

In pride of place by the stove was a brightly coloured, home made, picture looking rather like one of those race games where a dice is thrown to determine the progress of the player. I do not remember the finer details of the rules but each occupant, of the room, was represented by a flag and advanced one or more squares, as judged appropriate by his room mates, each time he committed some folly, act of absent mindedness, or illogical action. At the end of the road there was a sharp turn, the arrival at which indicated the owner of the flag was now 'going round the bend'. When the turn had been negotiated he was adjudged to be completely 'round the bend or 'wire happy'. One or two were on their second circuit!

It is on my conscience that I am not good at populating this account with people, and that is, I fear, the way it has to be. Not from any desire to protect their identities, hopefully that is not necessary, but from a complete inability to recall most of them except as, for the most part, exceedingly agreeable, albeit shadowy, persons. Had they not been agreeable it may be safely assumed they would be well remembered. A face may trigger recognition but only rarely the place it was last met and almost never its name. An incident may be clearly recalled, but not always details of the participants. The passage of time has, of course, something to do with such forgetfulness, but the inability to match names etc. to faces persists unimproved to the present day. Occasionally an escape route offers itself. I was greeted recently with the words, 'Hello Robin how good to see you again'. Without the least idea who it was, I replied 'Yes indeed,' and then had an inspiration. 'Did you have that beard the last time we met?' 'Why no, I don't think I did'. 'Well in that case, who the hell are you?' The problem is not always so easily solved.

The room I was welcomed into accommodated ten or twelve Kreigies. Bertie played, or was rather learning to play, the saxophone, and Jock (he had to be Jock being a Scotsman) Steele had been a butcher (who but a butcher uses a steel?) in Glasgow. He told the story of overhearing two youths discussing a proposed burglary, and deciding Tuesday night would be best because the Father taking confessional next day was known to be sympathetic with his penance's. On such trivia does fame depend!

The room was half way down the left-hand side of the corridor running lengthwise down the centre of the block, which had eighteen or twenty rooms. The block was in the top right hand corner, as viewed from the entrance gate, of six blocks in pairs spaced forty or fifty feet apart end to end, and rather more side to side. In addition, a larger block on the left contained the kitchen and a sort of store-room, used as a canteen for the sale and barter of goods, also as a suitably remote venue for aspiring musicians to practice. It was also used for the storage of sporting equipment including, I would suppose, the 'Wooden Horse' used for the famous, successful, and ingenious escape so admirably described by Eric Williams in his book of the same name. This escape took place sometime later, when most of the then occupants had been transferred to a new compound. Two unsophisticated lavatory huts, and a fire pond, completed the accommodation and facilities of the East Compound Stalag Luft III. I later, as I was prone to do, wrote a poem like this:

Sagan P.O.W. Camp
Take a largish lump of land,
Composed right through of sand.

Put a pine tree here and there,
Make the aspect really bare..
Have a hut or two erected,
Have a man or two injected.
Stretch some wire round the site,
Then some Guards to keep it tight,
And there, before your eyes
A Kreigsgefangenlager lies.

The main, and only, gate was at the North end of the Compound. It led into another smaller compound containing the Guard House, Cooler (solitary confinement cells for naughty prisoners), Sick Quarters, Parcel Store and other such administrative essentials, then to another gate leading out on to a minor road and to the Kommandantur where the camp Kommandant and his guards resided. To the South and East was a plantation of pine trees, in rigid rows, in which a clearing had been cut to make a site for the camp. The nearest edge of the remaining plantation was about one hundred feet away to discourage short tunnels. To the West was another compound, a good deal larger than ours, in which were the non-commissioned Air Crew prisoners. To ensure we stayed within the compound there was a perimeter fence consisting of two vertical fences of barbed wire mesh about nine feet high and five feet apart with tangled coils of barbed wire in great quantity between them. Some twenty feet inside the fence was the warning rail on posts eighteen inches above the ground. The ground was sand, black from the effect of rotted pine needles, to a depth of four or five inches and then yellow turning to white as the depth increased.

Christmas was not too far away and day by day the temperature was dropping. Low sand walls were formed around the sports ground to contain water squirted from the fire hose to form a shallow lake. This became a skating rink by next morning. There were even skates, some attached to boots and others of the clip-on type originating, probably, from earlier days when such things could be purchased, or provided from the protecting power, Switzerland, who were rather good at things like that. Snow, to the annoyance of the Goons, tended to make the Apells into impromptu battlefields with snowball fights between blocks, not at the Goons. That would have made them angry and damaged their dignity, resulting in reprisals for a moment's amusement producing no advantage or lasting satisfaction to us.

The Lageroffizier, or Camp Officer, Hauptmann Pieber, was an Austrian of kindly disposition, well tolerated and even liked. It was his duty to take charge of the Appells and to count those present, which he did by walking along in front of the lined up members of each block holding a clip-board in one hand and a pencil in the other, mentally muttering his five times table as he passed, wagging his pencil at each file. An NCO walked behind the block in exactly the same manner. When both reached the last file Hauptmann Pieber would call out, hopefully – 'Drie und achtzig?' to be answered by the NCO either with 'Ja Herr Hauptmann' or 'Nein, vier und achtzig', at which Herr Pieber would, with a shrug of his shoulders, about turn and start again at the beginning, every move being mirrored by his colleague. Appells were a two or three times a day occurrence and mostly passed off without any excitement. There were times, however, when things were very different, particularly if there had been an escape, or some reason for the Germans to impose reprisals, which they sometimes did by making the appell last a great deal longer than normal.

A small theatre had been made by joining two rooms into one. We, the new Kriegies, were able to see for the first time the amazing amount of talent, skill and overall expertise existing amongst our fellow prisoners. The smallness of the theatre made it necessary to put the show on for several nights, thus requiring the booking and issue of tickets, all contributing to the normal practices of theatre-going at home, and to the sense of occasion generated by 'doing a show'. The theatre-goers dressed in the best clothes available to them and supper was contrived to be a little more special and delayed to take place after returning from the theatre. The show we saw was a Christmas Revue with sketches of considerable originality, a dance band and a great deal more, leaving an impression of colour, noise and wit, and quite the best, almost civilised, evening yet spent as a POW.

The NCO's, in the adjoining compound, had a whole hut for their theatre, that is to say about ten times larger than ours. For some reason I was one of the lucky ones to be permitted, by special co-operation of our captors, to accept the invitation to visit their Christmas Pantomine. Their production was completely professional with special effects, lighting, transformation scenes, splendid costumes and scenery, a miracle of ingenuity, talent and, no doubt, some bribery and corruption of their guards. I do not remember having any criticism of the acting or script. It was quite wonderful and I would not have expected better in the West End.

Christmas day was enjoyed by all, I think. It was also the first time I was introduced to the potent properties of Kriegy Hooch and Wine, of which more anon. I probably enjoyed Christmas Day, I do not remember dis-enjoying it, so I must have done, since that was certainly the intention. Likewise New Years Eve 1943.

Some of the long-term prisoners had stories to tell of earlier camps when the Germans had as much to learn about British aircrew prisoners of war as the POW's had to learn about their hosts. I particularly liked the one about the German Kommandant who complained that coming into HIS camp was like entering a British Colony, where he felt he was not wanted! I am assured the following is also true: the camp was wired with microphones, which was soon discovered and at least some of the positions identified. Carefully a microphone was exposed and its terminals connected to the mains electricity supply. Switching on the current fortuitously coincided with the Kommandant showing off the system to a visiting senior officer who had been invited to '...come and listen to my prisoners talking..'. It is reported that no sooner had the visitor put on the earphones than the apparatus exploded! I do hope it really did.

Most inmates of Stalag Lufts would have taken the opportunity to escape if their name had been drawn out of the hat, or circumstances made it easy to do so. A small minority were passionately dedicated to escaping. It became their way of life, and possibly by absorbing their thoughts and energies, contributed to their sanity and tolerance of the situation. The majority, me included, found other things to occupy our minds and whilst prepared to help in any way suitable to our skills and talents, viewed the prospect of travelling through a hostile land without understanding the language, with some misgivings. The thought of going through, let alone digging, a tunnel was positively horrific. Most people know what claustrophobia is, and might occasionally have the odd twinge, but it would not have been the odd twinge with me. I should either have fainted in attempting to suppress the fear, or become hysterical, or both when regaining consciousness from the former. Some found happiness in sport, some in study, some in theatricals or in administration and some, like me, mostly in making things and being more, or less, interested in everything. Except, that is, those occupations in which there existed no aptitude whatsoever, such as, in my case, learning another language, or playing a musical instrument. There were a few who found nothing with which to occupy themselves and they became candidates for the 'Round the Bend Club'. Some committed suicide.

In the Spring of 1943 most, if not all, in the East compound were moved to a newly built compound a short distance to the West, beyond the NCO's camp and the German Kommandantur.

CHAPTER 27.

A New Compound.

April Fools day seemed as good as any other to move seven hundred odd prisoners about a quarter of a mile from the East camp to the newly built North compound. Every prisoner had to be searched, by the guards, to make certain no forbidden items came with him to sully the pristine newness of the new quarters. From the German point of view the idea turned out to be sound, sensible and rewarding for they discovered, no doubt with some surprise, no significant contraband after a whole days industrious searching. Two reasons must have suggested themselves, either there was indeed no forbidden matter or, it had by-passed the searchers. The former was a 'Happy Thought' and the latter not to be contemplated, so presumably they settled for the former and were happy. The Kreigies settled into their new home to the manner in which they had become accustomed. That is to say with a wireless set, tools, civilian clothes, forged documents, Reichmarks and all the other essentials deemed necessary for the successful existence of a prisoner of war, both within and, hopefully, without the encampment.

A fact of considerable insignificance, no more really than a tiresome coincidence, which, had it not been pointed out with some degree of friendly malice, I should certainly not have thought to mention, concerned the progress of the war. And the undeniable fact that from the day we, Jim and I, were shot down, we, the Allies, began to win the war! Up to that time efforts to do this had consisted of a great many heroic defeats.

Naturally everyone wanted to hear the latest news on the progress of this change in 'our' fortunes. The German newspapers afforded a somewhat biased view of any Allied success. Any juxtaposition of these two words would have immediately been struck out by the German censor, so it was a good thing we had a radio to receive the BBC World

Service. Almost every day a news bulletin would be received and it would be read to the occupants of every block each evening. It is not possible to overstate the gratitude and appreciation due to the makers, operators and custodians of the radio for their dedication and skill in keeping this invaluable piece of equipment safely hidden from the German searchers who, knew it existed, but never discovered where.

I was too newly a prisoner to understand the detailed ingenuity of fooling the searchers, but it was very apparent there were among us many pilots, navigators and air-gunners who, had they not been using their skills as aircrew, would have been expertly concerned, on one side or other, with the criminal fraternity.

The new compound, ostensibly similar to the one we had just left, had differences most of which were improvements. At the time of the move there remained a large number of pine trees dotted around, singly and in clumps, creating an impression of modest landscaping and reducing the otherwise bleak aspect. They were shortly to be removed but remained long enough for most of their lower branches to join stockpiles of firewood, and for me, and others of similar dedication, to bleed resin from them to use as a flux in soldering.

Pathetic gangs of ill clad underfed Russian prisoners were employed in clearing other trees by sawing them off just above the ground, stripping the branches and then loading the trunks and débris onto open-back lorries. There was little we could do to help them apart from the surreptitious passing of the odd packet of cigarettes, or pieces of bread or chocolate. They did not, even when such offerings were thrown amongst them, make a rush to grab for themselves, but left it to whoever might be nearest to pick it up, whilst the others looked their gratitude. They also evinced considerable humour by deliberately mis-understanding their guards and pretending to be very simple. One would walk, say one hundred feet from the lorry, pick up a twig and walk slowly back to place it carefully amongst the others, all the time looking puzzled as to why the guard was leaping up and down gesticulating wildly, making threatening movements with his rifle and shouting at the top of his voice. One of them, 'realising' they were expected to fetch larger pieces, picked up an entire tree trunk, stripped of its branches, balanced it on his shoulder and walked off in the wrong direction. The guard ran after him shouting and waving until, when only about six feet behind, the Russian 'realised' he was being called and pivoted quickly around. It is a great pity the guard ducked in time to have the tree swish by where his head had been. The Russian, with concern written all over his face, seemed to be saying. 'Oh my goodness it nearly hit you'! And no doubt thinking, 'damn! I missed.'

It had not escaped the notice of the compulsive escapers that here were lorries transporting, to freedom, large loads of pine tree foliage, in which, if they were hidden, they too might become free. Two or three tried dropping into the foliage from the roof of a hut, and one, I believe, hung on under the vehicle, but it only proved a shortcut to the cooler as the guards, on these occasions, were thorough with their searching.

The new compound contained fifteen huts in three rows of five. The huts were raised approximately two feet above the ground on wooden piles, thus permitting a clear view under the floor from one side to the other, except at fire places where there was a chimney to support, and wash rooms where the floor was concrete to contain drains etc. Needless to say these two exceptions were subsequently to be exploited. The washroom was the best improvement in the new huts, there had been no such luxury in the East Camp. There were also WC's, two in each hut, only to be used during the nights when the hut doors were locked shut, or in the event of sickness. Otherwise the accommodation was much as before, including small rooms at three of the corners in each of which, one or two, senior officers enjoyed a certain amount of seclusion.

In one such room, next to ours, in Block 122 lived Squadron Leader Wank Murray and his Canadian navigator who had set out to drop leaflets from a Whitley in September 1939. They were prevented from returning home through engine failure and had thus been amongst the earliest Air Force prisoners to come into German hands. S/Ldr. Murray was a very interesting person. As a regular RAF officer with a gift for languages, he had been sent to China to teach Chinamen to fly. In the process he had learnt to speak Chinese in addition to French, Spanish and Italian in which he was already fluent. He had not learnt German at the time he became a Kriegie so he set about doing just that and very shortly became Camp Interpreter, a position he held to the end of the war. He, too, liked making things including a Turbine Rotor, about two inches in diameter which, when subjected to a jet of steam or air, rotated extremely quickly producing a loud and very satisfactory screaming noise.

In the small room across the corridor lived another S/Ldr who, before flying bombers in the RAF, had flown the airliners of Imperial Airways. He reckoned he held the record for the journey from London, (Croydon) to Paris, by taking the longest time. Exactly how long is not remembered, but it was somewhere around five hours for the two hundred miles! A very strong head wind and the not very remarkable performance of the large four-engined bi-planes of the Hannibal type combined to produce a modest ground speed in the region of only thirty-five to forty miles per hour. He mentioned how strange it was, as he flew low to escape the worst of the wind, alongside the A20 to Hythe, to see motorcars overtaking him!

Another senior officer in a room of his own was admitted to be a little eccentric, and also very clever with tools of which he had accumulated a goodly number. He was constructing an air-conditioning system for his room. It was necessary to have an air intake in the floor, so he had bored a preliminary hole, which attracted the attention of a German guard, of that special variety dressed in blue overalls known as Ferrets, whose purpose in life was to snoop everywhere to discover tunnels etc. This one was, at the time, crawling around in the space beneath the hut. Upon spying the hole through the floor he poked his thumb through and the builder of the air-conditioning installation, assuming it to be a mouse, (or so he maintained) hit it with the mallet he just happened to have in his hand.

I believe Jim and I were the most recent Kriegies in the room to which we were allocated, in the new camp, and therefore benefited from the accumulated luxuries of the others. Such luxuries as a wind-up gramophone with a good supply of records, a home-made settee, a coffee grinder (no coffee beans but very useful for converting cracked barley into coarse flour), an iron cooking pot and many other little things like pictures, mugs, cutlery and a shelf of books. A room had been set aside as a Camp Library and very good it was too, containing reading matter of all kinds, including technical and reference books. All these came through the Red Cross and were available to everyone, whether their fancy was a detective story, or a desire to study some subject or profession. Indeed some Kreigies even sat exams in the camp to qualify, at least in the preliminary stages, for Degree courses in Accountancy, Teaching, Law, etc.

I attended two sessions of a German Language class before deciding this was no way to further the adoption of English as a world language. The sooner these foreigners discovered they could, only with difficulty, travel outside their own countries without speaking English, the better for me, certainly, and the peace of the world, hopefully. Some proof of the success of my theory was shown recently when on holiday in the USA a German said to me: 'Vy do ve Chermans have to speak English veneffer ve vant to go anyvere?' I did not want to offend him so I answered - 'Put it down to a happy accident of History,' then added, 'you may leave out the 'happy' if you wish'. He did not appear overjoyed at this honest and unarguable explanation and made no attempt to disagree, but this may have been because his command of English required some improvement.

The Cook House, as in the previous compound, was a large hut combined with other rooms of a communal nature. It was very good at boiling water in large coal fired boilers, and sometimes the water was adulterated with minimal quantities of meat and vegetables and called, 'soup'. At other times un-peeled potatoes went into the water, resulting in hot dirty water and boiled potatoes still in their jackets. If, maybe, they had been a little bad before boiling they were, afterwards, a great deal bad. Unadulterated boiled water was undoubtedly the forté of the cookhouse and twice a day one could collect as much hot water as there was. Suitable containers were provided for hot water collection and were of two types, a large china jug and a zinc jug marked 'Keintrinkwasser', that is to say, 'not for drinking water'.

The sanitary arrangements were much as before, with two modest sized huts, referred to as 'Aborts', under which were large brick pits covered by a floor and two rows of back-to-back seats perforated with the necessary holes. Each one was separated from the other by head height screens at the back and to either side, but open fronted, having no doors. The pits frequently had to be emptied for which purpose a large cylindrical tank on a cart arrived, euphemistically referred to as the 'Honey Wagon'. It was drawn by a horse with a civilian driver, whose duty it was to place into, and subsequently withdraw from the pit a pipe connected to the pump. The pump was hand operated and the whole business appeared remarkably unpleasant except to the horse who was pleased with the rest, and the driver who happily, so it appeared, carried out all these invidious duties without any means of washing. He would mount on to the tank, if it happened to be lunch time, produce sandwiches to eat whilst surveying, from his elevated position, the astonished onlookers, and possibly meditating as to why they might be giving him such a wide berth. Someone, one day, badly needing a pranger (Kreigie for hammer) and stole one of the iron pins designed to prevent the back wheels from coming off. The back wheel duly came off, causing the vehicle to collapse sideways spilling the contents at the first corner, unfortunately before the cart had left the compound, but at some distance from our hut, so it could have been worse.

At different times I was to become the Block Post Officer, and the Canteen Officer, the former consisted in walking down to Block 101, by the gate, collecting the mail for Block 122, sorting it into rooms and delivering. It was quite a pleasant job where I was happy to receive the credit for being the bearer of good tidings. But not so pleasing when someone discovered there was mail in the camp before I had been to find out for myself, thereby keeping them waiting a little while longer than might have been the case if I had been as conscientious as my counterparts in the other blocks. Canteen Officer I liked, no one minded waiting for whatever unremarkable largesse might be on free issue from the canteen. Everything was free from the canteen, arising from the fact that all POW's, theoretically, received pay at the same rate as their equivalent rank in the German forces. This amount was deducted from the pay due, and credited to them, back home. Fortunately the German forces seemed to be very poorly paid and only a fairly modest amount was deducted from the pay credited to us. I say, fortunately, because had we received our full pay we could have done no more with it than we were able to do with the smaller amount, that is to say, almost nothing. Money is surprisingly useless when there is nothing, or very nearly nothing, to purchase. The camp money was not, for obvious reasons, in the form of real currency capable of being used as legal tender outside the camp. It took the form of a sort of debased 'Monopoly Money' or superior cloakroom tickets, to which it bore a strong resemblance. In earlier days the prisoners had received this 'Lagergelt', or camp money, and were able to make some purchases, as I have already indicated, in the canteen. But it had now became the policy for the pay to go into a common fund from which bulk purchases were made of such commodities as became available, and these were then distributed, free of charge, throughout the camp.

Soap, as issued from the canteen, was not in great demand except when Red Cross supplies failed. Some of us liked to have the German version of soap to use for making molds, by carving into it a shape in which to cast molten solder or zinc. By this means it was possible to produce such things as German uniform buttons or other insignia. Soap is usually made from fat saponified with an alkali, but German soap did not appear to contain any fat and seemed to be mostly pressed dried clay. It was coloured and possessed a very 'loud perfume', always to be associated, from that time on, with a well-washed German. Safety Razors were in good supply but not much used, so I was able to get as many as I wanted. Not, as might be supposed, to be used as intended but, having discovered they were made of a zinc alloy (referred to as 'muck-metal'), they could easily be melted down to make any manner of useful things, such as steam engines. Tooth brushes with wooden handles and soft bristles were popular, but not for teeth cleaning, and tooth powder made, so they said, a fair substitute for baking powder if unable to persuade the Medical Officer to prescribe Bicarbonate of Soda.

There was rarely an issue of food, off the ration as it were, and therefore available for us to purchase. I remember a consignment of bacon sausage, usually very good but this time seemingly well past its 'use by' date and a trifle green in parts (probably why it was available). Few took their portion, so another chap and I had a feast by cutting away everything looking remotely 'off'. As neither of us had any ill effects it may be assumed that either we avoided the bad bits, or it was meant to be green anyway. The bulk purchase of several barrels of Italian preserved grapes, hopefully to be used in the making of wine, was not a success. The instruction to soak and wash well to remove the taste of the sulphur preservative was wildly optimistic.

They made quite good compost when dug into the gardens, the taste not being of consequence when used as a fertiliser.

The Red Cross individual parcels, and some other sources at home, made us almost independent of our captors and able to be choosy when it came to the poor quality goods, as used by the German people, and available to us from the canteen. Existence in a German Stalag without the Red Cross and other such agencies, would have been very grim and for many not even survivable. The Germans, it must be said, exhibited a greater degree of honesty in the safe transmission of parcels than did some of their counterparts in the UK. It had, on many occasions, been proved that the Dockers sometimes rifled the private, as distinct from the Red Cross, parcels. The honesty of the Germans may have had something to do with a mandatory death sentence if found in possession of a Red Cross parcel!

The first personal parcel, sent by my parents, contained my uniform, razor, toothbrush, soap, cigarettes, my pipe and tobacco, and assorted clothing, including a magnificent 'sweat shirt' obviously not new and not remembered as having been mine. Whilst exclaiming at my good fortune, Jim recognised it as being his! We had shared the same room at Horsham Saint Faiths' and it would seem that the packer-uppers of our effects - to be sent to our next-of-kin – had, at times, to guess which was whose, and sometimes they guessed wrong. Consolation, for me, was to hope when Jim received a parcel it might contain something of mine.

Red Cross food parcels emanated from Britain, Canada and the U.S.A. As might be expected the Canadian and American parcels tended to reflect the produce of countries not under siege by submarines. They contained such luxuries as butter, Spam, Klim (powdered milk), coffee, cigarettes etc. whilst the British were rather more mundane: Bully Beef, margarine, meat and veg, tinned cheese, dried egg, tinned bacon rashers, sweetened condensed milk and, never to be forgotten, Mortons Meat Roll. Not that there was anything to dislike in Mr. Morton's meat roll, indeed it was quite agreeable, but was suspected of having a very low meat content. I once saw it served up for dessert in the form of thickish slices covered by custard! It was produced for the sweet, without specifying the constituents, as a newly invented culinary masterpiece, and was well received. The British parcels were preferred for their variety and good food value, even by the Americans and Canadians, and when only one type was available, it was to be hoped it would be the British. An assortment of the three types meant we fared well, particularly, if there was a full issue of one parcel per head per week. This was very rare, mostly the issue was half this, and frequently less, sometimes none at all.

The American parcels contained a large tin of 'Oleo' margarine, which was dead white, but in the top of each tin was a small packet of red powder with the instruction to mix this thoroughly with the margarine, thus turning it to a desirable buttery yellow colour, should this be your preference. Apparently there was a law to prevent the sale of margarine masquerading as butter, or of an appearance where it might be mistaken to be butter. It had, as I recall, very little taste but made good fuel for 'fat-lamps, of which more anon. A 'D' bar might be almost anything, but in an American Red Cross food parcel it was a bar of extremely hard chocolate about four inches long, an inch and a half wide and one inch thick. It was of such concentrated goodness as to require instructions for the manner in which it should be consumed to avoid injury to the digestion. *'To be eaten slowly in about half-an-hour.'* Overheard: 'Why are you sitting there staring at your 'D'bar?' 'I'm waiting for half an hour, like it says on the wrapper'! As might be expected there soon came into being a competition to find who could eat a 'D' Bar in the shortest possible time. I think the winner did it in about one and a half minutes. There was some talk that he cheated by surreptitiously warming the bar beforehand.

The Parade/Sports ground, until recently a plantation of pine trees, had lost its trees, but left behind were all the stumps, not that this mattered for the 'Appells' where tidy ranks were seldom achieved anyway. There was always the happy anticipation that Herr Pieber might, with his eyes looking firmly left as he counted off the ranks, trip over an unnoticed stump. The stumps had to be removed before any sporting activity could take place, and to this end the Germans provided a remarkable piece of hand operated equipment, consisting of three stout wooden legs forming a tripod, some nine feet high. Two levers about fifteen feet long extended to either side from the top. When these were, alternately, raised and lowered, they lifted each time a vertical iron bar with a large hook at the bottom, engaged beneath a suitable purchase point in the root of the stump. Having dug down alongside the root to find a suitable purchase point for the hook the apparatus was placed over the stump, the hook engaged, and the levers operated, by a sufficient number of bods, to tear the root from the ground.

In spite of its elementary appearance it proved to be most efficient for the task, and it did not take long to clear the sports field, to the delight of the game fanatics. Some, such as me, viewed this with apprehension for, whilst we were all in favour of games, found them better suited to others who found close association with a ball less difficult. The trouble with a game fanatic is his incapability of curbing his enthusiasm to persuade anyone, however reluctant, to make up a team to enable HIM to play. He then has no qualms in blaming the ensuing fiasco on you, and forcefully gives his opinion of your presence as being the sole reason for his side losing. All however is forgotten and forgiven by the next time he is in the same predicament and needs one more to make up a side. I thoroughly enjoyed helping to pull out the stumps, not a ball in sight, and although there were to be times when some enjoyment was derived from that particular plot, it was never again to be as thoroughly enjoyable as stump pulling.

The first room in the new compound in Hut 122 was shared by Jim Lang (already introduced), Dick Iliffe, who was a friend of Jim's from pre-war, and an enthusiastic rugger player, who had been studying History at University as preparation to becoming a Lawyer. It was his theory that school taught the 'alphabet' of learning, University taught one how to learn (the subject was immaterial) and thus equipped, one then went on to learn the chosen vocation. A splendid system, I am sure, if the time and cash were available! John Madge, tall and thin and sometimes known as the 'perambulating split-pin', was frequently greeted on entering a room by some such remark as – 'Did someone come in? Oh dear, John I do wish you would not stand sideways.' Ken Jones, who loved Ballet and had a fine collection of Ballet and Classical music on records, producing for me an introduction to a lifetime appreciation and enjoyment. Harvey Vivian, a school master from Clifton College and married to Peggy Scrivens, a famous tennis player, who was at that time teaching the game to girls at Byculla School. Among her pupils was the girl I was to meet and marry some seven years later. Then there was Tiddles, the cat, where she/he/it came from, or even some months later, went to, remains one of those war time mysteries. It was black, learnt to like left-over vegetables, because there was precious little left-over meat or fish, and was very fond of milk, whether derived from powder, or Nestles sweetened condensed. It did not like being encouraged to go faster and faster between the ranks of shouting Kriegies on Appell. It was after one such occasion Tiddles kept running and was never seen again. Perhaps being a German cat she mistook the encouraging shouts to be of menacing intent?

I started to learn Bridge and became a moderately good player, having as a partner some time later an Australian Hurricane Pilot called 'Sport' - because that was the way he referred to everyone else. He and I once reached the top of the Block 'Bridge Ladder' and won the packet of cigarettes. Sport told this story:

'There I was flyin' my 'urricane low across the desert up and down the sand dunes when I saw this Arab on a camel. So I aimed straight at 'im and 'e fell off as I went over 'im, and I looked back over my shoulder and I laughed, and I laughed, and I 'it a bloody sand dune.' It says much for the Hurricane that he managed to get back to base with the propeller considerably reduced in diameter!

It was a splendid re-union recently when, thanks to the Australian Returned Servicemen's Association, who discovered him for me after nearly fifty years, that my wife and I stayed a couple of nights with him, and his wife, in Melbourne.

CHAPTER 28.

The Theatre.

On no account should it be supposed I was ever more than an extremely reluctant Thespian. When cast as Oliver Twist at kindergarten I received a sound ticking off from my usually very patient Mother for allowing (as if I had any option at the age of seven) the Teacher to apply black grease paint to the clean white shirt in which I had been sent to school. O.Twist apparently did not wear a clean white shirt. Such an experience for someone intending dedication to the theatre must have been off-putting. But having already discovered early in life that the worry of having to learn a part only to find this was but a preliminary to suffering a stomach full of butterflies before going on stage, it was the final straw. Mostly, but not entirely, I thenceforth managed to maintain a fair degree of remoteness from the Stage.

Building a Theatre was, however, another dimension and one I found, though in a very minor capacity, much to my liking. When we came into the new compound there was nothing more than a plot of sand designated to have a Theatre built upon it. It was not long before plans were produced and the work started. I do not know any of the procedural details, which must have been needed to obtain permission, materials etc. from the Germans for what became a building of considerable size, complexity and even sophistication. I heard it said the Third Reich was much in favour of 'Kulture' and as the theatre fell into this category it was allowed many privileges, including a mains supply cable for the electricity with copper conductors as opposed to the more usual aluminium. There was a projection room with, at least sometimes, a projector for showing German Films of considerable disinterest.

There were posh curtains, on proper tracks, an Orchestra Pit, and even a trap door in the floor of the stage! The Auditorium had a sloping floor of timber joists and boards supported on wooden piles driven into the sand, some two feet or more, below the floor level. This resulted in a rather large, and apparently wasteful, void which became considerably reduced, in times to come, by deposits of sand resulting from the enthusiastic efforts of the tunnel builders. The seating was most ingeniously and skillfully contrived from the plywood 'tea-chest' type boxes in which the Red Cross parcels arrived in bulk deliveries. These seats each had arm rests and sloping backs and achieved the near impossible by being not only splendid to look at but actually comfortable.

Standard wooden hut components were used to build the above ground structure. These were supported on brick walls enclosing the Stage area and the sloping floor of the Auditorium. The labour for the assembly and building work came from the surprisingly versatile ranks of the POW's, but where the money for the materials and fittings came from I never discovered. It may even, in part, have arisen from our unpaid, as already explained, pay. Some clever fellow designed a parabolic reflector for the floodlights, made from ingeniously interlocking strips of Klim (milk powder) tins. I must have made hundreds of these components, there being a large number of reflectors needed, each one requiring about fifty strips. Equal ingenuity resulted in a dimming system for these same floodlights. A square tin tube, made from biscuit tins, about two feet six inches long, sealed at one end, coated in pitch, except at the bottom, and filled with salt water was connected to the positive wire coming from the mains. The wire continuing to the lamps was attached to a tin plate on the end of a wooden stick. When this plate was placed in the water, in the tin tube, electricity flowed through the salted water to the plate and thus to the lamps. The nearer the plate on the end of the stick approached the bottom of the tube the less was the resistance and more brightly shone the lamps. It worked extremely well but was potentially a bit dangerous and if a use could have been found for boiling salt water, then there would have been a very handy by-product.

With such ingenuity plus enthusiasm and incredible talent the Theatre became a place of absorbing interest and occupation to hundreds of Kriegies as well as bringing a modicum of normality and civilization to everyone in the Camp on the rather special occasions when they went to see a 'show'. And such shows they were. I was no connoisseur, not being old enough to have made many visits to the theatre. Apart, that is, from Pantomimes, the Variety shows at the Hippodrome (by then a bombed out ruin), a few presentations of Shakespeare in the School Hall and a memorable visit to the Winchester Town Hall to see a wonderful presentation of the Mikado by the Local Amateur Operatic Society. I have heard from those with much more experience that the Stalag Luft 3 productions were of exceedingly high standard. For me they revealed another world where Prison Camps and Wars did not exist for sometimes as long as two hours, or more.

The Whitehall Farces like 'Rookery Nook' were great favourites in which the part taken by Robertson Hare in the London production was played with complete conviction by Peter Butterworth. After the war Peter made for himself a successful career on stage, films and television, as also did Rupert Davies, particularly for his portrayal of 'Maigret' in the television series. 'Arsenic and Old Lace' was playing in the Camp Theatre concurrently with being on in London and a newly shot-down Kreigie who had seen the London show reckoned ours was the better! The scripts for all the popular plays and musicals, both old and contemporary, appeared to be readily available and were performed as a continuous process to produce a show from London or America every four or five weeks with other, major classical and minor, productions in between. Of the Classical plays I remember suffering a severe fright when suddenly, in Macbeth, the skillfully made-up ghost of Banquo magically and unexpectedly appeared.

Harvey Vivian, the schoolmaster from Clifton College wrote a one-act play and persuaded me to be in it. I no longer recall any of the lines or even the title, which was to do with a character in a Pub talking to the Landlord when in comes a cockney newspaper boy (me) calling out 'E'ning Star 'n Standar'' (there now I do recall some of the lines), and becomes involved in a long complex dialogue with the customer. I know it was long and complex because I had to learn it! It ended, to much applause, when the man removed his hat to reveal horns signifying he was the Devil, thereby causing the curtain to drop, and me to heave a sigh of relief at having survived to the end without a major disaster. I am conscious of having done less than justice to Harvey's play, but it was generally reckoned to be good and very clever by the audience of the 'Theatre Club' to whom it was presented. Having now become a 'recognised' Actor I was automatically accorded membership of the Club, which included certain privileges, including the rather doubtful one of being available to any producer silly enough, and with the necessary powers of persuasion, or even a bribe of sufficient attraction, to include me in his cast.

One Producer, no less than the son of Sybil Thorndike, John Casson, availed himself of this opportunity and involved me in a very minor role as a Page Boy, in Shaw's 'Joan of Arc'. He was not to know, of course, that he would be remembered as the only Producer of this magnificent play where the audience found something to laugh at! The script called for me merely to announce the arrival of some important ecclesiastics, in this fashion – 'The Right Reverend, His Lordship, The Bishop of Beauvais, and two other - er –' (desperate pause while I prayed for the words to turn up before panic set in) '- er- 'irrelevant' Gentlemen.' It should have been 'Reverend' and had it been so, then neither I nor, maybe, anyone else would have recalled that splendid production.

In ancient Rome when Claudius was doing very little to improve the ethics of his subjects, there lived a royal lady, his wife, of great beauty and no discernible morals, called Messalina. Two talented inmates, following the precedent set by Gilbert and Sullivan and inspired by the interesting reputation of this lady, (and helped by the novels of Robert Graves, 'I Claudius' and 'Claudius the God') wrote an Operetta. The original lyrics and music were of such quality and enjoyment that it not only ran for twice as many performances as usual, to allow everyone in the camp to see it twice, but was seriously considered for the London stage. It is a great pity this never happened. I believe there were reasons/difficulties familiar, maybe, to the world of the Theatre but certainly none of these would have concerned the propriety of the script which would in no way have been offensive to the Censor of 1946, let alone today. It was witty and tuneful and required a large cast of competent actors, who were also able to sing. The barrel of available talent had to be scraped to the extent where I became a vitally insignificant participant. To be precise, I was a slave, who, with two others had to carry on the Emperor in an open Sedan type chair, with poles for handles, and place him, not too gently, upon the stage. The jolt of the 'not too gentle' placement called for the three slaves to sing in chorus – 'Your pardon Lord we crave'. This was the entire extent of our 'speaking part', and we couldn't do it! So deep had they delved into the barrel that not one of us could summon a note, certainly not the half dozen or so required to sing our line. The problem was solved, to the complete satisfaction of everyone, by the orchestra doing the singing for us, and very well they did it too. On the first night, following the producer's admonition, we slightly overdid the 'not too gentle' bit and the chair broke.

During the run of 'Messalina' I noticed Peter Butterworth, who had one of the leading parts, as might be expected, showing concern for the quality of his voice by shyly and surreptitiously taking large doses of cough syrup, of which he appeared to have a substantial amount. I discovered later, what he had known for some time, that this Cough Syrup was about one hundred percent proof alcohol. I can only suppose the officer in charge of medical supplies was a fervent supporter of all things theatrical in general, and Butterworth in particular.

Revues and Variety shows gave opportunities for the extroverted, but up 'till then frustrated, soloists to tell their jokes, sing their songs or play their instruments. It must be to the credit of those who organised and, presumably, vetted such talent for me to have no recollection of a bad act. John Casson, as well as being a superb all round actor and Producer, showed he could also be a very entertaining conjuror. Everyone particularly enjoyed the trick where he showed the audience a small painting of a bathing beauty, in a two-piece costume, walking down towards the sea. He rolled the picture and, putting two fingers into the top of the roll, pulled out a little Bra, he then did the same to the other end and pulled out a pair of pants. To an audience full of anticipation he then unrolled the picture only to discover the tide had come in and the lady was now up to her neck in the sea. I have seen the trick done since but never to a more attentive audience. German Officers frequently attended and appreciated the performances, although some of the humour was not always to their liking and some not understood at all. There was the time a comedian was giving his version of a news broadcast at the time of the stalemate of the Eighth Army, advancing up through Italy, at Cassino:

'Here is the latest bulletin from the Italian front. The British forces have advanced one foot'. (loud cheers from the audience and puzzlement on the faces of the Germans who quite correctly did not think a foot was very far.) *'Upon the foot being struck by shrapnel it was rapidly withdrawn. That is the end of the Bulletin'.*

The Germans found this very funny until they realised they were not the only ones laughing. Why the British should be laughing at such a humiliating story seemed beyond them, so no doubt supposing they had missed something to their disadvantage, they stopped laughing.

Stuck in my memory is a cabaret turn in which two American G.I's in Paris, following instructions to speak French to the natives and both being in civvies, meet in the street and, mistaking each other for Frenchmen, had a conversation beginning thus:

'Bonjewer manure, ou ay votre domi-silly?'

'Mon domi-silly ay dons ler Champs A-lousy', and so on - fortunately I do not remember how.

Competent musicians appeared to abound, and likewise those who wished to become competent by constant practice. Fortunately it was usually possible to have them do this remote from the general camp population, but if one happened to be doing something in, or near, a practice area then you realised what a painful process was involved in becoming a musician. We all enjoyed the concerts given by the orchestras, from the classical through the entire range of the lighter musicals and dance music. One chilly Spring evening when there were still some clumps of Pine Trees in the compound, a group, growing larger by the minute, gathered in one of the clumps to listen to an impromptu solo trumpet recital given by a recently shot down Texan. He was absolutely wonderful and was encouraged to keep on and on, until, with little daylight remaining and becoming very cold indeed, he announced: 'Ah'm sorry folks, ah cain't play no more on account ah'm workin' up a sweat shiverin''.

A very lost bomber on a night training flight ran out of fuel, the crew bailed out and two or three of them managed to meet up. Having discovered themselves to be in hilly country they set about finding some kind of habitation. They realised there was a possibility, exceedingly remote of course, that they might not be in England, which gives a good idea of their 'lostness', and so they decided to be careful in making any rash approach to the first person they met. After a while a cottage turned up with chinks of light showing through the shutters and considerable chatter coming from within. They listened intently and decided it was not English being spoken, maybe French but they were by no means certain of this and then one of them, who should have known better, exclaimed:

'It's Welsh in'it?, we're in Wales look you, there's good, boyo lets go in'.

Now this was a real possibility for they had last been flying towards the West, which is where Wales is, and although nowhere near where they had hoped to be it was at least better than it might have been and a great encouragement to wishful thinking. So in they went, only to find their language recognition was no better than their navigation which, no doubt, accounted for my hearing the story in a German Prisoner of War camp!

To land in Germany in mistake for Wales, even if it was dark, might seem a bit unlikely but it usually came about from the simple error of setting the course on the compass with Blue (south) on Red (north), whereas it should have been Red on Red. The result was to make the aircraft fly a reciprocal course, that is, exactly in the opposite direction.

CHAPTER 29.

Tin Bashing.

Tin Bashers were accepted, with reluctant enthusiasm, as a desirable nuisance by the other members of a room in which these highly skilled members of the community happened to live. For those unfortunate enough, or perhaps worse ignorant of, or even perhaps never to have met a Tin Basher, a few words of explanation. There are those amongst us who find complete satisfaction and relaxation in innovating, making and repairing things. Sometimes the things are useful, even desirable, but this is by no means an essential quality. The finished artifact is of little importance compared to the pleasure and anticipation experienced during its design and manufacture. I know about these things because it did not take long to discover I was a Tin Basher just waiting to happen, and the model aeroplanes and boats, Meccano, working guns, and loud explosions of my youth had all been an apprenticeship to the achievement of this status. The significant raw material was tin-plate, derived from the containers of food in the Red Cross parcels and foraged from the rubbish bins when insufficient could be obtained directly from our own parcels. Since a 'tin' was rarely just as one wanted it, a certain amount of persuasion was needed to make it assume the desired shape, hence the word 'Basher'.

Tools had to be improvised, as anything resembling a real tool, for instance a file or hacksaw, would instantly be confiscated as, quite understandably, it would be suspected of being used to aid escape. My tool-kit came to consist of, a pen-knife with one largish blade and a nail file, a pair of nail scissors, quite adequate for cutting tin-plate, with specially ground points making it possible for them to be used as drills. My best tool was a table knife with a heavy solid aluminium (or an alloy of some sort) handle. The blade was modified by having the tip snapped off and sharpened, thus producing a chisel about three-eighths of an inch wide, for cutting tin or wood. It could be used as a screwdriver and re-sharpened, using the cement hearth as a whetting stone. Further up the blade from the chisel end, the next inch and a half of the blade on the sharp side, was serrated by placing the sharp edge of someone else's knife across mine and hitting it firmly with a heavy object at intervals of about a sixteenth of an inch. This produced, on my knife, a series of teeth able to perform as a remarkably efficient hacksaw. It will be understood the process automatically, and at no extra cost, made two hacksaws, one on my knife and one on the other fellows. I expect he was rather pleased about that. The handle of the knife, being solid, fulfilled the function of a 'pranger', that is a planisher or hammer for dressing the tin into folds and shapes and generally hitting things where moderately gentle force was required. The upper part of the blade, between the handle and the beginning of the hacksaw, was kept sharp to cut sheets of tin into strips etc. This was accomplished by pushing the blade through the crack between the slats of a stool, in such a way as to bring the chisel end against a batten beneath the stool, thereby serving as a fulcrum. The blade could then be used as a sort of guillotine, or one bladed scissor, to chop sheets of tin with great facility. The blunt part of the back edge came in very handy for scraping the paint from the tins prior to cutting them up. So much for the knife, though it did have one other use, I had to eat with it.

As the sheets of tin were not of any great size joints had to be made and it was often necessary for these to be waterproof. Soldering was the best option if fluids were to be contained, but was no use for ovenware as solder melted at the temperature attained by hot fat. Solder could be obtained from melting 'silver paper'; in those days it really was TIN-foil, later it became aluminium foil and was no use at all. The best source of solder was from Bully Beef tins. These were sealed with a disc of tin soldered into a recess in the bottom with no concern, I am happy to say, for the generous, and wasteful, amount of solder used in the process. Bully Beef tins were not generally sought after as being useful in any way, either as receptacles or as raw material. They tended, therefore, to be thrown away by the majority who were only interested in the contents, and had no conception of the treasure hiding on the bottom. It was only necessary for me to make an occasional tour of the rubbish bins to keep well supplied with solder.

Melting the solder away from the tin was not difficult, but was rather smelly, and was done on the communal cooking stove. The molten solder was cast into sticks in a mould made from a folded newspaper, the most unlikely of materials. It tended to scorch a bit but worked very well. Flux was mostly Resin, either from trees, when there still were some in the compound, or from a member of the orchestra's string section, who might be persuaded to part with a block of the stuff. Occasionally a 'killed acid' flux could be obtained, if one knew the right people. With this it was possible to solder metals not already 'tinned' as the tinplate was.

Soldering is usually associated with a soldering iron, and naturally we had no such thing, and even if we had the source of heat would have presented a problem. We used a blowlamp, not the paraffin pressure type, but a very effective homemade device whereby a thin jet of air was blown through the flame from a pyjama cord wick immersed in de-watered fat. This produced a very hot thin jet of flame about two inches long. The air-jet pipe was made from a sheet of tin, rolled around a pin at one end and a pencil at the other. It was about a foot long and took a great deal of making, and thus became quite the most precious component of the soldering outfit.

The jet-pipe was never put away connected to, or even near, the lamp because when the Germans searched our rooms they would take away any kind of fat-lamp as being an item associated with tunnels. The pipe on its own meant nothing to them. I never had to make another pipe but I had so much practice in making replacement lamps it only took fifteen minutes to manufacture a replacement. The big end of the blow pipe was held in the mouth, rigidly clenched between ones teeth, to which it fitted comfortably after a time, thus leaving both hands free to hold and manipulate whatever was being soldered. The heat at the tip of the flame was such as, if careless, to burn away the tinning and render it no longer possible to make the solder 'stick' to the burnt area. Hours would be spent watching a tin of fat bubbling away on the stove to drive off the water, thereby rendering it suitable to use in the lamp. Watching was essential to prevent the fat over-heating and catching alight when deprived of its water. Subsequently I found it was sufficient to melt the fat, leave it to solidify, bore a hole through the fat to the bottom of the tin and pour away the water, which had separated and sunk to the bottom!

Baking tins and roasting dishes could not be made from small sheets of tin soldered together, so the small pieces were joined to each other by some kind of welt. The edges to be joined were folded to interleave with each other, or via a jointing strip, and then hammered flat. This did not produce a watertight joint but after being used a few times the fat, or other fluid, leaking through the almost tight joints and carrying finely divided pieces of whatever was being cooked, eventually made the joints entirely leak-proof. At least so far as is necessary when baking, roasting or stewing.

Other tools of importance were those used for woodworking. A mallet was made from a piece of hardwood, Walnut I think, salvaged from a chaise-longue and provided with a handle. I made a rather superior frame saw from the slats of the same chaise-longue. A piece of twisted Red Cross string tensioned the blade, which had been made from a length of the steel tape used to bind crates and large parcels and on which I had, with my nail scissors and considerable effort, cut teeth. It proved a very efficient tool, surviving many searches by dint of being completely dismountable into its several components to look like a bundle of sticks. The blade could not be disguised and had to be hidden. On one occasion, after a warning had been received, it survived a frisking from the Gestapo hung from the waistband inside my trousers. It was a good hiding place but hurried movement was to be avoided. A sort of disposable tenon saw could be made from a piece of tin, say six inches long and three inches wide. One long edge was folded over a few times to form a stiff spine and the other edge was given teeth by making short - about an eighth of an inch - cuts at right angles with a pair of scissors. Surprisingly it lasted very well.

Many useful and even essential articles were made from tins and tin-plate. From a simple mug, requiring no more than a folded strip of tin, to preclude all sharp edges, bent to the correct shape to form a handle and soldered to a tin of suitable size and shape. To a Coffee Percolator, large enough to serve twelve people, complete with a glass dome to view the 'perking'. The ground coffee came in either the Canadian or American parcels. When made in a Percolator it gave off the most delightful aroma - to the very considerable envy and dismay of the Germans who were unlikely to be invited in for a 'cup of coffee', unless, of course it was intended to bribe, or otherwise, corrupt them. For the most part they had only smelt, or tasted, ersatz acorn coffee since 1939. Coffee made from ground beans is, incidentally, an extremely effective stopper-up of leaks. Even quite large imperfections in the soldering would, after a while, become tight. I used coffee grouts, with complete success, in the radiator of my Jowett car when I came home to find it still leaked a bit after soldering the split caused by frost. Probably the largest cooking utensil I made was a Double Boiler which helped considerably in preventing the burnt porridge, to which we had become accustomed, and made possible the production of Bread Puddings, which required, so I was informed, all-day steaming.

A sheet of tin, suitably stiffened, if attacked with a largish nail to make lots of holes, became a grater, and if a chisel, like the end of my knife was used, then a shreader resulted. Fortunately there were other more important things to make than kitchen utensils, such as steam engine models and boats to sail on the fire pond. I will try to curb my enthusiasm for this positively enjoyable aspect of being a Kreigie as I find, to my amazement, there are some who do not find such things interesting or even totally absorbing.

The first model boat was designed to look and behave like the sleek Bermuda rigged craft so familiar to the happy carefree days in the Solent before the war. It was a modest venture, some eighteen inches long, made of paper strips in many layers, glued over a wood framework and painted to protect the paper from the water. The glue was a sort of size, completely soluble in water, and the paint was proper oil paint. Where it came from I do not remember, maybe - and there was nothing unusual about this - I never knew. Its availability was the only important factor, who stole it or where it had been stolen from might have been interesting, but was not in the least important. Some ingenious character had designed a keel for model sailing craft, which he maintained dispensed with the need for a rudder, and would, automatically, keep the boat on a course to suit the set of the sails. I used his design and it worked! If the sails were set correctly it would even run before the wind; anyone familiar with model sailing boats lacking any automatic steering device, or in this case even a rudder, will know this is not what usually happens. The boat floated and sailed well enough to compliment its design, in fact it was the fastest on the pond, but not for long. The paint must have been an ersatz product not intended for even brief immersion and it was not long before the glue and the paper proved their unsuitability and became soggy, to the extent that further trials were consigned to the stove where the released calories complemented the coal ration. Many years later and with infinitely better resources I built a bigger and better sailing model with the same keel arrangement, and it still worked!

I designed and built a more ambitious sailing boat with two masts, a ketch, having a composite construction of tin keel and frames, planked with wood veneer, obtained by delaminating a piece of three ply from a Red Cross crate. The planks were fastened to the tin frames with slivers of tin bent over, i.e. clenched, inside and out. The hull was covered with cloth and hot wax from German boot polish. It was not a very elegant boat: the wood veneer won its argument with the tin frames, causing an upward bend in the hull resulting in a 'hog-back' which is, aesthetically, as ugly as it sounds. In all other respects it worked well and with the patent keel would go before the wind, mainsail out to one side and the mizzen out the other. It also had the unique ability, when tacking or sailing across the wind, to turn about on reaching the far side of the pool and come back on the other tack without relying on its owner to rush round to meet and turn it. This ability was not so much a function of the boat as of the pool. The sloping brickwork sides went down into the pool, from ground level, at forty-five degrees for a few feet, and then became vertical. This resulted in the forward projecting part of the patent keel striking the slope before the hull. Momentum caused the bow to plunge into the water, and the boat to pivot around. The sails were stiffish paper and perfectly adequate as long as the rain stayed away.

My first steam engine was single acting with a slide valve held on to the port face with elastic derived from a pair of underpants. The cylinder was part of the handle from a safety razor, the shaft, crank etc, were bent up from the brass hooks designed to support the belt at the waist of an Airman's uniform jacket, and other parts came from bent tins and solder. The flywheel, for example, was a boot polish tin given weight by being filled with strips of tin coiled round and round inside like a clock spring. Tubes were made of tin rolled around a piece of fence wire and soldered down the seam. A suitable tin served as the boiler and a fat lamp as the fire. Steam pressure was low for several reasons. Underpants elastic is not very strong, the cork keeping the steam in the boiler was not exactly of the highest technology and above all a fat lamp, whilst very good at soot making, is not so good at providing heat, unless given a forced draught, which it did not have. Taken with the considerable heat losses, particularly when driving a boat across the pond out of doors, tended to result in a struggle by the steam to reach the engine from the boiler before becoming condensed back to water. But it did work, spluttering and plodding its leisurely way across the pond, and what more can one ask than that?

The boat was all metal, made from about ten cocoa tins, flattened, welted and soldered together before being cut out, bent, and bashed into the shape of a boat some two feet long and eight inches beam. It looked very like a Tug but without, in the least, being capable of emulating one.

A toothbrush holder came my way. This was a brass tube three-quarters of an inch in diameter and about seven inches long with fitting caps at each end and quite obviously asking to be turned into the cylinder of a steam engine. The conditions attached to its acquisition were twofold. I would not be getting either of the end caps, and two inches of the tube could be mine only if the remainder was returned to its owner. My hacksaw-table-knife proved entirely adequate to satisfy this condition and in due time there emerged a working steam traction engine. Without going into detail it is, I hope, of interest to give a list of some of the materials and their sources: the cap of a trumpet valve became the cylinder head; parts of a trombone formed the eccentric and slip ring; the piston valve cylinder was a short length of the handle of a Gillette razor; the piston was cast into the cylinder from melted down German razors and the crank shaft, was again, the ever useful belt hook. Klim tin lids became the big back wheels; a talcum powder tin was the boiler and eventually the finished product seemed and looked good enough for a test run.

The test track was the central corridor of the block; the fuel German boot-polish, which was more plentiful than butter or margarine. Having filled the boiler with boiling water it did not take long to raise a head of steam, just long enough, as it happened, to suspect that an inferior brand of burning oily black boot polish was not going to be welcomed by the inhabitants of the adjoining rooms. With an almost authentic chuffing noise the traction engine went sedately down the corridor obtaining, by its motion, a modicum of draught to the fire, thereby encouraging it to burn better. The speed increased, the smoke screen became all pervading, and nearly impenetrable. Fortunately the little traction engine, which was after all the only point of interest, was still visible ahead of - and therefore clear of - the smoke screen it was laying.

The loud cries of appreciation from the small audience, assembled to watch the trials, brought some of the occupants of adjoining rooms into the corridor, who after some initial panic, and being re-assured the block was not on fire, suggested, quite firmly, that we should seek appreciation elsewhere. Not wanting to appear unreasonable I picked up the poor little engine, whose only crime was to smoke rather heavily, by the wheels, which were the only parts cool enough to handle, and took it outside where the breeze fanned the flames to a modest inferno. For one short glorious moment the speed became positively impressive and then all the solder joints melted, until, with a last defiant burst of steam, flame, smoke and smell it disintegrated into its individual components.

Such an end was in no way to be regretted. If it had not worked that would have been sad, but it had worked and now the tale of its inspiration, construction, performance and destruction could be told without running the risk, either of being required to give a repeat performance or, having to produce evidence to prove the conception and construction were indeed as immaculate as the tale had led the listener to believe. This, however, was not the end of the engine. It was rebuilt from the salvaged bits with the intention of providing power for a paddleboat. The rebuild was an improved conception from the original, having its framework components and flywheel, not of tin but cast in solid metal obtained from melting down German razors. The molds were made in cardboard and proved entirely satisfactory, at least for a one-off. The paddleboat never materialised, owing to the state of the war in general and the Russians in particular. I brought the engine home with me, and still have it. For many years it was incapable of movement owing to the razor metal seeming to 'grow' and the piston thereby becoming solid within the cylinder. Recently I cut out the piston, made a brass one and it now works again.

Wind-up gramophones were fairly common, in fact it seemed as if there was one in most rooms. I don't remember seeing a new machine and it might have been they all dated from the earlier years, prior to October 1942. A pleasant illusion of luxury was induced by playing ballet music, or some similarly gentle and soporific record, at bed time. There was a snag, the gramophone did not switch itself off when the needle reached the bit at the end of the track where an eccentric circle causes the pick-up to waggle to and fro, and in a more sophisticated machine, switch off the motor and stop the turntable. Not a very big snag one might suppose, but most irritating for the person who had been honoured with the choice of the record, and the responsibility of ensuring his choice lulled everyone to sleep – not to be woken again by the scratchy noise of the needle at the end of the track. The only way to prevent this was to leap out of bed at the appropriate moment, or sit by the machine throughout the performance.

I solved the problem with some thread and a few tin components. No longer the indefinite 'whirr-whirr' going on 'till the spring ran down, now there was only half a whirr, followed by a sharp clunk and silence. Progressing from the experience of another tin-bashing colleague I evolved a method of mending broken gramophone springs. As time went by this became more and more of a problem and no spares ever became available. The mend was achieved by taking the two ends of the broken spring and hammering them into hooks in such a way as to enable them to engage with each other but allowing the join to flex without bending the steel of the spring. This was necessary because to form the hooks the temper in the steel had to be removed, which was done by pushing the broken end through a potato before putting it in the fire and making it red hot. The potato limited the heat to the short length projecting, thus not spoiling more of the spring than necessary. With the temper removed the spring could be cut and trimmed with my nail scissors prior to forming the hook.

Removing a spring from its case and then returning it - before becoming an expert - can be quite exciting, gloves and an apron are a good idea. The springs were originally packed in graphited grease, very messy stuff, much of which, unfortunately, did not survive to go back with the mended spring. Rather than risk a dry spring a mixture of German Brilliantine and powdered pencil leads was substituted. It never gave any problems and I could always recognise a machine I had mended by the smell of the Brilliantine, being both overpowering and unmistakable. A spring could be joined about three times before it would no longer last out a ten inch, seventy-eight r.p.m. record. Using this method I never had a spring break twice at the same place. German Brilliantine was in plentiful supply as a free issue from the canteen. I believe I may have been the only one to have found a use for it.

The stoves in the rooms were enormous and the fuel supply miniscule, so we devised a system to by-pass the stove by burning the meagre ration of coal in a German jam tin, lined with clay stolen from the perimeter of the fire-pool. The jam tin - about a foot high - was in front of the stove and had a flue of Klim tins zig-zagging up the front of the stove and disappearing into the top door to connect back with the main flue. A small fire in the jam tin not only could be used for cooking but all the heat normally lost up the chimney, or in warming the bulk of the stove, came into the room from the Klim tin flue.

A word about Klim tins. They could have been specially designed to be useful, even essential, in a POW camp. The dried full-cream milk powder was splendid stuff, but the tin became a source of raw material, not only for its tin-plate, but because the can, which was opened by a key winding away a strip of tin, then exposed a spigot upon which the released lid would then fit. This spigot could also be used to engage into the base of another can, from which the bottom had been removed, and so on, one tin on another forming a pipe of indefinite length. It would then become the air supply line under the floor of a tunnel; the improvised flue to a home made stove, or in shorter lengths and with the joints soldered, a coffee percolator etc. etc. Such was the universalistic appreciation of the container that an officer of Oriental origin, American/ Chinese, with an unpronounceable name, was known as 'Klim-Tin'.

So far this chapter has concerned itself with some of my tin bashing activities. There were many others in the camp who not only did the same sort of thing but, in many cases, did them a great deal better. A model yacht, of infinite detail, even to having a lift-off deck exposing the fully furnished cabins; a Glider with a wingspan of four or five feet, carrying on its back a rubber powered bi-plane. When the glider was towed up to the limit of the line the bi-plane was thrown forward, on a spring-loaded catapult. As the glider started its descent the powered plane went on climbing until the motor ran out. Both, having been set to fly in a large circle, hopefully, to avoid going over the wire, would arrive back on the ground at about the same time. The rubber motor came from a football bladder, carefully cut into strips. Another glider was last seen, still gaining height, slowly disappearing towards Berlin, and another flew beautifully, and very fast, into a room in a nearby block without waiting for the window to be opened.

A working wall clock was made with carefully cut tin gear wheels, meshing with lantern pinions made from used gramophone needles. It kept good time although, to overcome the inevitable friction of parts slightly less than perfect, the driving weight - a tin full of sand - was rather heavy, producing a 'tick' with which it was almost impossible to live.

Some genius with a length of electric flex made an immersion heater from two discs of tin, tied through and on either side of a cotton-reel, with the two wires of the flex joined one to each disc. The device was hung from a piece of wood, into a jug full of cold water, connected to the mains electricity and, standing well clear, switched on. The cold water, two or three litres, boiled in a very short time. Such was the success of the contraption that all who could acquire the necessary length of flex - this being the difficult bit - copied the design until some, mutually agreed, staggering had to be adopted to prevent all the lights in the camp going dim at 'brew-up time'. Great care was always required, particularly when the water container was of metal. I never knew of anyone being electrocuted, maybe this was because the huts were of all wood construction and this gave an insulation from earth?

There was this Lancaster going to drop bombs on Berlin when it was hit by anti-aircraft fire, causing a fire in the rear part of the fuselage. The pilot turned to the teller of the tale, the bomb aimer, and told him to go and put the fire out. He, being a prudent fellow, took his parachute from its stowage and clipped it to his harness, then he gathered an extinguisher and went to attend to the fire. The extinguisher did no more than irritate the fire: the rest of the story is best told in the words of the bomb aimer, and if you can imagine the Australian accent it will much improve my attempt to re-tell his tale.

'I couldn't ask the Skipper what to do because there wasn't any inter-com plug, and there was damn all he could do anyway, so I said to myself, 'you're on your own Cobber, be clever, and then I had a beaut of an idea and I opened the 'atch in the floor, and in came the wind and blew out the fire. I was so bloody pleased with meself I went to tell the Skipper, forgot I'd left the 'atch open and fell through the bastard thing!'

He did remember to pull the ripcord and floated down amongst the Bomber stream, to either side, above, and below, thinking, 'those lucky devils are going back to bacon and eggs and a comfortable bed and I don't know where I'm going'. But he was the lucky one. The aircraft he had saved from burning never did get back to England, and neither, as far as he knew, did any of the crew survive.

CHAPTER 30.

Escaping.

In any account of Prisoner of War life, it is, I dare say, obligatory, to include something about escaping, indeed there are excellent books devoted entirely to this aspect, and I have much enjoyed reading a great number of them.

Professional escapers, of which there were many, were not, by any means, the majority. The majority, of which I claim to have been part, were at all times available to the escaping fraternity to do the more mundane tasks and to give the benefit of their, in many cases, highly specialised skills. If, as a reward for labour or skills provided, an invitation was given to join an escape attempt then most of the majority would, with subdued enthusiasm, have had a bash. The selection, of those so invited, gave priority to German speakers, or other native continentals like Poles, Czechs etc. who could be more convincing when posing as Germans or foreign workers. This put un-pushy people like me far down the priority list.

It was not, of course, a pre-requisite for an enthusiastic escaper to have any skill with languages. Such a person would concentrate on travelling in the dark and trying to avoid any contact with the population. This was known as going 'hard-arse' and enjoyed a good success rate, possibly better than the well-qualified escaper possessing beautifully forged documents, money and the ability to communicate. Harvey Vivian, who I have already mentioned, having taught German at Clifton College, spoke it immaculately and was therefore a perfectly equipped candidate for whom no effort was spared to get him outside the wire. On two or three occasions this was successful but each time he was discovered and brought back, having aroused suspicion by speaking German better, and more correctly, than any German!

The first job the Escape Committee gave me was to sit in, and at the end of, a cold draughty corridor peering out through a split in the woodwork into the dark for hours and hours. I was required to keep a Log of the periodic sweeps of the searchlights operated from the Goon Towers. It was all in aid of an attempt to discover if there could be any recognisable pattern, which might be exploited in the event of a night-time escape attempt. I also had to log the movements of the 'Hundfuehrer', (the guard patrolling within the wire and accompanied by a large ferocious Alsatian dog). I came to the interesting, and useless, opinion that the Goon with the searchlight was as bored as the Goon with the dog and even if either had a pattern to guide their duties it had long been forgotten. I was more bored than either having neither a dog or a searchlight with which to play.

Another erstwhile student Architect and I were entrusted with the task of making a full survey to enable a scale plan of the camp to be drawn. We were given a sheet of Imperial size cartridge paper and nothing else. Pencils, erasers, drawing pins and a twelve-inch ruler we had already. If we had possessed a tape measure or chain it would have been quite useless. The survey had to be done without the knowledge of our captors, who would certainly have found something strange in two officers stretching a tape around the perimeter, and between the huts, calling out measurements for the other to write down.

Red Cross string was knotted together and carefully measured with the twelve-inch ruler to be one hundred feet long. Chalk marks were made one hundred feet apart in the corridor of our block so that my colleague and I could then walk over this distance many times and establish the number of normal paces we each took to cover the distance. This gave us our individual factors to convert paces into feet. Thus equipped, and with concentrated expressions of unconcern, we paced the camp in every direction to obtain all the necessary dimensions. The Plan, during its production, was rolled and stored, when not being worked upon, in the piano in a room set aside as a sort of chapel. On one occasion, whilst fetching or returning the plan, we found it occupied by an individual who complained bitterly, in a powerful cockney accent - which may have been Australian - at the disturbance of his meditation. This individual was a character whose presence in the Camp was a bit of a mystery. He certainly never flew anything, sailed anything, or marched with the Army. I think the war caught up with him in the desert where he might have been in the NAAFI or even something like the Salvation Army and was sent to us entirely on account of not knowing where else to put him.

An Admiralty manual of some sort, purporting to contain all the knowledge ever likely to be necessary for a sailor, in the section devoted to splicing ropes, made it quite clear it was not possible to splice 'round' or 'square' Sennit. This gem of information rarely surprises anyone because it is not easy to find anyone who has the least idea what you are talking about. Sennit is rope, or braid, plaited instead of being twisted. Sash cords, clothes-lines and the rope used in place of a Huygans chain in a thirty hour Grandfather, or long-case clock are usually Round Sennit, and also the short piece of rope used for closing the open end of a Kit-bag. Short pieces of rope have very limited application and as quite long pieces were needed to haul containers of sand from the bottom to the top of a tunnel shaft, and also to pull the trollies along the underground railway, some clever fellow with the supreme benefit of ignorance, and uninhibited by the statement contained in the Manual, of which he had never heard, devised a slightly tedious, but completely satisfactory, method of making end splices in Kit-bag cords. This produced ropes of indefinite length, limited only by the supply of Kit-bags. A four-inch nail, with its head replaced by a wooden handle, became a Marlin Spike and a select group of us could be found outside on a Summer's day sitting happily, well, sitting anyway, around a pot of water and a box of spuds, splicing innumerable kit-bag ropes and being ready at a moments notice, if warned by a 'stooge', to sit on our handiwork and resume peeling the potatoes.

There are two types of 'Stooge'. The one mentioned in the last paragraph was one of a comprehensive system placed strategically around the camp in such a manner as to be able to signal to each other the presence and position of Guards, Ferrets etc., within the compound, and then, individually warn the groups involved in nefarious activities. A written record was kept of all German personnel inside the wire and it was not unknown for the German authorities, who had not been able to prohibit the practice, to consult this list when checking on the whereabouts of their own people. On one occasion this led to a couple of Ferrets doing a spell in the Cooler for being out of the compound when they should have been in! The other type of stooge was the individual in each room appointed each day to carry out the household tasks of cleaning, cooking, fetching and carrying. I was never over fond of being selected to 'stooge' in either capacity.

When a tunnel was under construction, and I scarcely remember a time when one was not, a great difficulty arose in disposing of the spoil, which was white sand. It could not be spread over the ground owing to the surface sand having become black, presumably as a consequence of many years accumulation of fallen pine needles. Black is not an easy surface over which to spread white if you do not wish it to be noticed. So, where to hide the white sand? and how to get it to wherever that might be? A short-term solution was in the roof space of the hut from which the tunnel was being dug, thereby disposing of the second problem as well as the sand. The limitation of this method became noticeable when the ceiling started to collapse. Good dispersal places were the perimeters of games areas and, particularly, the Appell area, where the two or three times daily shuffling of over a thousand restless feet had worn away, and intermixed, the black surface with the sub-strata a few inches down. This had resulted in a loose yellow-grey top-sand into which the well-scuffed addition of white sand was virtually unnoticeable. The Appell area, around the football pitch, was, as might be expected, in full view of some four Goon boxes, so the dispersal had to be completely surreptitious.

Two types of bag, to be worn beneath the clothing, were ingeniously devised and issued to, or made by, the willing workers. The chest bag, worn beneath a pullover and a battle-dress blouse, tended to make the wearer look a good deal better fed than his colleagues, and was used to transport sand where the destination was not under scrutiny by the guards. The other type was the leg bag, two of which were worn, one inside each trouser leg, suspended by braces from around the neck. The bottom of each sausage-like bag was closed with a nail, used as if it were a large pin, to which was attached a length of string ending in the pocket. When the string was pulled the nail came out, the sand poured from the trouser leg and a bit of not too obvious scuffing allowed dispersal by this method to take place in full view of the guards. The same method was equally successful in taking the sand to gardens where the gardener would dig a small pit, as gardeners do, and the nonchalant passer-by, whilst stopping for a chat and to admire the daises, would pull the strings and fill the little pit with white sand. Tiring of the chat he would move away as the gardener, anxious to repair the damage, covered over the now non-existent pit. Some of the gardens, particularly those furthest from the perimeter goon-boxes, became higher and higher and attained quite a good altitude. If the dispersal point was hidden from the view of fixed or regularly patrolling guards, and not requiring any subsequent disguise, like in a roof or under a floor or even in a no longer needed tunnel, the sand could be carried in bulk, in boxes, with pole handles, disguised to appear legitimate by placing a layer of potatoes over the sand. It is not easy to appear natural when carrying a load of sand, as if it were potatoes, which would have weighed some three times less than the sand.

There are three ways of getting from inside the wire to freedom on the other side. Over the wire, through the wire, and under the wire. Over was difficult, dangerous and only rarely resorted to. One athletic character, figuring he would not be seen if he was under the Goon-box, made a quick dash across the forbidden area between the warning wire and the perimeter fence. He leapt into the supporting structure of the Goon-box and swung like a trapeze artist over the wire and down onto the path outside. regrettably taking rather longer than had been hoped. For obvious reasons this courageous attempt had to be made in daylight, and although the wire was successfully surmounted, he was seen by the Goon in the next box down the line. He was met on the other side by a guard who had been given sufficient warning to be waiting for him as he landed. Perhaps he was fortunate to have been intercepted before he was able to make a dash for the trees some forty yards away, and give target practice to at least two machine guns and two rifles. The guard escorted him good naturedly (and why not? He had done his duty without ever being in danger or having to panic) to the main gate, and thence to the Cooler. Their progress, around the outside of the wire, was accompanied by applause from those inside, and the whole incident became an agreeable anecdote of a spectacular attempt by a brave man being frustrated by a, this time, tolerant enemy. It could easily have been a tale of tragedy.

Through the wire had two variations, openly and comfortably as an Officer and a Gentleman via the gate or stealthily, uncomfortably, and dangerously, with wire cutters. The former could be dramatically successful as on the occasion when a second party of prisoners, destined for de-lousing, accompanied by a proper escort of guards, followed the first out through the gate after a decent interval. But instead of getting de-loused - which neither they or the first party really needed - they turned smartly off the road and into the woods where they rapidly became civilians, with forged documents to prove it. The 'guards' also removed their homemade uniforms and discarded their wooden rifles, bayonets and cardboard pistol holsters, collected documents and other escaping gear from their erstwhile charges and also became civilians. Yet another, equally bogus, party hoping for a similar success, was stopped at the second gate by a guard who explained to his officer how clever he had been to become suspicious when realizing three parties in succession seemed a trifle unlikely. The officer, knowing there should only have been one party, nearly had a heart attack on being faced with the uncomfortable fact that a large number of his prisoners, with no excitement at all, had just walked to freedom.

Tom, Dick and Harry (not forgetting George) are not always the unidentified attachments to the principal characters in a tale or situation. In Luft 3 Nord they were tunnels and their story has been told, and filmed, as 'The Great Escape'. The book by Paul Brickhill, is not only very well written but is, by my judgement, essentially factual. The film, on the other hand, relies heavily on the imagination of the Producer, and only a little on the facts. In the film, it is even the wrong tunnel which is successful! Why this should be I have no idea, the only improvement needed to the story, in the film, was to stick to the book.

'Tom,' started from Block 123 beneath a concrete area into which a hole had been cut and then sealed with a beautifully made, flush fitting, concrete cover with 'wavy' edges to appear as if there were cracks in the concrete floor. There were some Polish officers who were wonderful craftsmen in many materials, and one named Minskewitz, who excelled with concrete.

'Dick,' was started in my Block, No.122, from the central sump in the concrete floor of the Wash Room. The sump, covered by a grating, was around two feet by two feet, or maybe a little less, and about two and a half feet deep. It normally had a foot of water in the bottom below the outlet to the drain, coming from the basin wastes and the floor wash-down. One entire side of the sump was removed and in its place a concrete panel, made by the Polish officer, could be removed to give access to the tunnel shaft. It could then be reinstated even when the tunnelers were working down below. The joints were waterproofed with a mixture of soap and sand, thereby allowing the water to be replaced and contained in the normal way, rendering the tunnel trap almost undiscoverable. Indeed it never was discovered.

'Harry,' started in Block 104, from beneath the hearth of the stove in Room 23, again made possible by those skilled with concrete. The entire hearth, about four feet square with the lighted stove upon it, could be lifted and placed to one side. A temporary flue of Klim-tins carried the fumes from the stove back to the chimney during the time the hatch was open. In the film this tunnel was, with much drama, discovered, whereas, in fact, it was the successful tunnel through which seventy-six officers went under the wire.

'George,' started from the Theatre, which is all I know about George.

'Tom' was well beyond the wire when discovered, somewhat unfortunately, by a German guard impatiently waiting for his more skilful colleagues to complete searching Block 123. He had no idea he was standing over a thirty-foot deep shaft, but during a fidget his rifle butt struck the floor and produced a hollow sound unlike the sound from other fidgets on other parts of the same floor. Thus found the tunnel had to be destroyed but the usual methods, collapsing it from above by driving a heavy vehicle over it, or emptying into it the contents of the honey cart, did not seem plausible because of its size - thirty feet deep and about two hundred and sixty feet long. So the Germans decided to blow it up. A unit of noticeably reluctant army Sappers was produced, of which one or two, even more reluctant than the rest, were ordered to crawl the entire length to lay dynamite charges. Then, presumably to avoid damage to the hut, which was after all Reich property, they replaced the concrete cover, and retired to a safe distance with the detonating apparatus. A considerable crowd of prisoners gathered to witness this exciting operation. We cheered wildly when the concrete cover, to prove the effectiveness of the dynamite, came sailing through the roof, until, inevitably obeying the laws of gravity, it ran out of puff and returned to earth back through the roof of the hut and at some distance from the exit hole. This was small compensation for the loss of the tunnel but the shamefaced misery on the faces of the explosive experts was better than nothing. My account of the discovery of 'Tom' is, as I remember it being told to me at the time. Paul Brickhill tells it slightly differently. I prefer my version but his may well be more accurate.

'Dick', under our washroom floor, and for all I know still there to this day, was used as a secure hiding place for those essential things not permitted by our guards. When it became likely that 'Harry' was seemingly the best hope for success, and to hurry things up, 'Dick' was also used for hiding the excavated sand, speedily, easily and safely.

'Harry', from under the stove, one wintry night in March, came to the surface, through the snow-covered ground, outside the wire. Unfortunately - or, as things turned out, should that be fortunately? - just short of the tree line, thereby slowing down the rate of exits, and only seventy-six of the hoped for one hundred plus went into the woods to start their chosen method of travelling to a neutral, or occupied, country. Three made a 'home-run', fifty were murdered, on the orders of Hitler, by the Gestapo, and the survivors were returned, some to us and a few to other prisons. It bears repeating that the Germans responsible for our custody were deeply ashamed of this dreadful atrocity committed by their countrymen and it was, maybe, because of this that the inevitable reprisals were never very nasty.

Reprisals were not punishments, they were collective impositions caused for good (German) reasons, of management, shortages of manpower, exigencies of war etc. It was sheer coincidence their juxtaposition with an annoying - to the Germans - incident made them appear to us to be like punishment. They manifested themselves as extra Appells, prolonged Appells, none, or lesser parcel, issues, increased block searches etc. To implement such measures the German officers and men invariably became involved in unpopular extra duties and the reprisals, as a consequence, tended to fizzle out fairly quickly. For some reason, after the success of 'Harry', it was decided to hold the Appells along the North side of the compound instead of around the football pitch. This meant all the blocks lining up in a straight line along the warning wire in front of the main wire between the compound and the Vorlager containing the Coal Store, Hospital, Cooler etc. Beyond the Vorlager, outside the camp, was a minor road along which it was the custom for a squad of the Arbeitskorps (Work Party) to march, shovels at the slope, to and from their daily toil, singing lustily – 'Ai-ee-ai-oh,- ai-oh,- Ai-ee-ai-oh,- ai-ee, Ai-oh, ai-ee Ha- ha-ha-ha-ha-ha....'. At which point we would join in the merriment with hysterical laughter, more 'he-he-he' than 'ha-ha-ha', from a thousand odd voices, to the beat and tune of their version. This caused them to lose their step and stop singing, so we would sing for them the song from 'Snow White'. 'Hi-ho, Hi-ho its off to work we go...' Appells moved back to the football pitch.

It was, naturally enough, those who stayed behind in the camp who suffered the reprisals, not the escapers, who were either on their way, or in the Cooler. Maybe it was reckoned by punishing the majority, they - the majority - might prevail upon the minority to give up these foolish escapades and thereby bring peace in Camp and goodwill between captors and captives. In fact there was very little complaint when the cause had been worthwhile, as in the case of a successful escape. When the cause had been a bit of 'goon-baiting', like camouflaging a hole into which a guard might fall and hurt himself, then the short-lived amusement did not equate with the resulting reprisals, and only irritated the entire camp who had to endure them. But worse the Germans too were irritated and an irritated German is more likely to be ever watchful to find some misdemeanor upon which to vent his exasperation. This tended to make things very difficult for those engaged in clandestine operations. Some types of 'goon-baiting' were fairly harmless, as when the Germans were convinced there was a tunnel being dug and were unable to find how the spoil was being hidden. Some helpful fellow placed a number of bottles on top of his locker, subsequently found in the next search and confiscated, containing coloured liquid with a label to identify it as 'Earth Destroyer'.

Never let it be said the Germans have no sense of humour. An American in our block managed, one night, to cut his way through the wire only to be arrested on the other side and taken off to the Cooler. Next morning when the Appell was taken inside each block, because of bad weather, the English speaking Unteroffizier allotted to count us, looked up and down the ranks before exclaiming – 'Ah I see zer is no 'Love' amongst you' - that being the name of the would-be escaper.

For those skilled in deception it was not difficult to falsify the count at the Appells. This could be used either to make it appear all were present when in fact someone had, unbeknown to the guards, got away, thus giving the fugitive a better start. Or, on the other hand, it could be made to appear, by making the count come short, that an escape had taken place when it had not. This latter device was used when it was known the Germans were going, as a reprisal, to make the count last a very long time. We made sure they were kept very busy, and in a state of panic as succeeding counts failed to produce the correct answer. When we were as tired of the game as they, then they were allowed to get it right.

I made a few water bottles for the 'hard-arse' escapers to take on their travels made from pilchard tins. Being oval they were about the right shape and, when soldered open side to open side, had a good capacity. The bottom of a pilchard tin lends itself to being beaten out to become either concave or convex depending upon whether it is attacked from the outside or the inside. The tin with the concave side fitted well to the body when worn at the belt and the convex outer side meant this had not been achieved at the expense of reduced capacity. A tube at the top with a cork completed the bottle. There were never any complaints, maybe because none of my customers ever got far enough to taste the contents, but the tang of fish in a tin is almost impossible to remove, it seems to permeate the varnish coating and even the metal. I also made a portable heater where a wick floating on fat in a tin would heat another tin of water, or soup, and the one would fit inside the other to be carried until next needed. The golden rule was to allow the fat to solidify before placing it back with the other baggage.

From the German point of view I enjoyed being classified as having an unblemished record of undetected crime and as a consequence had little direct contact with Ferrets. Few of them could manage much English and none ever discovered me doing anything 'verboten', so why should we bother with each other? They were of all types, good at their jobs and pleasant, or in some cases unpleasant, in the doing of it; corruptible and incorruptible; clever and a bit dim. The likable types were usually those who were punctilious in the carrying out of their duties, which they did fairly and politely. One such we called Charley. His family lived in Hamburg and although they suffered severely in the devastating air-raid on that city, he was not granted compassionate leave to go to their assistance. He was a bit surprised the next day when he came into the camp to be given the suggestion that if he were to prod around with his iron spike in such-and-such a locality he might find something to his advantage. He was duly persuaded, and quickly discovered, about a foot beneath the surface, the trap of a tunnel with, beneath it, the beginnings of a shaft. There ensued the usual 'Goon Panic', in rushed steel-helmeted guards brandishing machine guns, to hold back the interested and surprised - very surprised - inmates, whilst ferrets of all types examined this latest example of Kreigie ingenuity. Charley was of course, congratulated on discovering the tunnel, particularly at such an early stage of its construction. Most importantly, he was sent home on a weeks leave, that being the normal reward for finding a tunnel. If we had not known that, there would not have been much point in digging him a tunnel!

When the Gestapo came to search us, as after the tunnel break, not only did they prove not very good at it, but we had been given due warning from our guards who were a great deal more frightened of them than we were. Our lack of fear was entirely due to ignorance. A tin of instant coffee in a Kreigie's locker was no crime but if one was discovered in the belongings of a guard the Gestapo took the view he had been bribed - they were probably right - and the consequences could be rather nasty. Therefore, whenever coffee, cigarettes etc. came back into the camp with the request that they be put innocently with our belongings until after the departure of whoever was frightening them - almost certainly the Gestapo - it was only prudent we too should take steps to ensure the success of any search, arising from the same reason and directed towards us, would be equally frustrated. The same system would work just as well in the opposite direction, that is, items of contraband from our rooms were entirely innocent when found in a German locker.

There were some very ingenious hiding places in the camp. Boards forming the wall surfaces could be made removable to expose the cavity within the thickness of the partition, and then held back in place with elastic bands. This method served well for a long time but was eventually discovered. A tame Goon informed us of this discovery and that a special search was to be made to raid all such caches before we knew they had been rumbled. A policy existed in the camp, in anticipation of just such a contingency, never to use a new hiding place until an alternative was available. With this prior information, all the wall caches were emptied and in each was placed a note, stating in the much-used journalistic idiom of the German newspapers at that time – 'Plan maezig gereunt'. Probably not spelt like that, but meaning – 'Evacuated according to plan!'

It is difficult not to believe there is some kind of pre-destiny or fate hanging over all of us. Consider Jim and I, we survived without a scratch yet in the other Mosquito shot down at the same time and place by the same fighter, both were killed. Remember the Australian putting out the fire and falling through the hatch to become the only survivor of his crew? And there was John Russel, piloting a bomber on the thousand raid to Cologne when the port engine and wing root were set on fire by flak. He told his crew to bale out, his parachute was placed on his lap by the bomb-aimer on his way aft to jump, and whilst he was holding the plane steady for them all to get out, the wing fell off. He was thrown out from the cockpit, his parachute still unfastened on his lap. He remembered no sense of urgency, casually reaching out and retrieving the parachute from mid-air where it was accompanying him on the rapid fall to the ground. He hooked it to the harness, checked it was properly fastened and pulled the rip-cord. The 'chute opened, he swung once, hit the ground and sprained his ankle! I seem to recall he was the only survivor. Logically, because of his intention to be last out, he was most likely to have been the only casualty.

Kismet, fate, pre-destiny, luck? Maybe. Logic? Almost never.

CHAPTER 31.

Day by Day.

Time, we are assured by Einstein, is relative. To what is not always quite clear, but it is certainly relative to established social standards in so far as rising in the morning and retiring for the night are concerned. Few would disagree that for a gentleman of leisure - we were all gentlemen by definition, and of leisure, by force of circumstance - to have to be on parade by 8.00 a.m. was unreasonably premature, and to suffer the lights turned out at 10.30 p.m. was reminiscent of the nursery. These, however, were the strictures placed upon our day by our captors, with which we had no intention of abiding. In consequence, by the very simplest of devices, we changed to more civilised timing, thereby proving Einstein to have been correct and relativity to be relative to whatever base suits you best at the time. Camp Time was adjusted to be one hour ahead of German time meaning, first Appell was now at 9 a.m. and bed time was 11.30 p.m. It is a happy thought that the Goons had to be on parade to count us at the unearthly hour of eight o'clock, and we did not have to be there until nine!

Camp-time applied to everyone within the wire, even the Germans had to acknowledge it as fact, but there was one individual who found even the modified times to be uncivilised. So he set his watch three, I think it was three, hours ahead of camp-time, maintaining that no Gentleman of leisure would dream of rising before mid-day or retiring before two in the morning! Apart from a few impolite remarks from his roommates concerning his occasionally odd meal times this worked for him and for them. It was called 'Foo-time', that being the name he, not inappropriately, answered to.

All this interference with the clock had no effect upon the seasons and in due course came Christmas, Ice-hockey, Football, Rugger, Cricket, Softball, other seasonal games, and a few unpredictable events, until Christmas was back again. Christmas is a good place to start, if only because the three that happened whilst I was there proved to be really rather enjoyable. If this account, of Christmases, should seem a little vague and a bit on the fuzzy side, then it may be assumed that is how they were. The essential prerequisite was the appointment of a syndicate 'Brew Führer', who would commandeer the block bath tub - a wooden article oval in shape built by the skills of a cooper, about four feet long by two feet wide, and eighteen inches deep. He then collected, from all syndicate members, the necessary ingredients. These came, mostly, from the Red Cross parcels and consisted of dried fruits - raisins being preferred but currants, prunes, apricots or whatever, being accepted, and sugar. It had been found unnecessary to obtain yeast as the raisins had sufficient, occurring naturally, on their skins to get the brew going. The fermentation process gave off a not unpleasant smell, which was a good thing if you happened to live in the room with the Brew Führer. He would tend his brew and with expert eye, and taste, decide if it needed more of certain ingredients or required stirring, and in due time concede it was ready. The result was a brown wine, very cloudy - until strained through multiple thicknesses of, clean(ish), underclothes - and not unpleasant to taste.

From wine, not, it has to be admitted of a sought after vintage, could be obtained Brandy. This is a very up-market description of a spirit, which although tasting no better than the wine - was, in fact, a great deal worse - would speed up the Christmas spirit, thereby making the taste of only secondary importance. A German jam tin containing the wine was placed on a stove and brought almost to the boil, the vapours thereby driven off were guided through a rubber tube into a trombone (without the bell end) immersed in a pitch-lined wooden trough of water. This elegant Still condensed the vapour into alcohol of exceedingly high proof and quite disgusting flavour. An expert (there was always an expert in the offing) explained this foul taste was a consequence of over, or under, heating the wine causing the 'fusel-oils' to be vapourised with the alcohol. As any dictionary will tell you fusel-oil is '...a nauseous oil in spirits.' I commend the dictionary for its accuracy. It was not possible to control the temperature accurately to the correct fraction of alcohol, due to the lack of a thermometer. Such control as was possible consisted of listening intently to the jam tin and assuming anything in excess of a gentle burble was too hot. It was also the expert's opinion that the rubber tube was 'not a good idea', although the obtaining of such a rare commodity, it had to be admitted, was much to the credit of someone.

On one occasion, when everyone was supposed to be out on Appell, I was left in the room pretending to be too ill to venture outside, but really to listen to the gentle burble of the jam tin. A guard put his head in through the open window. 'Vass ist dass?' he inquired. My German was not up to an explanation of 'vass das vass', so I filled a spoon with the clear fluid dripping from the trombone, went across to the window and shoved it into his mouth. After a moment of startled apprehension his eyes sparkled and with a big smile he exclaimed! 'Ah, Schnapps, goot'. I have since then never fancied to try any drink described as Schnapps. If a spoonful of the spirit was set alight it would burn with a pretty blue flame until the spoon was empty, except for a single drop of water(?) or something pretty nearly neat spirit. Nothing would disguise the taste, black coffee came nearest and had the happy side effect, for days after the merrymaking, of inducing mild inebriation whenever coffee was taken. If the 'Hooch', as it was known, became a regular thing at times other than at Christmas or, maybe, a birthday, then it did happen that blindness, fortunately of a temporary nature, could result from the impurities present in the distillation. Hence the expression 'Blind Drunk'?

Christmas was preceded by setting aside quantities of specially hoarded food and drink, decorations were made and hung, seats were booked for the Pantomime, and if a vacant room was available it was converted to look as much like a Pub as ingenuity could contrive. The canteen, one year, purchased quite a lot of German beer in barrels, which, in hindsight, may have been the first attempt in the world to brew an alcohol free beer. They had also been pretty mean with the taste and colour. It did not even modify, let alone, disguise the taste of the hooch! The day was mostly an increasingly hazy round of making visits, and being visited, each call requiring the acceptance of food or drink until all was gone. As a seasonal gesture, by our captors, we were allowed to roam around the camp until much later than the usual time for being locked into our blocks, or was that at the New Year? Or maybe both. It was a long day, a long time ago, and the Brew-Führer had done his job very well!

January and February, in Silesia, are pretty chilly and it was possible to make ice rinks upon which the Canadians and other experts could play thrilling games of ice hockey and upon which we the unskilled could attempt to emulate them. It has been a lasting pleasure to recall two teams of 'barely able to skaters' sitting, sprawled or otherwise fallen down, in their excitement to get at the puck, which sat unscathed on the ice yards away from any of them. The expertise acquired by me in Canada availed little as I could still go better backwards than forwards.

In winter it is customary to play soccer and rugger. Left to my own devices I would never go out of my way to get involved in either, but they tended to involve me, usually it seemed, to our mutual disappointment. But it was assumed by some of the experts that I was exactly of the right size, neither too tall to be a freak, or too small to be a midget, but precisely a normal average height of five feet six. Eminently suitable, therefore, to be a Hooker in the front row of the scrum between two freaks, to whom I clung, suspended, with both feet off the ground. It was moderately successful if not entirely enjoyable. Harvey Vivian - who seemed to crop up rather frequently to interfere with the peaceful enjoyment of my enforced leisure - was our enthusiastic coach. He came up with the bright idea of changing the front row freaks to normal size people. The cunning of this was to oppose the other side's front row freaks by normal sized people, thereby obliging them to bend to an extent where they had no 'push' left in them and we, thus, invariably won the ball. What happens, you might ask, if the opposition arrived at the scrum first and obliged us to reach to their height? No problem, we fell over, as you might expect, and made sure we were first up.

They made me Captain of a Soccer side. I think there were five divisions, each of some ten teams, and it will come as no surprise to learn my team was lowly in the Fifth Division. The reason they made me Captain was because I had previously played the game and therefore knew the rules, which was a rather rash assumption. There were Australians, Americans, Canadians, a Frenchman, Czechs etc. and it has to be admitted we all enjoyed playing against others of similar skills to our own, including the Poles. Having raised a team composed only of their nationals, they were inclined to the belief that to lose was not only a disgrace to their country, but quite impossible. To maintain the peace and quiet we always let them win, which was not at all difficult. It was noticeable that spectators would turn out to watch our games, in almost the same numbers, as they would to watch the First Division. Genuine ignorance coupled with intense, mostly good-natured, enthusiasm are two splendid ingredients for the spontaneous entertainment of a discerning audience.

Field hockey was something I had never played. It looked fun and as it seemed to require more of the hands and less of the feet I gave it a try. But the ball knew I was unsettled by its presence and the referee kept blowing his whistle, and crying 'Sticks!' at me, as he did also to most of the others. All in all it was not the fun it might have been, but proved to be dangerous and painful. The last time I played was also the first!

Winter evenings are reputably long and dreary, but they never seemed so. There was no radio, none of us had ever seen television, no pubs, dances or, indeed, any of the outside entertainment one could have found in any of our hometowns, and yet I do not recall being bored. The evening meal - a rather important event - was late'ish and the, before-bed-time brew-up, of tea, cocoa or whatever else was on offer, was a reliable event to look forward to, after reading, studying, writing, drawing, painting, listening to records, playing bridge or some other game. All rather remarkable when compared to the leisure facilities (time-wasters!) available today.

Cricket and softball held enjoyment for many. Handball, which I enjoyed, is a game most of us had never come across before, played by two teams one on either side of a head-high net, with a soccer sized ball. Only the hands are used and the ball must not touch the ground. With such a high net the freaks had some unfair advantage over the normal size players.

One late Spring morning, almost as soon as the block doors were unbarred, the majority of us were woken by the playing of a fife and kettledrum, accompanied by a picturesque rabble, including Red Indians, singing 'Yankee Doodle Dandy'. They marched around all the blocks brandishing a Stars and Stripes, intent upon waking up, and reminding 'Limeys' and others not fortunate enough to be Americans (but particularly Limeys) that today was the Fourth of July. It was indeed a sight to see. Great care had been taken to make costumes and Flag, completely authentic, together with the fife and drum, and the whole impression was a chunk of eighteenth century history transported through time to Silesia. Unfortunately there were no tea chests to throw into the Hudson River, but there were lots and lots of the descendents of the subjects of George the Third and these, when encountered in ones and twos, were ceremoniously thrown into the Fire Pool! There were no fire-works either, but there was 'Fire Water', masquerading as 'Hooch', which enabled the celebrations, with much noise, and by the light of fat lamps, to continue long into the night. Next morning on Appell it was noticed the Rebels had suffered many casualties, all in the head, and very sore too.

Soon after this time the Americans were taken away from our compound to be re-housed in a new camp adjoining to the South. Future celebrations of Independance Day were glimpsed and heard, by us, but not suffered.

If there are Bed Bugs around it becomes of first importance to get rid of them. Thankfully I never came across one, and I believe this applied to most of us, but there was, of course, the time, already mentioned, when by pretending they existed an ingenious escape occurred, but otherwise I recall no problem. This happy state of affairs did not seem to exist in the barracks occupied by our guards, at least not in one where they tried to remove them from the cracks and crevices of the wooden building with a blowlamp. They were one hundred percent successful, producing as a monument to their folly, a magnificent bon-fire, fuelled exclusively by the block and its contents, and it may be presumed - the bedbugs. A blazing building is really not much to laugh at, but we found it amusing.

A Prison Camp is not a good place to have toothache. Possibly there are no 'good places' to have toothache, but it was not too bad a place either. When I was afflicted, a one-time medical student, subsequently a pilot, and now a POW, who dealt with such minor disorders in our block, prescribed Asprin, to be dissolved slowly upon the painful spot. It worked rather well, but would have been a great deal better if there could have been more than three a day, which was all he could spare from his meagre stock of medicines. Bicarbonate of Soda was prescribed for indigestion but it was also in extremely short supply. Not because of people complaining of indigestion, but in reality there was no other source of Baking Powder, except Tooth-Powder, which also seemed to work, but left behind a taste not normally associated with a cake.

The Camp Hospital was in the Vorlager, that is, the compound intermediate between the main gate and the free world. At Luft 3 I never visited the hospital, only the dentist, who had a surgery in a Room of 101 Block. It seemed to me, when eventually it came to a visit, to be reasonably well equipped with a proper chair and all the usual instruments of torture, including a drill, and gas apparatus. The dentist was a New Zealand army officer, taken prisoner in the desert. He was, in my opinion, a most agreeable person, and a fine dentist. Needless to say this opinion was formed subsequently to my visit, prior to which I had no idea what to expect, or what the next half-hour or so would produce. A short inspection preceded the verdict. Five stoppings required, and the root, from which the Horsham St. Faiths Dentist had removed the top, to be pulled out. The removal of this root might, it seemed, relieve the congestion of teeth in the area, and thereby alleviate the pain, from the impacted Wisdom Tooth, the cause of most of the recent discomfort.

While the injections for the extraction took effect, he drilled and stopped the five cavities, and then yanked out the root. The whole visit had lasted twenty minutes. The usual agony of drilling was much diminished, owing to the injections progressively taking effect, and the root was no bother at all. I asked him why it was he could do treatment in twenty minutes that would require at least three visits at home? 'If', he answered, 'I were to treat my patients at home as I have treated you, they might complain and go somewhere else next time, but also, I should only be able to charge for one visit, not three.' His first reason did not impress me, I had never had such a painless session, but it could not be denied he did have a point with the second. Nearly two years later a dentist, at home, on being asked to inspect and probably replace the German ersatz rubbish, which had been used to stop the cavities, remarked that he wished he had some of the 'rubbish', which was better than anything he could get. And so it proved. The stoppings outlasted anything in my experience, either before, or after.

In July 1944, the war was becoming, from our point of view, much more interesting. All the news was, with few exceptions, good news. Italy had been invaded, the Russians were getting closer each day, 'D' Day had taken place a month before, and the bridgehead was becoming firmly established. From the German point of view, the news, however misrepresented on the radio and in the newspapers, tended to be 'bad news', inducing noticeable changes in the attitudes of our guards. For the most part they now conceded that defeat was possible, even likely. This was particularly so in those guards of unpleasant disposition, some of whom were only waiting for the end of the military restraints that prevented them from ill-treating the prisoners, which would follow a German victory. Significantly these types no longer laughed when told their name was going on the Black List.

The Invasion of Europe had been eagerly anticipated for, what seemed, a very long time. Some Kreigies had made formal 'Vows', specifying the 'Penance' they would perform when the invasion was announced as a *fait accompli* on the German Radio. Which Deity they invoked, in their vows, I do not know, but certainly one was enthusiastically cheered as he went towards the loud speaker, on his knees, along the furthest straight line distance from which it could be seen. Another was equally encouraged to keep the promise he had made - to carry his bed for a full circuit of the perimeter.

Unfortunately for the World, and particularly for those responsible, an attempt to assassinate Hitler was not successful. The day following the publication of this news was curiously memorable in the Camp. At morning Appell the guards, who always accompanied those with the ability to count, were seen to be smarter in their bearing, and, when the occasion demanded, 'Heil Hitlering' each other with the Nazi salute. Hitherto the military salute, as used by us, had been customary (unless you happened to be in the SS, or some other equally fanatical group). As Herr Pieber made his way towards us, past each block of lined-up kreigies, it seemed we heard sounds of merriment. When he reached us he came smartly to attention before the Block Commander. With a goodly clicking of heels he snapped off a Nazi salute, and with resignation muttered, as the predictable outburst of laughter burst over him – 'I am sorry

Chentleman, I haff to do it zis vay, zey are vatching me'. One had to feel a little sorry for him as he went on to the remaining blocks, knowing the same reaction would meet him each time.

Apparently, following the attempt on his life, Hitler, or his minions, had ordered the Nazi salute to replace the military version, as a sure measure of restoring confidence, patriotism and faith in the Nazi party! It did not work with us, nor anyone else, as far as we could discover. Most Germans were, by this time, no longer very fond of the Nazi party in general, or, Hitler, in particular. Many were, indeed, anxious to tell us they never had been Nazi's, or even liked Hitler.

Christmas 1945 came and went, in came the New Year, bringing the almost certain hope that it would be our last behind barbed wire. January brought low temperatures and much snow and the Russians getting nearer by the minute. Something was undoubtedly going to change the existence to which we had become accustomed. The manner of this change did not show up on any crystal ball.

Would our Captors shoot us? A not unlikely option. Would we be handed over to the Russians? A prospect not viewed with enthusiasm, but better than being shot; or would we be moved? This last did have some virtues, in so far as the only direction for such a movement had to be to the West, and that was where home was. Speculation was rife, and some preparations were made for a mass breakout, and/or resistance, to any attempt on our lives. In the meantime there were still tales to be told.

'A disabled bomber made a crash landing on water. They did not know whether the water was the sea, a large river, or a lake. It was very dark and the landing was accomplished with skill, no damage to the crew, and the aircraft still in one piece, floating on the calm water. But bombers do not float well, or long. Quickly, the dinghy was thrown out, it self-inflated and the crew transferred from bomber to boat without even getting their feet wet. They tried to paddle away using their hands as paddles, not having discovered those provided. The distance between boat and bomber stayed exactly the same, then it was realised there was a tethering line. 'Cut the cord', cried the Captain, 'before it sinks and pulls us under'. A knife could not be found, mild panic, until someone, delving beneath his flying kit, produced a penknife from his trousers pocket. The cord was cut and, being anxious that so much time had elapsed, one of the crew leapt over the side to swim and pull the dinghy away from the aircraft which, remarkably, still did not seem in a hurry to sink. After a few frantic strokes the swimmer made a discovery, he stood up and walked! Not <u>on</u> the water (he wasn't that type) but on the bottom, towards where he hoped the shore might be, towing the dinghy in about two feet of water!'

Some Royal Navy officers were of the Fleet Air Arm. Strictly speaking they could have been expected to be with their colleagues in a camp for Naval Officers, but the Germans were a little confused as to whether a sailor arriving by aeroplane should be classified as a 'flieger' or a 'mariner'. As a consequence, a few finished up with us. One such, he looked just like the sailor on a packet of Players cigarettes, had a fund of tales, two of which have stayed with me.

In a large warship, anti-aircraft practice firing was carried out by shooting at a drogue, towed behind an aeroplane - flown by a very brave, or just unfortunate, pilot. To give realism to the exercise, it was assumed the ship had lost all electrical power. The emergency supply, to run the predictors etc., was generated by the Band of the Royal Marines who, it was assumed, would not be called upon to play music whilst under attack by enemy aircraft. They were therefore mounted on bicycles, somewhere adjacent to the bilges, from which the front wheels were missing, and a dynamo took the place of the back wheel. The time arrived for the 'shoot' to begin, but the aircraft, with its drogue, didn't. When, eventually, it did, the officer who knew how to operate the, for those days, sophisticated predictor apparatus, had left on a call of nature and left everything in the, as yet unskilled, care of the raconteur. No sooner was he on his own than the drogue arrived. It must be mentioned the stand-by operator <u>had</u> received some instruction and was aware of the principle involved. He twiddled hopefully, the band peddled madly, and not being able to delay matters further, the command was given to 'Fire'. He was in the bowels of the ship, and until the 'phone, from the bridge, rang he was not to know how successful he might have been. 'You bloody fool,' yelled the telephone, conjuring visions of a shot-down drogue-towing aeroplane, Court Martials etc., 'you've shot off the drogue'. It might be supposed this would call for congratulations all round, but not a bit of it. They had been late starting, there was no possibility of getting another drogue, the day was wasted - well, not quite! It had been well demonstrated that 'where ignorance is bliss, 'tis folly to be wise'.

The other story concerns a practice torpedo shooting exercise. The sea was a bit rough when they set forth in the cutter to retrieve a used torpedo, or it might have been a whaler, anyway it was an open boat of wood construction, propelled by some eight sailors with oars, and steered by an officer - in this case, the storyteller. It is necessary to know a little about 'practice torpedoes'. They are just like the real thing but have no war-head, and when the engine stops they float in a vertical position, nose up, with about three or four feet projecting above the surface, thus enabling them to be spotted, approached, and captured. Now, it is a well-known fact that a torpedo, once given a taste of liberty, is most reluctant to be re-captured. In a calm sea the torpedo is at a distinct disadvantage. It just floats there waiting to be caught but when the sea is a bit choppy, as it was this time, with a swell of some three feet or so, then, by borrowing energy from the waves it becomes re-animated. It rises on the swell, descends as the wave passes, and owing to its considerable inertia, continues going down until, buoyancy overcoming inertia, it accelerates upwards to burst through the surface. This sequence, once established, continues for as long as the swell lasts, or the torpedo is secured and towed back to the waiting warship.

The boat was rowed towards the intermittently appearing objective, which popped up twenty feet away. By the time the spot was reached it had, naturally, disappeared. After a short wait there it was again, twenty feet to port - obviously changing course under water and not going straight up and down. Down it went again, the boat was rowed to the exact spot, they waited peering out from the boat not knowing in which direction it would next appear. And while they were all looking out it popped up behind their backs, up through the bottom of the boat, then back to the depths, leaving a large hole admitting a great deal of water. The frantic row back to their ship, accompanied by attempts to stop the in-rush by sitting in, and laying across, the hole, together with much bailing, enabled the ship to be reached as sinking became imminent. There was just time to hook on the falls, from the davits, at bow and stern, as the ship fortuitously rolled towards them, then rolled away lifting them out of the water. At least that is what should have happened, but the boat full of water being too heavy stayed put and the davits bent down to meet the boat, instead of vice-versa. Net result, a dozen soggy sailors, a pair of ruined davits, a whaler with a very large hole in its bottom, and a very expensive lost torpedo.

By January nineteenth the Russians were within striking distance of Breslau and Posen, and the likelihood of moving prisoners from Sagan became very much a possibility. We were told the German High Command was confident the Russians would be held at the River Oder, and no move was contemplated. On the twentieth the Oder was reached and crossed South of Breslau. The Kommandant, still insisting no move would be necessary, gave qualified permission for rucksacks to be made, but forbade the digging of slip trenches for protection in case the Camp should come within the battle zone.

CHAPTER 32

Goodbye Luft 3.

Something was going to happen, and obviously, whatever it was, could not be long delayed. Either, we stayed put with our guards, and who knows what that might lead to, or, we might be marched to the West, by the Germans, or to the East, by the Russians, if they arrived before the Germans made up their minds. A march, in whatever direction, was more than likely in the offing, so a great manufacturing of back-packs, of all shapes and sizes, got under way. The most usual was made from a Kit-Bag, to which straps were sewn. I made mine by adapting a pair of Service braces, which were of considerable substance and well suited to the purpose. Despite the Kommandant's ruling to the contrary, a few sledges were made, duly discovered, and confiscated. Footwear was overhauled and many unaccustomed faces were to be seen as their owners took rare exercise around the circuit to train for the march ahead.

January 27th 1945 witnessed much confusion. In the morning the Kommandant told the Senior British Officer that he had been told, by the High Command, that the camp at Sagan was not to be evacuated. This contradicted the inference to be drawn from our knowledge that two days emergency rations had been issued to the German personnel, and sick persons in the various compounds had been moved to the Main Camp. Having started the day by denying the possibility of a march, they ended it by ordering the different camps to start evacuation, variously by eight, nine or ten p.m., depending on which compound they had so (mis)informed. The prior notice of the proposed move varied from two to four hours relying, apparently, on the whim of the particular German officer responsible for the individual compound. No rations were to be issued for the march, by the Germans, but each prisoner would be allowed to take one Red Cross parcel.

The shortness of notice could have been expected to be the cause of much confusion. The fact it did not do so was entirely the result of having modified the German optimism, with our own, more realistic - and opposite - brand of expectancy, leading from our belief that the Russians were not going to be stopped at the Oder, or anywhere else short of Sagan.

We could have walked out of the camp almost immediately. Rucksacks were already packed, it only remained to dress appropriately for the weather, and, hopefully, consume as much of our food stores as we should be unable to carry. The Germans, however, possibly as a result of believing - you would have thought they had known better by now - their own propaganda, were nowhere near ready. Some, indeed, had to be rounded up in the town where they had been enjoying a carefree, well-deserved relaxation from their daytime duties. It soon became evident to us that even the most pessimistic deadline for the start of the evacuation, had no chance of being met. With time to spare we were able to remove the multiple layers of clothes, designed to resist the very cold night outside, but now becoming more and more uncomfortable as, with carefree abandon the fuel ration was burnt in the stove, and the room was enjoying a temperature it had not known since mid-summer.

There was now a chance to re-assess, and re-pack, the essentials deemed indispensable for the journey ahead, and for the final destination. Carefully padded and protected by my notebooks, arising from my studies of 'History of Architecture', went my tools and latest Steam Engine! Followed by more mundane things, such as, socks, a change of clothes, mementoes (if not too heavy and mostly of the paper variety) tobacco, cigarettes and food: not forgetting the blanket, made into a roll, fastened externally to the top and sides of the rucksack.

The deadline was under constant revision, so we started to build a sledge. It was just about finished when an announcement was made by the guards to say sledges would be allowed on the condition they did not hold up the march. Our sledge was rather superior, and very simply made. A chaise-longue, the largest part of which had served well as the seat of a home made settee, formed the body of the sledge, and bed-boards, properly shaped and nailed to either side became the runners. It was a splendid contraption, about four feet long and two feet wide, with a handle at the back in the best tradition of sledges pulled by dogs in the Yukon. Ropes were made from torn sheets, which allowed, in the absence of dogs, four or more kreigies to take the place of a team of huskies. There was plenty of wood available, the barrack blocks were made of it, and as we helped ourselves to battens and boards there arose, as might be expected, a sufficiency of nails for the manufacture of the sledges. We now had a fine sledge, but it soon became apparent there was more waiting in prospect as the time for departure was constantly put forward. A chaise-longue, in addition to the larger central portion, has two similar smaller pieces at each end, so, with the extra time, these were also turned into sledges.

Eventually the various compounds began to leave. The Americans went first, between 9.30p.m. and into the early hours of Sunday the twenty-eighth January, to be followed by us, the North Compound, between 1.00 a.m. and 3.00a.m, and then the other compounds, until the camp was empty by 7.00a.m.

When dressing for the march there were two considerations, first, keeping the cold out, and second, leaving, as far as possible, a minimum amount requiring to be packed and carried. Fortunately these considerations are complimentary to one another. I wore, on my top half, two vests, two shirts, a pyjama top and a pullover beneath a battle-dress blouse, uniform tunic, and a jacket I had made from a blanket, plus the wooly lining of a flying suit. On my lower half two pairs of trousers, over pyjama bottoms, over long-johns, two pairs of socks and a pair of service boots. This was all concealed beneath an Airman's double-breasted greatcoat, held together at the front by string, there being no hope of using the buttons, let alone the overlap of the double breasting. A balaclava, a scarf, and my treasured peaked cap, completed the cladding, but for ease of access a tin mug and eating implements dangled, on string, from a redundant buttonhole. My height still exceeded my width, but not by much.

As we left the camp we collected our quota of Red Cross parcels, which went on the sledges together with our rucksacks. It proved no trouble at all to tow our worldly possessions over the frozen ground. Others, without sledges, were not so fortunate and becoming overloaded by the parcel issue, threw much of it onto the road verges, from whence it was retrieved by German civilians.

The arrangements made by the Germans were wholly inadequate in so far as guarding the columns, or caring for those who, for whatever reason, fell out, and might die of exposure if not given attention. The guards, who were for the most part on the elderly side, found it was all they could do to look after themselves. Almost no attempt was made by them to patrol the column, tending to concentrate on looking miserable and complaining bitterly. It seemed a German soldier had his equipment packed for him, presumably to distribute items of military necessity throughout the unit. A guard near us, discovering the reason he was walking with a pronounced lean to the left was entirely attributable to a large side pack full of ammunition, emptied the lot, with suitable German expletives, over the parapet of a small bridge, into the stream beneath. Thenceforth, he became more or less, perpendicular.

Another had brought along his bicycle, which he was not permitted to ride - to do so might well have been impossible for practical reasons. I suspect the equipment hung around him, plus the required instant availability of his rifle, and the walking pace to which he would be committed, may have been beyond the skill of a competent young man, and he was neither of these. He struggled for a mile or two, pushing the bike, trying to make it relieve him of some of the weight hung around him, until the bike met the same fate as the ammunition, by being discarded at the roadside. Most of the guards were ordinary, pleasant people, not over bright and certainly, in their present situation, not at all happy, so it is not very surprising that many of their prisoners were sympathetic to their plight. Often a German pack traveled many miles on a homemade Kreigie sledge, with the grateful guard taking his turn at pulling. Not for a moment expecting his offer to be accepted, a prisoner enquired – 'Like me to carry your rifle, Fritz?' Fritz was delighted and for a short time the prisoner strutted along with a rifle, and the guard enjoyed a short relief from its weight. The humour of the situation was enjoyed by all, but the consequences of discovery, by someone less simple than the guard, could have been serious, both for us and, more so, for the guard. The rifle was happily relinquished (it was becoming a bit heavy anyway) and reluctantly repossessed by Fritz.

Not all the guards were so old, or so benevolent, a few were on the fanatical side. A column of Americans had one such, who became violently excited if someone stepped sideways out of the column. He threatened he would shoot the next person to do so. There is always someone who accepts such a threat as a challenge, and here was no exception. A quick step sideways, very short pause, and back again, by which time a bullet was on its way, going harmlessly past where the American had been and carrying on to hit the next guard down the line between the shoulder blades. By the second day many guards were unfit for duty, and one was so severely frost bitten, it was later rumoured he had both his legs amputated.

I once saw a horse-drawn open cart, apparently used to follow the columns and to pick up the sick and stragglers. The occupants were in no way to be envied. How they managed to retain any heat, huddled on the bottom of an open cart, I do not know, it was bad enough walking, where at least some warmth was generated.

Somehow our column became intermingled with some Americans, probably late starters or stragglers as their compounds had started ahead of ours. There was a very prominent gap, very noticeable even in the gaggle of general disorder pervading the march. The cause turned out to be one ingenious American who, instead of going to the trouble of building a sledge, had the brilliant idea of towing, at the end of a piece of string, a frying-pan. It was no ordinary frying-pan, being of considerable size, about two feet in diameter, and well able to accommodate his pack, a Red Cross parcel, and other oddments to fill the crevices arising from putting square things in a round hole. There was also the added advantage of having his favourite cooking implement with him, wherever it was he was going to be. Frying-pans do not make good sledges, they slide extremely well, almost no friction, but have no disposition towards maintaining direction. The gap in the ranks equated to the, considerable, length of string and the radius of the circle thus imposed by using the American as its centre. The long string was apparently needed to enable the puller to have time to get out of the way when the pan, responding to a downward slope, overtook him thereby becoming as far ahead as it had been behind.

The first dawn revealed a scene of almost total depression. The countryside - not a building in sight - stretched undulating white and bare to the horizons, with only the straight road appearing and disappearing forever into the distance. The thought that our destination, wherever it might be, was beyond that horizon, would have been utterly depressing had that been all there was to look at, but there was a saving grace. We carried our little world with us, furnished with enough chat and incident to ensure boredom was not to be a consideration. Aches, pains, blistered feet, and cold, yes, they were not going away, but I can honestly say that apart from the first depressing sight of the road stretching out for ever, I never again found, amongst the varied emotions of incarceration, depression to be of any significance.

By great good fortune and through the kindness of Jim Lang - and Lord knows how he came by it - I have a report of the march compiled by Group Captain D. E. L. Wilson, the Senior British Officer, dated 20th February 1945. It makes, for me, fascinating reading after all these years and recounts many incidents and happenings of which I was not aware at the time, or since. These I shall ignore, except where they fill in some of the overall detail and sequence of the things I do remember.

At around eight a.m. our bit of the column arrived at a place called Halbau, seventeen kilometres (ten and a half miles) from Sagan, where it had been intended we should rest. But, as no provision had been made for the issue of rations or even water, the 'rest' lasted only about an hour before the march resumed towards Freiwaldan, eleven kilometres (seven miles) away, to billet for the night. At Halbau the civilians, almost entirely women, for the most part appeared friendly, and many came out to give us hot water and food - but very little food. The groups, or messes, with a good German speaker, were able to do better by bartering cigarettes, coffee, or soap, for vegetables, sometimes bread, or even eggs. Often these German women would refuse to take anything in exchange for the food. The guards tended not to interfere in these transactions, and indeed, often assisted, but there were always exceptions. I witnessed a guard threatening a woman who was pouring coffee into mugs. She responded vigorously by telling him she had a son who was a prisoner in Canada, who had written to say he was being well treated and she wished to make some small gesture of appreciation.

Freiwaldan was reached about noon. No adequate billets, or rations, were available and after about an hour standing around on extremely cold feet, an 'authentic rumour' instructed us to make our own arrangements with any of the local inhabitants who might be willing to take us in for the night. I walked over to a lady and her daughter, just about to enter their house, and in a carefully rehearsed bit of excruciating German asked if she had a room for the night. That is what I thought I said, but by the horrified and frightened look on her face, she might have understood something quite different. Or maybe she did understand but did not fancy, as a lodger, the nearly spherical and exceedingly scruffy object before her. It was never put to the test for, at that moment, a guard turned up and poked a machine-gun in my face, gesturing for me to return to the other side of the road. I don't think the rumour had reached him! Objections to us being in the town, either from the civilian or military authorities, led to the march being resumed.

At five p.m., and six kilometres further - thereby bringing the days march to some twenty-one miles, and making the time we had been without proper food or rest to over fifteen hours - we arrived at Leippa. This was a village consisting of, as far as I was concerned, a large barn, a lot of snow, and a mass of half-frozen, very tired, un-fed POW's. Coming into the village we saw some Americans huddled into the snow, wrapped in everything they possessed, blue with cold, and apparently going to spend the night there. Obviously they had arrived before we did and it seemed a mystery why they had not been put under cover, as was to be the case with us. Maybe they had reached the point when they were unable to take 'just one more step'. There were many such who, had it not been for search parties sent back by our people, would certainly have died where they had fallen, before next morning. A barn was made available and I was lucky to be among the seven hundred who were squeezed, immediately upon arrival, into a space previously calculated to hold, at most, six hundred. Others were not so fortunate and were obliged to spend hours standing in the snow, until a parole was given promising that no one would attempt to escape during the night. Other barns were then found to accommodate the thousand or so, who would otherwise have been forced to pass the night in the open. Even so, sixty officers spent the night in straw, in the lee of a farmyard wall. Some suffered frostbite and vomiting, for neither of which was there any medical assistance forthcoming from the Germans.

Our barn was lofty, draughty and bare. The floor was concrete with no more than the odd wisp of straw. In the dark we did our best to emulate sardines and, after a cold snack, wrapped everything we had around us. Trying not to be the one on the outside, we prepared for the night. No sooner had we composed ourselves when the doors opened, not making, it has to be admitted, a great deal of difference to the inside temperature, and a bread ration of a loaf between three men was distributed. Distribution was indiscriminate, that is to say, the distributor stood inside the doorway and threw the loaves, two hundred and thirty of them, blindly into the darkness in every direction. It was obvious when yours, or maybe someone else's, arrived because it was quite painful, the German loaf not being of the soft crumby type. There was no water, but snow sufficed.

They told us the temperature that night dropped to '30 below'. Whether this was Fahrenheit or Centigrade was only of academic interest, it was extremely cold! I have detailed the multiple layers of clothing donned before leaving. Add to this a blanket providing two, not very thick, layers over me and it might be wondered if any of my heat could have escaped, or any cold found its way in. Wonder no longer. The concrete beneath and the nothing above sucked out any heat I generated, and it was only to either side that tightly packed colleagues formed any kind of mutual buffer. I slept and I dreamed; I rarely remember dreams but this one, in subject if not in detail, is never going to be forgotten. I dreamt I was back studying Architecture and being constantly frustrated in the design of hot water systems, which never worked properly!

During the night it became necessary for me to visit the bathroom, in this case an euphemism for a farmyard covered in deep snow, and more coming down by the bucketful. This venture was not popular with those between me and the door over whom, in going and coming, I tripped and stumbled. Others, it seems, pretended they were already in the bathroom.

The resumption of the march was delayed the next morning by an extremely inefficient bunch of guards trying to remember where they had put their charges of the night before. The delay was further prolonged by an ineffectual attempt, on the part of the Germans, to make a count of the prisoners. Eventually, with it still freezing, the march resumed at eight a.m., Monday the 29th January. A short distance along the road we came across a farmer loading milk churns, for collection, on to a platform at the roadside. I went across to him, holding out my mug in one hand, and in the other a couple of cigarettes. Without hesitation he filled my mug with milk and refused the cigarettes. This had not gone unnoticed and it took only a short time before his churns were empty, a large number of mugs were full, and he, eventually, was persuaded to accept a bar of soap. When asked why he would not accept payment he shrugged his shoulders, explaining that the Russians would be there shortly and they would certainly, neither pay for anything or be grateful, whilst we had offered to pay, and there was no doubt of our gratitude. I often wonder how he fared.

Arriving at the town of Priebus, at eleven-thirty, a half hour rest was decreed and we discovered the people of the town to be, as before, friendly and willing to provide water, but there was still no provision by the Military. The Senior British Officer had consented to an extension of the parole on condition billets were found for the next night. So it was, when arriving at Muskau at six p.m., Monday 29th Jan. there occurred, for the first time, some evidence of organisation by the Germans. Billets were provided in a Cinema, a Glass Factory, a Riding School, a Stable, a Pottery, and a French P.O.W Camp. The Group Captain's report states: '...except for the Riding School conditions were tolerable.' I cannot argue with this since our Mess was in the Riding School! It was, nevertheless, quite the best place, so far, in which to spend the night. It was dry, the weather had become not so cold, but the floor of the Riding School, whilst soft and suitable for the feet of horses, was a bit on the damp side. There was little light, no heating, no facilities for cooking and no sanitary arrangements, unless you can accept a largish field as fulfilling that role. The Riding School was part of a large country estate, the home of Von Somebody, and included a factory and many other buildings, one of which had a bathroom with, apparently, unlimited hot water produced by the waste steam from the factory. Not many people knew about this, I only stumbled across it whilst exploring the new surroundings, soon after arrival. Joining the modest queue I enjoyed a hot bath, which was, if you don't count the wooden (brew-fermenting) tub, the first, in over two years.

Although told the stay in Muskau would be for only twenty-four hours, it was not until ten forty-five p.m., Thursday, 1st February, in complete darkness, that the columns re-assembled to move off towards Spremberg, where a train would complete the journey. A sudden and complete thaw the previous evening had made it doubtful the sledges would still be viable. We made a start with ours but even out in the country there was insufficient snow, and so, reluctantly, they had to be abandoned. For the first time we now had to carry our rucksacks, where they were designed to be, on our backs, and for the first time I knew what it was to become very, very weary, rather quickly. Some clever people managed to barter soap, cigarettes etc., for prams, wheelbarrows, or small wooden handcarts. We were not so clever and had to make decisions as to what should be discarded. The exhausting effects of the previous marches, the darkness, the hilly nature of the country, but above all the absence of the snow, made this march the most difficult stage of the journey, both for us and our guards.

There were occasional halts at the roadside, no food or water, just halts, when your pack could be removed, allowing a short regeneration of energy to take place. During one of these stops I sought to improve my knowledge, and at the same time, cheer up an unhappy looking guard standing alone, leaning on his rifle. I approached poised to inquire of him the bore of his rifle, which I thought would be an easy question for him to answer and might, therefore, put him at his ease and bring a smile to his gloomy face. I knew how to ask the time in German. You say 'How many hours, is it?' So, pointing at the muzzle of his gun, I said (in German) 'how many millimetres, is that?' He thought for a moment, eyeing me up and down, and then muttered – 'Zere kleine' (very small). He then made it plain that in payment for this confidential information he expected to relieve me of my wrist-watch. I suppose he was a frustrated soldier, never having been in a position to do any looting and saw this as an opportunity to catch up before the war ended. He did not get my watch, neither did he appear any less miserable for my intervention.

Seven kilometres short of Spremberg, at around six in the morning, at a village named Graustein, a halt was made before the intended resumption of the last lap, in five hours time. Dry barns with lots of straw, and farmers doing their best to provide everyone with hot water, made this the warmest, most comfortable four or five hours sleep of the entire march. This providing you weren't, and I wasn't, beneath the chap who, seeking more exclusive quarters, went up into a loft and, marveling at the softness of the straw beneath him, found this was due, in large measure, to there being no floor boards. If it had not been for the chap he landed on I don't suppose we should have heard of his adventure. As it turned out we heard very loudly. Eleven thirty saw us on the move again. My pack was getting to be so heavy I even contemplated jettisoning my steam engine!

Spremberg was reached at three o'clock in the afternoon. Accommodation for all of us was provided in, what was stated to be, the reserve depot of the Eighth Panzer Division. For the first time soup was provided, also hot water, and our mess, like many others, was able to have a sort of meal - from the food brought with us - in almost normal surroundings, if you accept the lack of table and chairs as being almost normal. Assuming the worst was now over we started to make arrangements to pass the night when, to our dismay, the order was given to march again, and at four-thirty that afternoon the column set off for the station, about three kilometres away.

Arriving at the station we were confronted by our train, not drawn up alongside the platform - there was no platform - but standing in the middle of a wilderness of lines. It consisted of cattle trucks behind a large, panting, steam locomotive. My tour of Germany, so far, had experienced First Class, very briefly, in Holland; Second Class down to Frankfurt; de-graded Third Class, up to Silesia; and now, it seemed, by cattle truck to our destination. This, they informed us for the first time, was to be Marlag and Milag Nord, a camp on the Luneburg Heath, near Tarmstadt, about thirty kilometres from Bremen, and three hundred miles from where we were. It was most encouraging to realise, in train class terms, we had now, by successive stages, reached rock bottom. Any change in the future had to be an improvement. A cattle truck, as most will know, is designed to take ten horses, or forty men, neither of which are 'Cattle', so why is it a Cattle Truck? There were not enough trucks so the luxury standard of forty was often exceeded, and possibly, by reason of the German ability to become confused with higher numbers (forty is quite high) some trucks had a little less than forty. Happily ours was one of these.

None of the trucks were clean, and in many cases manure, indicating previous occupants had been cattle, horses, and people, had to be cleared away. In our truck it was possible, by head to foot interleaving, for all to lie on the floor. For no other reason this made the journey more comfortable than the third class, wooden seats, in the train from Frankfurt to Sagan. But this was by no means the case in other trucks where the best they could manage was to sit, using every square inch of floor space and wedged one against the other. Added to this there were those who were unwell, with vomiting and dysentery, resulting in conditions of dire unpleasantness for all in the truck. It was only possible for us, in our truck, to express sympathy when told of these wretched conditions at the rare stops, when we were allowed out on the track for indeterminate periods. One of these stops, in some kind of marshalling yard, witnessed the spectacle of hundreds of us, crouching and standing to obey the calls of nature, in full view of the occupants of another train of cattle trucks. Men, women and children, going in the opposite direction, miserably immune to the sight we provided, and possibly, with hindsight, on their way to the horrors of a concentration camp. What other reason was there for this overcrowded train of human misery to be going East, when everyone else was trying to go West?

A bread ration was issued, together with some Red Cross parcels, brought from Sagan, but no water. This was promised at a place called Falkenberg, reached at one o'clock on the third of February, but never materialised and, waterless still, the train went on with the promise of a rendezvous with a field kitchen, organised to draw up alongside at Halle. Here at last was to be an example of that much vaunted, 'til now unnoticed, German operational efficiency, and to be fair it very nearly happened. At around nine-thirty Halle turned up, and so did the field kitchen, but a Hospital Train from the Russian front had been there before us and nothing edible or drinkable remained.

At the outskirts of Hanover, about seven-thirty on the morning of the Fourth of February, a longer stop than usual enabled a majority to obtain water from houses, or in our case, from the engine. It was slightly oily and hot but not unpleasant. This was the first 'issue' of water for thirty-six hours, since leaving Spremberg. The nearest I had been to getting a drink in that time was by having the good fortune to find myself near to a generous individual, in the truck, who had given me an onion. He spoke German and had been able to barter some cigarettes for onions during the march. Even an R.C. Padre parted with his supply of Holy Water to assuage the thirst of his companions. The shortage of anything to drink certainly reduced the need to obey the call of nature, but did not altogether remove it. An empty tin was found for the afflicted person which, after filling, was then passed hand to hand over the recumbent occupants (who hoped the track was smooth and the tin not too full) to the chap standing in the corner, beneath a small opening. This provided the only means for ingress of light and air, and by the same token, the only exit for any object small enough to go through. He would reach up and empty the tin, with no means of knowing, and more than likely not caring, where the contents landed. Again I was lucky a person of my normal height could not reach the vent, so I was not considered suitable to be the tin emptier. A splendid job for freaks!

The train arrived at Tarmstadt at five in the afternoon of Sunday the 4th of February. It rained as we marched the two to three miles to Marlag and Milag Nord, and that was the best bit of the journey, between the train and the shelter of the camp buildings. A long semi-paved, narrow access road lead to the camp gates, and there we waited, cold, soggy, and miserable for up to eight hours while a search of each individual was carried out before entering the camp. In the style of many previous searches, efficiency decreased in direct proportion to the time elapsing. Had the original pace of one person per minute persisted it would have taken thirty hours to search each of the one thousand nine hundred odd arrivals.

I sat upon my kitbag/rucksack, not doing my notebooks any good at all, as I later discovered. A kitbag is not as waterproof as I had supposed but, happily, no damage was done to the Steam Engine. The traces of Luneburg Heath Mud are still to be seen on the kitbag, which is still around – somewhere!

CHAPTER 33.

Hallo Marlag-Milag Nord.

The Compound, with which we were to be concerned at Marlag-Milag Nord, consisted of twelve wooden living huts, recently evacuated by Prisoner of War Other Ranks, from the Royal Navy. In the same way as we had not been too fussy of the condition in which we had left Luft 3, the previous occupants had also been less than particular and had practically gutted the huts. There were no light bulbs or stoves in many rooms, and no movable equipment left in the kitchens. Beds remained for about a quarter of the new residents, but no mattresses; a very inadequate number of stools, benches, tables and lockers, and very little else.

Wood straw was immediately provided en-masse to each room where, in the absence of beds and mattress covers, it went on the floor to become a large communal bed for all in the room until beds and covers eventually arrived some weeks later. In the meantime, whilst things were generally better by comparison with the rigours of the march, there was no fuel to dry out clothes and bedding, Red Cross food supplies were becoming scarce, and German rations inadequate.

Soon after our arrival I did a little exploring and found the communal washhouse, in which I noted a cloud of steam arising from a naked Kreigie prancing around under a shower. Hot water!, I thought, I must have some of this before it runs out. I rushed back to gather my things and returned with a towel and soap, shed clothes and waited, in the surprisingly short queue, to plunge under the stream of hot water. The steam, I discovered, arose only by virtue of the warmth generated in the individual beneath the water, which proved to be just warm enough to prevent it from becoming ice. Never join a short queue, you may be disappointed!

A day or two later we did get taken to a shower house, a short walk from the compound, and enjoyed the first proper wash in hot water since leaving Sagan (for many), and for me since the bath at Muskau. The event is significant also for the walk to the shower house, not that we needed more walking, but by going past fields full of swedes it was possible for a large number of those, very disappointing, vegetables to go back into the camp with us. We ate a great many swedes in the weeks to follow. They fill you up when eaten, become water, and leave you hungry again in about half an hour. This was the only time in my captivity I suffered any pangs of hunger. Others, who even under normal circumstances seemed always hungry, were absolutely starving.

This new camp was a complex consisting of a compound for Officers of the Royal Navy, another for Ratings - this was now ours - and a compound for Merchant Service prisoners on higher ground close by, on the outskirts of the village of Westetimke. There was an Ostertimke as well, presumably somewhere to the East. No longer was the outlook confined to a clearing in a plantation of fir trees. There were still trees, in clumps, on the near horizons of the undulating heath land and in the village. The near view was, of course, barbed wire and Goon Boxes, in which the guards were now no longer in the bluey-grey of the Luftwaffe, but in the dark green uniforms of the Kreigsmarine; the equivalent I imagine of our Royal Marines. They wore greatcoats nearly touching the ground, had rifles of a corresponding length, with bayonets more like swords, and could well have been mistaken for the leftovers from some long forgotten war. An impression reinforced after a closer examination of the individuals, all of whom were on the elderly side.

After a while beds and other items of furniture began to turn up. Wooden bunks, as before, and tubular metal folding camp beds with sprung canvas bases, quite obviously too comfortable to have been intended for prisoners of war. Indeed, they had been intended for the Africa Corps by whom, happily, they were no longer needed, having been booted out of Africa, and nearly out of Italy. But there had to be a snag somewhere, fortunately not a very big one this time. The beds were not double-deckers and the floor space available meant that either there would be no floor space, just a sea of beds, or conversion must be made to turn them into double deckers. Beds designed to fold do not take kindly to being supported one above the other. Fortunately each bed had three square hoops for the support of mosquito netting attached to it. These, when suitably manipulated up and down, lashed together and reinforced with a couple of pieces of wood, (redundant to the stability of the hut,) became, after one or two disasters, very comfortable bunks. The demise of the Africa Corps, and the daily shrinking needs of the Armies in the East and West, brought other benefits to us by way of Black Bread (Pumpernickle) and tinned meat. Some trading activities with the Villagers produced eggs and vegetables and these improvements, including a better supply of Red Cross parcels, brought to an end the period of the great hunger.

In Silesia the noise of Allied bombing on Berlin, and more rarely on nearer cities, had reached us on many occasions, but there was never the sight of, or even the sound of, an Allied aircraft. It was very different in 1945 on the Luneburg Heath between Hamburg and Bremen. In the darkness the sound of the heavy bombers was an almost nightly occurrence. On one occasion a large number of American Flying Fortresses, in perfect formation and at a great height, went over leaving white con-trails in the sky, and litter on the ground, some of which fell within the barbed wire. Discarded long-range fuel tanks sounded like bombs on their way down and could have been equally as painful. Mostly there were empty chewing-gum papers, wrappings of bulk packages of cigarette cartons, used book matches, "Camel" and "Chesterfield" cigarette packets and Coca-Cola bottles. In fact everything you might expect, in the way of rubbish, from an airborne army of young Americans. The sight of these flying Armadas was extremely impressive and must have been very frightening and demoralising to the Germans when they were seen apparently unopposed above the Fatherland.

The heavy bombers of the RAF, flew at night and were thus invisible to us on the ground but not, unfortunately, to the German night fighters. When night attacks were made on Bremen or Hamburg we would see streaks of machine-gun tracer fire originating from nowhere and aimed at nothing. Except that sometimes a steady red glow would start small, then get bigger, brighter and bigger still as it fell earthwards, which is how a blazing aircraft appears from a long way away on a dark night. An expert opinion from a confirmed optimist would deduce, from the size of the blaze, that it could only be a shot-down fighter, and sometimes he might well have been right.

One day the sky over us in broad daylight was full of Lancasters. Great big black bombers, in contrast to the silver of the Fortresses, in a formation that was also very different. It was not as if there was no formation at all, the fact that something like fifty plus aircraft could be seen at one time, all going in the same direction, tended to indicate a formation of sorts, at any rate a mutual aim or purpose. But there could be no doubt the Air Force definition of 'Formation Flying' was not met by this straggle of aircraft. Unlike the Americans who had a leader, a navigator and a bomb-aimer, from whom the others in the formation took their initiative, each RAF bomber had its own navigator and bomb-aimer, who were accustomed to act independently on their own initiative. This I suspect is exactly what they were doing and, being daylight, was not something that was going to make them change from the established order of things. If someone were to tell me they had all pasted blackout paper over every window except the one under the bomb-sight, I would find this a very plausible reason for the way they behaved. There were hardly two at the same height, and from the lead 'plane to the last must have been eight to ten miles, and likewise from side to side. The war was nearly over, the Luftwaffe was not much in evidence, and I do not recall any opposition being offered to the gaggle of bombers within our field of view. One can only suppose they knew what they were about, which is a happy thought.

The previous inhabitants of the compound left behind a number of homemade cookers of a type, not unknown, but not common in the previous camp. Our Mess inherited one of these in good working order. It worked like a forge with a small fire in a recess, about the size of a coffee cup, formed in clay and enclosed in a large tin. It was blown from below by ducted air generated from a centrifugal fan rotated at high speed by a large hand-wound wheel driving, via a belt, the small wheel on the blower. Fuel was the problem as wood tended to be consumed rather quickly. The issue briquettes were better but the ideal was coke and this could be had by minutely scavenging the cinder perimeter path. With four or five of these machines in the centre corridor of a block, all bringing a pot to boil for the evening 'Brew,' visibility was reduced to nil, and the atmosphere - probably poisonous - certainly very unpleasant, which was why they were in the corridor, not in the rooms.

Having enjoyed myself converting camp-beds to double-deckers, building an oven to take the place of the room stove and having my first fried egg (bartered from the locals) since becoming a kreigie, I became ill. The Doctor prescribed chlorodine, which has the most medicine-ly taste and smell of any medicine, and therefore ought to cure anything, but although I found the medicine to my liking, it failed to cure my ailment. Whilst languishing on my sick bed, waiting to be diagnosed as having Jaundice, the war carried on apace with the British Army getting closer each day.

Our captors, not wishing to have their guests removed from them, marched all those capable of marching, to Lübeck on the Baltic Sea. Happily I was not considered capable of marching, indeed, not even of walking. I was laid upon a two-wheeled hand-cart, together with all my worldly possessions, and with a complexion of an interesting shade of yellow, pushed between the curious, and even envious eyes, of my colleagues who were preparing to set off on another march. I was on my way up the hill, to the Hospital in the Merchant Service compound, where I became known as 'the canary', (thereby making proper acknowledgement of my colour and the means by which I had come to be a guest of the Reich). There I would remain until such time as it took for me to get better and return to my usual colour, or the war ended, whichever was the sooner.

At the time, and for all I know even to this day, there was no magic cure for Infective Hepatitus, as they now told me was the correct name for Jaundice. By giving the ailment such a complicated and important name the patient could hardly be surprised that no one had yet found a cure. Rather in the same manner as the early makers of pocket watches used precious metals most beautifully engraved and decorated, as if to compensate for their poor time keeping. As far as I knew there were no other sufferers of the illness. This was strange because the effects of the march were blamed for me getting it, and not only was I far from being the only marcher but I had survived in a great deal better condition than many others. I am not complaining, just curious. Had things been otherwise I would have been marched off to Lübeck, with all the discomforts and danger encountered by those who were not so fortunate, and been delayed two or three weeks before release. Nor would I have experienced toasted 'white' bread (the first for two and a half years) without butter or margarine, the only food I was given or indeed wanted. Jaundice is not an illness to be recommended. I felt very poorly and at the time it is most unlikely I would have thought fate had dealt me any sort of a good turn.

The Ward was a standard wooden bungalow with, at a guess, some twenty beds. The Doctors were all Prisoners, mostly from the Army and the Patients were, with few exceptions, seafarers mostly from the Merchant Service, as would be expected with the Hospital being in a Merchant Service Camp. In the RAF the Captain of an aircraft more than thirty years old would have been a rarity. In the Merchant Service it would have been rare for a ship's Captain, or for most of his Officers to be under thirty. So it followed that the beds around me were occupied by older men with afflictions more likely to be met in middle age, like gall stones requiring surgery for their removal. Such operations were well within the competence of the Hospital; two, possibly three, took place while I was there. One to the Captain in the bed next to me, who had been through it before and was, somewhat surprisingly, looking forward to the event with pleasant anticipation. The anaesthetic was administered by an injection causing rapid unconsciousness for a limited time, usually sufficient to carry out a minor operation, before the patient woke up. If by mischance the operation was still going on when the effects wore off then, as it was not possible to give another injection, chloroform, ether, or whatever, had to be used. This would be a disaster for the elderly ship's Captain who did not look forward to waking up feeling, and being sick from, the after effects of the chloroform, ether, or whatever, instead of the anticipated after-effects of the injection - which he described as being '...the best 'free drunk' in all my experience'. On this occasion I regret to recall time ran out and the pleasures of a 'free drunk' were replaced by the misery of sickness, or, maybe in this connection it should be, a hangover, with none of the pleasure of the night before.

Another Captain, or he may have been an Engineer, was more fortunate. He awoke in the ward, after a similar operation, very happy indeed, sang a song or so and announced: 'Mush 'ave a pee, goingsh to the headsh', and started to get out of bed.

'George', (that was his name,) said the orderly firmly, 'you have just had an operation and you can't get out of bed. Here use this bottle'. He pushed him back down on the bed and handed him the bottle.

'Go away, I'msh all ry an' I c'n walk', pushing away the proffered bottle.

'George, you must use the bottle'. Again, it was thrust into his hand. George took the bottle, examined closely its white, bulbous, vitreous enamel form and, with a neat underhand bowling action, he hurled it across the ward shouting; 'Bloody Depth Charge!' and fell back fast asleep. When he woke he had no recollection of the incident. Come to think of it, he may well have been a Sub-mariner.

While I was getting better, the British Army was getting nearer and the Royal Air Force was, to the best of its ability, spreading alarm and confusion behind the German lines. We were behind the German lines, and clearly identifiable by day with 'P O W' in large white letters painted across the roofs. The enclosures also had wire with Goon Boxes at regular intervals, which helped to make identifying us from the air fairly certain, but this was not the case at night. Fighter planes and fighter-bombers roamed virtually unopposed ahead of the advancing armies, shooting at, and bombing anything showing a light, or illuminated by a flare. By this time the sounds of distant battle, and sometimes bomb bursts not so far away, had become part of the scenery, as it were, until one night four very loud bangs made it quite clear that if we were not the target we were mighty close to it. The compound at the bottom of the hill had been occupied by refugees after we left, and they had not been fussy enough about their black-out. A stick of bombs, from an intruding Mosquito (so they said) had severely damaged one hut and caused some casualties. It was a good job the quality of the bomb aiming had left a great deal to be desired! We were to learn later there had also been casualties, caused by allied fighters, among our colleagues marching towards Lübeck.

By the time I was fit enough to wander around a bit the war was getting very close to Westetimke. Dreadful stories came from the locals of young boys left dangling from lamp-posts in the town, having been hung as deserters, and left as examples to others, after running foul of the SS and Gestapo. A bunch of 'boy-soldiers', rigged out in a hotch-potch of uniforms, with rifles, which most were dragging - not carrying - went by closely, on the other side of the wire. 'Tommy soon come,' muttered one of them, 'then ve vill be behind der vire and you go home'.

Whilst expressing this admirable sentiment he somehow made it clear their only objective, in going towards the enemy instead of more sensibly in the opposite direction, was to surrender at the first opportunity and achieve the, now highly desirable, status of a Kreigsgefangener. I don't suppose the eldest was more than fourteen years old. The excitement, and patriotic duty, of being a Hitler Jugend, let alone becoming a Were-wolf, had quite evaporated in the reality of a lost war.

Another of the little known advantages of being afflicted with jaundice comes to light when one is told – 'No, I am very sorry but you cannot get out of bed and help to dig slit trenches, they will have to manage without you'.

The trenches were dug, without my assistance, and the time came when all the camp occupants spent most of a day huddled in the bottom, safe from the variety of missiles, travelling with lethal intent over and through the Barrack blocks, whilst a battle was being fought over us. This is not to be construed as meaning we were the Prize. We just happened to be in the way, and the Germans, sensibly, but without the instincts of gentlemen, put guns and tanks behind and close to our compound, hoping thereby to inhibit the Guards Armoured Division - our potential liberators - from shooting at them, for fear of hitting us. This ploy may have been the reason nothing heavy came near us, only machine and small arms fire. The temptation to look out of the trench to see who was winning resulted in one fellow having his cap sent spinning by a stray bullet. It also allowed me to witness a German tank, about a hundred yards away in the field between our wire and a belt of forest, from which shots were coming, aimed at the tank. The tank stopped, three or four men came out and started to run for the cover of trees ahead of them. We cheered, another German tank had bit the dust. From the far trees a machine gun opened up, aimed at the fleeing tank crew, so they turned around and ran back to the comparative safety of their abandoned tank, scrambled in, started the engine, and drove off. Maybe they had wanted to surrender? There didn't appear to be anything wrong with the tank, and they probably drove off to find a safer place at which to surrender.

By the end of that day the Germans had gone and there was a very large tank, a Churchill I think, parked outside the now open, gate. The guards had been happy to exchange roles and one at least, without the monumental cost of a Nuremburg trial was summarily dealt with by being escorted on a one way trip into the woods by a couple of our liberators. They had asked if there were any of our guards who had behaved towards us in such a way as to deserve severe punishment. One was pointed out as having been responsible for the killing of at least one prisoner, and possibly another. The one, where I remember the circumstances, had become mentally unbalanced – 'wire happy or, round the bend'- and had climbed on to the roof of the hospital where, with voice and gesture, and in the glare of at least two searchlights, he exhibited the nature of his distress. Two emotions were possible - it was funny if you didn't know he was 'round the bend', and sympathy, if you did. The German guard saw it as an opportunity to kill one of the enemy - and did so. There was no possibility of the episode being an escape attempt, since the Hospital block was within the guarded perimeter fence, and there was certainly no attempt to be clandestine by the prisoner. This all happened at Luft 3, and why this particular guard stayed behind instead of going with the rest of the Luftwaffe guards to Lübeck I do not know. It could have been at his own request, knowing, as he must have done, that the free for all chaos of the inevitable release would provide opportunities for revenge by the people he knew had promised to do just that. By staying behind he may have hoped there would not have been anyone to 'put the finger' on him.

If, all these years later, it may be thought such instant justice was barbaric, it should be remembered that these soldiers of the Guards Armoured Division were, by the time they reached us, no strangers to the horrors of the Concentration Camps, or the behaviour of the fanatical SS on the battle field. A tank crew told of when they were accepting the surrender of a trench full of SS Germans. When the tank Commander came out through the top of the tank, one of the Germans fired a Piat anti-tank weapon and blew his head off. In instant reaction the tank was repeatedly slewed round at the rim of the trench, causing it to collapse, continuing until all the Germans were buried alive. There were no survivors.

With the gate open and the guards gone small parties went into the town and countryside to liberate chickens, ducks, etc. I saw a pig, legs tied together and with its throat cut, suspended beneath a pole being carried to a one-time Butcher who, no doubt, soon recalled the long unpractised skills of his calling.

My recovery had reached early convalescence, but not well enough to join in the process of liberation. I thereby missed the opportunity to get hold of such memento's as officers daggers, bayonets, coal-scuttle tin-hats, cameras, watches and such-like desirable objects; but well enough to wander carefully around at increasing distances from my hospital bed. Hospital patients were to be evacuated right away, so next day I found myself in an army ambulance, glad to be well enough to sit beside the driver, instead of in the back with the more seriously sick.

CHAPTER 34.

Stalag to Student

We were taken, in three or four ambulances, to Celle, a journey of some fifty miles. We traveled over roads, which until a few days before, had carried German traffic strafed by artillery and from the air, which had not improved the surface of a seemingly minor road, having probably had only minimum maintenance during the war years. The driver, nevertheless, drove quickly, explaining as we bounced merrily along: 'We do not usually drive at this sort of speed over bad roads. Some of the poor fellows we carry are dreadfully wounded and we try to make the journey as comfortable as possible. But you chaps, although sick, are not wounded and in pain, and a bit of bumping up and down won't hurt you. Besides I expect you'd prefer to get to a good meal and bed without waste of time. There is also the matter of German soldiers and 'were-wolves', not yet cleared from the woods on either side, and at this speed I hope they'll find it more difficult to hit us!'

I found his reasoning entirely reasonable in every respect. No one did shoot at us, perhaps because bouncing ambulances make difficult targets, or, to give the benefit of the doubt, because they were ambulances. The only people to be seen at the verges of the road were occasional scruffy, ill-clad gatherings, of both sexes, seated hopefully near something cooking over a fire, or wandering with no apparent enthusiasm or purpose. They were the freed slave-workers of the Third Reich, now become displaced persons, at liberty to return to their homes, if they had any. In the case of those from countries like Poland and Czechoslovakia, there was no certainty of home still being there, even if they wanted to return.

At Celle, a large hall had been commandeered for use as a hospital. Its use, formerly, appeared to have been as a 'Drill Hall' or 'Party Headquarters', as long red banners with a large black swastika in a white circle, so essential in every Nazi scheme of decoration, still hung round the walls. First thing on arrival was the indignity of being de-loused by having the long spout of an over size 'Flit-gun' poked up sleeves, down trousers, up coats and down collars. This was done by an orderly pumping vigorously to inject white clouds of DDT powder designed to seek out and kill all bugs with which, it was assumed, we might be infested. We were not, but that made not the slightest difference. The orderly, who knew exactly what he had to do, was immune to all protests and bored stiff.

An Army Sergeant gathered our little party, of ten or twelve, and led us into the hall. As we were obviously 'walking wounded' (and apparently not even wounded) he attempted to get us into ranks of three before marching us to wherever it was he had in mind to put us. He found it difficult, and confusing to be confronted by a group of mixed ages in a variety of uniforms, Naval, Air Force, Merchant Service and, in the minority, a couple wearing army battle dress but with seagoing type hats. Each of them carried some form of un-military baggage, (he was not to know these contained, in each case, the entire worldly possessions of its owner). Neither did the motley collection he had inherited seem to be in the least amenable to discipline, not at any rate when administered by a Sergeant, in the army. It began to dawn on him that his disreputable charges were not of the Army or any other kind of fighting servicemen within his present experience. When they verbally remonstrated with him, the sound of their voices was reminiscent of one of his own officers, indicating they were not from the ranks of whatever service they were from.

An immaculate Army Officer, from his insignia a Captain and a Doctor, approached, and in the high pitched voice of an actor caricaturing the 'typical' British Officer, exclaimed - 'Sergeant, who are these people? This is a Hospital, not a Refugee centre'. The Sergeant came splendidly to attention with a smart salute, showing great respect for this caricature of an Officer whom I had instantly thought to be a bit of a twit - which only goes to show how wrong first impressions can be.

'Sir!' barked the Sergeant, 'they have just been released from a Prison Camp'.

'Oh! Horror, horror, horror,' exclaimed the Doctor, throwing his arms high in the air, (perfectly in 'twit' character). He too it may be assumed had seen what went on in the concentration camps. 'Prisoners? British prisoners? We must get you home as soon as possible'.

The gist of this dialogue is somewhat as written, the 'Horror, horror, horror" bit is one hundred percent fact. It is not something one would be likely to forget, and even less likely to invent!

Our 'caricature' Officer, led us around the hall, passing soldiers with 'walking wounded' type wounds. Having received first aid they were sitting on chairs waiting for whatever it is that happens next to the walking wounded. He seemed to know all of them, and how they were afflicted, inquiring after their well-being as we passed. It soon became apparent that he commanded enormous respect from all who had met him. A soldier he did not know came limping towards us.

'Soldier, what's the matter with your foot?' he enquired.

'It's nothing really, Sir,' the soldier replied with a smart salute.

'That is for me to decide, sit over here'.

There and then he called an orderly, examined the wounded leg, gave instructions for treatment, apologised to us for the delay and proceeded to find a room large enough to hold the dozen beds for our party. He arranged a hot meal and commandeered the cinema next door for our sole entertainment during the afternoon. He did everything to make our stay as comfortable and as short as possible. It was as if he waved a magic wand, red tape vanished at the sight of him, the impossible took no more time to arrange than the easy, and with all that, never did he neglect the care due to, or the welfare of, his real patients. He became to us, then, quite the most wonderful person it had ever been our good fortune to meet, and I still think so. Next day he arranged for us to be on an aeroplane to take us to Brussels.

The aeroplane was a Dakota, fitted out as an ambulance with double tier stretcher beds down either side. We sat on the floor between them. It was a very salutary experience to come out of a Prison Camp, and be among the mangled, wounded, young soldiers, of whom we had, at times, been less than grateful when it had seemed they were rather a long time in coming to fetch us home. Some of their wounds were quite dreadful.

The Hospital in Brussels was staffed by British Nurses and Doctors who, it seemed, had been warned of our arrival. We were led, in all our scruffiness, down the centre aisle of a large ward, between the beds on either side, each occupied by a wounded serviceman, to a small separate ward just big enough for our little party.

'This,' said the Sister, welcoming and congratulating us on being released from captivity, 'calls for a little celebration'. An assortment of medicine and tooth glasses appeared accompanied by a couple of bottles of Champagne taken, (and I know this because I went with the Sister to the little room at the other end of the main Ward to help with the carrying,) from a large refrigerator in which I glimpsed a number of Bed-pans! I still wonder why this was a good place to store Bed-pans?

The Chief Medical Officer expressed his welcome and arranged for us to be docketed and documented. He provided us with Monopoly money, (or so it might have been by the number of noughts on the Bank Notes) and a Pass to get out of the Hospital, which stipulated that we be back again by ten-thirty that night. Finally he arranged for transport to take us into Brussels to enable us to spend the money and enjoy our first freedom from any kind of supervision, hostile or benevolent, for, in my case, two and a half years. A wander round the shops in the late afternoon proved, at least to me, that shopping then, as now, held little attraction. A visit to a Bar, however, restored faith in both money and freedom.

The time passed all too quickly and enjoyably, until, being mindful of the stricture on our Pass and not wishing to let-down the kind man who had so generously arranged the money etc., we just managed to catch the last tram back to the Hospital. We arrived only an hour late, at about eleven-thirty and the 'kind man' was pleased, probably relieved better describes his feelings, to see us back. He tended to agree with us that ten-thirty was, perhaps, a little early. To-morrow, if we were still there, he would stipulate eleven-thirty as being a more realistic time for people in our circumstances. More bottles of Champagne were discovered hidden among the Bedpans, and so to bed.

Next day we awoke about mid-day for breakfast in bed, followed a few hours later by Lunch, and sometime after that, it being apparent no-one was going to take us anywhere else, the tram took us back into the City. We did not waste any time in the shops, deciding instead on a night-club type of establishment, which welcomed us to a table in a corner and a little back from the perimeter of the small dance floor. One of our number spoke sufficient French to be elected table interpreter. A round of drinks was ordered and, despite being so early in the evening, a difficulty arose as to how much each owed in respect of his chosen drink. The problem was solved by pooling all our money, which formed a very impressive heap in the middle of the table. The waiter was instructed to help himself to the cost of the round, and to continue to bring drinks and help himself until the money was gone!

Two things I recall of the ensuing evening. The girl with whom I was dancing stared at the ceiling in puzzlement when, in an attempt at conversation, I inferred that there were 'beaucoup de peuples'. I was never quite sure when 'plafonde' should be 'plancher', or vice-versa. On this, the only occasion I had attempted to use French out of the class-room, I had chosen the wrong one. The second thing was the Proprietor getting a bit up-tight and refusing to allow some of his pot plants to be taken as gifts to be presented, by us as a measure of appreciation, to the custodians of the Champagne (and Bed-pans), our kind nurses.

As on the previous evening explanations were needed to account for our return an hour later than stipulated. This time, I am happy to say, the reason was a great deal more convincing, even if it did not rate too highly as an excuse. We tried unsuccessfully to persuade the, by now, completely disillusioned kind man, that our lateness was entirely a consequence of our anxiety to have a 'thank you' gift for our Nurses. This caused us to miss the last tram and we had to hitch a lift in the back of an Army truck. He, possibly dreading what might happen if he let us out again, arranged for our departure next morning. There was really no reason for him to have worried, all our money was gone.

Another Dakota Hospital plane enabled us to experience the emotion felt by all returning Britons when sighting the White Cliffs of Dover. We landed, on the 2nd of May 1945, by a large Hospital, at Wroughton near Swindon. Because we were some of the first British Prisoners of War to be brought home we were greeted in a similar rather extravagant manner as at Celle. This was agreeable to us, but also embarrassing to be the centre of attraction for Doctors and Orderlies, who we thought should be better employed attending to the wounded. One of our number snapped at a Doctor – 'Don't worry about us, attend to that poor fellow over there', pointing to a soldier on a stretcher with his smashed face all wired together, ignored for the moment by the Medics, and moaning piteously. The Doctors were, of course, hardened to such sights, and I am quite sure the treatment they provided was none the worse for that, but we were not.

Despite being actively convalescent and not very ill, they put us to bed, took temperatures, woke us at the crack of dawn, and tried to turn us into proper conforming patients. A day was spent by us insisting we were not ill enough to be patients, and certainly had no intention of conforming, but all to no avail. As also were our efforts in trying to convince anyone who looked even moderately important, and who would listen and take notice, that all we wanted was to go home. The nearest we came, on the first day, was a telephone call to our families but without being able to predict when they might expect us. However, a solution was found the next day, undoubtedly because of the considerable nuisance we made of ourselves. It was suggested that if we were to discharge ourselves, entirely at our own responsibility, they would provide us with rail passes to wherever home might be. And so it was, forms signed, passes issued, trains looked up, and off to the station without time to make another 'phone call.

I arrived at Portsmouth Town Station at around midnight. Public transport had packed up for the day, so I went to the RTO, remembering how they had helped me get from Waterloo to Portsmouth without a ticket back in '41. This time they excelled themselves and I found myself in an Army Jeep, driven I believe by an Army Red Cap, all the way to Denmead. My knock on the back door of the farmhouse, at around one am, brought Mother, in her dressing gown, to see what the noise was about.

'Who is it?' she called.

'It's me, Robin'. The door was flung open, a great big hug, nothing said, what was there to say? Just the deep down solid contentment of returning to the heart of an affectionate and loving family.

I just managed to catch, and thank, the jeep driver before he succeeded in slipping away from what he saw as an emotional scene, with no further part for him to play. Mother offered him a cup of tea, or coffee, or anything he fancied, but he obviously felt rather surplus to the occasion and drove off into the night.

Father put in an appearance, his slightly embarrassed smile conveying his relief, happiness and contentment at the very satisfactory outcome to a worrying and unpredictable two and a half year episode. My brother, Bill, was also at home having only just come on leave from his duties as First, or it might have been Second, Mate on a merchant ship. He was still sound asleep, and remained so until next morning when he helped with the serving of my breakfast in bed. My homecoming was as joyous and enjoyable as could possibly be imagined by everyone concerned, with the possible exception of the chicken who, accompanied by a long-stored bottle of champagne, had an important part to play in the Celebration Dinner.

A couple of days later, the 7th May 1945, the sun shone on Denmead Farm and on where I was sitting in a deck-chair, on the one-time tennis court, now a lawn, when Mother, who had been listening to the Radio, rushed out to tell me the war was over. Today was V.E. Day. It was indeed a happy time, both sons home, and the war ended. True there was still a problem with Japan but that was half a world away, and our side seemed to be getting the upper hand, maybe that too would be over before they required our assistance?

When one is not yet twenty-four years old, and life has suddenly reverted to a sort of normality, it has to be admitted, when thinking back over fifty years, that normality, however satisfactory, does not leave many memories. I have to confess that the priority of greatest importance, and therefore most to be remembered, was again to be the possessor of my splendid seven h.p. Jowett. It had been driven down from Mareham to Portsmouth by two Airmen, who, so they said, 'enjoyed' more of an adventure than they had bargained for, when volunteering for what had seemed a splendid way of going home on leave, which happened to be in that direction. They arrived at the farm without warning, from where Father persuaded them to follow him to his office on the outskirts of Portsmouth, at Cosham, where the car was put in the garage to await my return. Father had propped it off the ground on bricks to prevent damage to the tyres, but unfortunately had not thought to drain the radiator. Things could have been worse as only the bottom of the radiator had split open at a soldered seam, not the cylinder blocks, which would have been disastrous. It did not take long, after towing the car back to the farm, for me to make a Kreigie style blowlamp, remove, repair and put back the now watertight radiator. In fact it was not quite watertight, but used coffee grouts soon sought out and stopped the leaks. I re-seated the valves, borrowed the battery from my brothers Scott motorcycle, turned the engine over a couple of times, and switched on. To my considerable astonishment it started first swing! For five pounds I bought another similar Jowett, one year newer than mine, (1930) in which the frost had been less kind and had cracked the cylinder blocks. I mixed the two cars, retaining the best of each. The body of the newly bought one became a luxurious chicken house, and mine looked exceedingly elegant with imitation leopard-skin seat covers! When I sold the car, for forty-five pounds, (it had cost ten) a couple of years later, it became the only car, up to the present time, on which I made a profit.

They sent for me again, early in June, to report to a place called Cosford. This turned out to be a vast complex embracing, as far as I was to discover, every activity, excluding aeroplanes, from Recruitment to Demobilisation. On arrival somebody wanted to know how, why, where, and when, I had become a Prisoner of War, together with relevant information and opinion consequent thereon. Somebody else persuaded me to share with him a bottle of 'plonk' red wine on the night before the obligatory Medical Examination, designed to ensure I was absolutely one hundred percent fit before being discharged, thereby hoping to avoid any come-back for a disability pension at a later time.   Jaundice, Champagne, Belgian night-clubs, a long leave, and most decidedly half a bottle of 'plonk', are poor preparation for a medical examination.   When the eye Doctor asked me to read the eyesight test card, I said, 'which card? Where?'   And when the stomach Doctor prodded me in the stomach I said 'Ouch', it was exceedingly painful.   The result of the examination, not surprisingly, found me unfit for release and prescribed four weeks rehabilitation, consisting of four successive classes in which the exercises etc. became more strenuous as one approached the goal of one hundred percent fitness. There were five classes actually, counting the one at the bottom, which was a class for cripples. I was in the next class, one above.

The first day each of us was given a card. Only one day was needed to discover this card served to denote your presence at the classes. If the Instructor had the card, you were there, if he did not have the card, you were not there. So, if the card was not collected at the end of the day then you were there next morning, even if you happened to be staying at the 'Kings Head' in Shrewsbury, which three of us made a habit of doing. We returned each Thursday to collect our cards, buy the Doctor a large gin in the Mess, so he would remember us with affection next morning when we assured him there was absolutely no need for him to make an examination. We were so benefiting from the exercises we could easily manage the next class, or even jump one! He never let us jump one, but he always promoted us to the next class without bothering to make an examination.   After four quite enjoyable weeks, during which I did one hours PT, a short cross country walk, an hour or two swimming, a visit to 'Chances' glass works, (most enjoyable) a dance or two on the Station, and several train journeys to and from the 'Kings Head' where we enjoyed, at a much reduced rate, a small dormitory containing four beds.

As returned Prisoners of War we enjoyed a certain status, amounting almost to hero-worship by the Recruits, and respect tinged with reluctant tolerance from the smartly attired Penguins, (non-flying officers) who administered the Station. We had not succeeded in acquiring much noticeable smartness, but we were Officers, albeit scruffy ones, having achieved, mostly by default, the not to be despised rank of Flight Lieutenant. Although our uniforms were a mixture of battle-dress and ragged well-worn 'best blue', most had medal ribbons beneath their air-crew brevets. This all went to prove something, even if the buttons were a dull brown, tinged with green, advertising for all to see the parsimonious attitude of the Air Ministry in not providing Batmen. The new shoes issued from the stores were most uncomfortable, so I wore a pair of black, elastic sided house shoes, which just lasted out the duration of my rehabilitation.

I wonder why it is that I still have a piece of official looking paper, described in the top right corner as - R.A.F. Form 2520/119 and calling itself 'FIRST CLASS RAILWAY TICKET R.A.F. - NOT TRANSFERABLE', 'To be detached only by Ticket Collector' etc... stamped twice, signed and dated 31 JUL 1945. It authorised a journey from RUGELLY - crossed out (wherever that might be) - and re-written - COSFORD To PORTSMOUTH ?

The possession of this ticket might suppose it was never used, but that is not so. I arrived back home, complete with a de-mob suit - which served very well in the garden and workshop, except for the 'pork pie hat' worn only once at a Fancy Dress dance. The priority for demobilisation was arrived at via a formula compounded from: Age, Length of service, Overseas service (including as a P.O.W.), Compassionate grounds, including sickness, and the importance of your civilian job to the national interest. The calculation of this formula produced a number of 'points' to define your place in the queue, the higher the better. In my case 'length of service' was high, (over four and a half years) i.e. a good thing, my age was low, not a good thing, and had it been only these factors in consideration then my release would have been many months hence. Fortunately time as a P.O.W. counted as overseas service with double points, or something like that. This farsighted provision brought my points exactly to the total for those being de-mobbed at that time.

I was offered a permanent Commission, but chose to go back to being a 'student with a difference'. I was older, and more experienced in the ways of the world and its inhabitants, than many of my fellow students who were as I had been five years before. I had a car, a gratuity, and Post-War Credits, which when honoured twenty odd years later, purchased a Radio Control for the model aeroplane my son was building at the time. Quite the best thing about being a student again was that this time it was entirely my own decision, unlike previously as something expected of me as the eldest son following in Father's footsteps. I am happy to say it was never regretted.

*   *   *

Forty five years after the flight home in the Dakota ambulance I retired and obtained my first Passport, enabling me to take to the air once again, this time in Concorde, with my wife, to begin a five and a half month holiday round the world. It was the first time Liz had flown!

The End.

POSTSCRIPT

Fifty-one years after being shot down, that is to say on the 11th October 1993, I was in my cellar workshop when Jim Lang telephoned from his home on Vancouver Island to mark, with mutual congratulations, the anniversary of that moment in our lives when it had suddenly seemed possible we might now have a future in which anniversaries could be celebrated. I was still musing on how thoughtful and kind he had been to do such a thing when the telephone went again. This time it was Aad Neeven from Holland who had chosen this moment, being well aware it was our anniversary, to tell how a friend of his, Eric Mombeek, had come across some German records for the 11th October 1942, in which he had found, and Aad Neeven had translated into 'normal language', the following:

"*Corporal Gunther Kirchner of the 5th. squadron of (Jagdgeschwader 1)*
at 18:20 hours did shoot down 1 Mosquito, 2 kilometres out of Utrecht,
and shot-up one other."

(This has to be us, but I am surprised he did not claim the other Mosquito. Even this was subsequently explained.)

Aad Neeven, in his follow up letter to the 'phone call, as well as providing the translation, also gives this additional information:

'You were his third victim. The aircraft belonged to II/JG1 ...I think...from Katwijk. Enclosed you will find the picture of the Pilot. It was taken 'at readiness' for scramble at Schiphol. Unteroffizier Kirchner received the Iron Cross, 2nd. Class, after his first victim, a Wellington, on the 23rd. July '42. On this picture he is seen wearing his decoration and sitting in the sidecar of a BMW motorcycle together with Uffz. Schmid. The nice thing is that the sidecar has the "Tatzelwurm" (Tapeworm) painted on it. This was the squadron emblem. For the 5th. Staffel it was painted red. He, Uffz. Kirchner, was killed on the 19th April 1945 when his aircraft, a Heinkel 162 (jet) crashed for unknown reasons when he returned to base, shortly after he had shot down a Spitfire.'

Also in the letter he expressed having had a reluctance to tell me about his findings in case I might not have wanted to know who had shot us down. To this I replied, after thanking him profusely for the photograph and the information:

'I have always reconciled being shot down with the almost certain knowledge that had it not happened my chances of surviving another two and a half years of operational flying were pretty slim. So, whilst never consciously wanting to know who was responsible, now, thanks to you, I do know what he looked like and in a strange sort of way feel gratitude towards him.'

POST-POSTSCRIPT

Another letter from Aad Neeven cleared up the mystery of the other Mosquito - claimed as damaged by Unteroffizier Kirchener. It had come down in the sea, seventy kilometres West of the Hook of Holland, and, as we had always known, there were no survivors.

One day at the end of March, fifty-one years after becoming Prisoners of War, Jim Lang and I went back to Holland to be met by Aad Neeven and two of his colleagues. They had been engaged in making very thorough research into the 'Air War' over and on Holland, and were now prepared to set aside a day to share that part of their findings where Jim and I had been involved.

First we were taken to the Gas Works in Haarlem where the gas-holders we had damaged but failed to demolish, had now been pulled down to make way for a more efficient energy plant. The Manager, J de Prinse, went to no end of trouble in making us extremely welcome. He sent us on our way with the gift of a bottle of wine apiece, and it occurred to me to be a trifle surprised that had he been the manager in 1942 he would have been our target!

We visited the aerodrome at Soesterberg, now a museum, where Jim had been taken after capture, and then to the Police Station in the village of de Bilt - now a dwelling - where he was taken next. Their research had been so meticulous as to identify a house, in Utrecht, where a part of our Mosquito - probably the engine cowling that had passed me on the way down - had landed on the roof. The house was now lived in by a crippled lady whose father had been killed by the Germans. She struggled to her front door to thank us for getting rid of the Germans. The field where our Mosquito had finished up was also identified and we were taken to it. When this location was plotted on the map and a line drawn to connect it with the house in the town, then continued on to the East it crossed over a lake and the moated 'Fort bij Vechten' - which I now found to be the name of the place upon which I had landed.

When we all arrived at the Fort - still a military depot - it was to find that access was strictly forbidden to all but the military. There were two policemen on motorbikes, with guns and if you should manage to get past the policemen, there were soldiers on guard at the bridge crossing the moat. All of this proved no obstacle to our determined guides and we were, after short negotiations, allowed to explore the Fort both from the outside and the inside.

With little effort on my part, it is all rather wonderful to realise how the gaps in my story, concerning the bombs on the Gas Works, and more particularly the details of who shot us down and where, have come to me. Albeit a bit late in the day, but very deserving of my gratitude and thanks for the persistence of Aad Neeven and his colleagues, John vid Maas and Wybe Buizing, in tracking us down, providing me with the information and giving Jim and I a very memorable and nostalgic day in Holland.

APPENDIX.

ADDITIONAL INFORMATION RELATING TO OUR PARACHUTE DESCENT INTO HOLLAND.

For the map of Utrecht and the contemporary reports I am, as usual, indebted to Aad Neeven. I have plotted on the map the places where the aircraft and the engine cowling(?) landed, as well as the fort where I landed. Here, in translation, is a report which identifies these places:

After the war, to assist the R.A.F. in finding missing airmen, reports of crashes were submitted from all the municipalities to the military government of Holland. From one such report dated 31st October 1945 is the following:

> *'Sunday 11 October 1942 on or about 18.45 hours.*
>
> *In a paddock bordering to the municipality of Vleuten, a burning aircraft came down. It is unknown what has happened to the crew. A part of the cabin(?) fell on the house, Zuiderzeestraat 2. Pilots helmet in the Robert Schumanstraat.'*

(The document - of which the above is only one item - is from the Burgemeester of Utrecht).

Another report refers to Jim's capture when he gave himself up a week after being shot down:

Dayreport Police de Bilt-   of Sunday 18th. October 1942.

21.10 hours. Reports at Overberg at the Police Station an English pilot named Jim Lang: Born at Vancouver on 15 - 5 - 1913 commission number 106223.
The relevant organizations are warned by Heer I van P.
He will be collected by the German Military Police of Utrecht.

AN APOLOGY.

When Aad Neeven read this manuscript he was very kind in his comments but had three complaints. His name was not spelt with an 's' at the end, IJmuiden is spelt with capital 'IJ', (he kindly added '..in all English publications it is misprinted, but not now in this one!). And he was a bit upset that I should have hinted he had an accent and pronounced W's as V's.

I apologised as follows:

'I do not at all wish to offend you, but at the same time a 'typical British' reader would understand, instantly, that here is a Dutchman speaking exceedingly good English. It is to be looked upon more as a 'device' rather than being accurately phonetic. Journalistic licence! - something like that?'

I can only add that his spoken English is devoid of V's for W's, his accent barely perceptible and his idioms rarely at fault. Likewise with his written English just now and then you realise this is not an Englishman writing, even if its only because the grammar is better!